The Environment: Between Theory and Practice

Erratum

The last sentence on page 213 should read:

Instead, my contention has been rather modest: that socialist changes in production relations may yield good results for the environment.

The Environment: Between Theory and Practice

Avner de-Shalit

OXFORD
UNIVERSITY PRESS

OXFORD

UNIVERSITY PRESS

Great Clarendon Street, Oxford ox2 6dp

Oxford University Press is a department of the University of Oxford.
It furthers the University's objective of excellence in research, scholarship,
and education by publishing worldwide in

Oxford New York

Athens Auckland Bangkok Bogotá Buenos Aires Calcutta
Cape Town Chennai Dar es Salaam Delhi Florence Hong Kong Istanbul
Karachi Kuala Lumpur Madrid Melbourne Mexico City Mumbai
Nairobi Paris São Paulo Singapore Taipei Tokyo Toronto Warsaw

and associated companies in Berlin Ibadan

Oxford is a registered trade mark of Oxford University Press
in the UK and in certain other countries

Published in the United States
by Oxford University Press Inc., New York

British Library Cataloguing in Publication Data

Data available

Library of Congress Cataloging in Publication Data

De-Shalit, Avner.
The environment: between theory and practice / Avner de-Shalit.
Includes bibliographical references and index.
1. Environmental policy.   2. Environmental protection.
3. Environmentalism.   I. Title.
GE170.D465 2000   363.7—dc21   99–057190

ISBN 0–19–829769–6
ISBN 0–19–924038–8 (Pbk.)

1 3 5 7 9 10 8 6 4 2

Typeset by Hope Services (Abingdon) Ltd.
Printed in Great Britain
on acid-free paper by
T. J. International Ltd
Padstow, Cornwall

DEDICATION

My father was a professor of nuclear physics in the 1950s and 1960s until he died, very young, in 1969. As a scientist he was very enthusiastic about the promise of technology; but at the same time he was rather anxious over what he thought very likely to happen—the invention of a machine that would perform like a human being—and he feared the irresponsible misuse of technology, especially nuclear energy. As a young lecturer—he was not even 30 years old at that time—he initiated a series of meetings and correspondence with the then Israeli prime minister, David Ben-Gurion. The result was an astonishing exchange of letters. Nowadays I expect prime ministers are too busy to engage in such philosophical discussion, but Ben-Gurion was an exception in many terms. The first letter he wrote to my father (13 January 1957) ends with the optimistic assertion:

The most advanced and sophisticated machine will only perform the will of its creator; but there is almost no limit to the mind and intellectual ability of the human being—which is the only reason I believe that nuclear research is possible.

Notice, however, that even this statement reflects a certain doubt. According to Ben-Gurion, nuclear research is both necessary and possible, owing to the boundless possibilities opened up by the human mind and intellectual ability. And what, the question implies, if this belief in the human being is mistaken?

As one who lives in the Middle East and experiences the hatred, terror, violence, and political stupidity so prevalent in this area, I find this a chilling thought. I therefore wish to emphasize that I write this book, whose subject is the environment, justice, and democracy, because I still believe that men and women are capable of reason and that it is important to struggle towards these goals, and that we should not relinquish hope of a better world. And yet, I write this book feeling so much more anxious than my father did forty years ago.

I therefore dedicate this book to both the children of Israel and the Palestinians, in the hope that they will live without war and bloodshed, and in a world that is safer and more reasonable in environmental terms as well. I hope that they will learn to respect each other and the Earth that is their home.

ACKNOWLEDGEMENTS

Writing acknowledgements makes me very uncomfortable because I feel that there is little I can call my own in the book. The truth is even worse, because there are several writers whose works have had a profound impact on me, even though I have never met them, and even though I do not necessarily agree with everything they say; among these are John Dryzek and David Pepper. Others whom I did meet, and quite often, and from whom I have learnt a lot are both environmental philosophers and theorists, in particular John Barry, Andrew Brennan, Andy Dobson, Tim Hayward, Eric Katz, Andrew Light, and John O'Neill, and political and moral theorists, particularly Daniel Attas, Dan Avnon, Brian Barry, Bob Brecher, Michael Freeden, David Miller, Saul Smilansky, and Gayil Talshir. Most of the above have also read parts of this book or discussed my thesis with me, and I am more than thankful to them. To Holmes Rolston I am indebted for writing very detailed and extremely helpful comments on one of the chapters. I was lucky to have two very helpful referees and I am happy to thank them here, and also Dominic Byatt, my editor in Oxford University Press.

A great deal of this book was written at the Oxford Centre for Environment, Ethics and Society, known as OCEES, at Mansfield College, Oxford. I had a great time there as a visiting research fellow in 1995/6 and, in the summer of 1997, as an associate fellow. I would like to thank Maurie Cohen, Michael Freeden, John Muddiman, Antonia Layard, and Bhaskar Vira, not only for the intensive and endless discussions we had about our work, but more importantly for the supportive, friendly, and warm atmosphere they helped to create. Many thanks also to Nina and to Anne Maclachlen, and to the director of OCEES, Neil Summerton. From Maurie and from Darell Posey I learnt that philosophical arguments are not enough; one needs anthropological evidence to back these up, and it has always been incredibly exciting to discuss this with them.

I would like to thank my colleagues and students in Israel for their comments and suggestions and for allowing me to take up their time with my questions on the environment in a place whose only concern seems to be security and the fragile future of its democracy. In particular, I would like to thank Shlomo Avineri, David Heyd, Emmanuele Ottolenghi, Moty Perry, Moses Shayo, and Amos Zehavi, all of whom read parts of this book or discussed these ideas with me.

Several chapters grew out of papers I presented on different occasions: in New York (American Philosophical Association), Lancaster (philosophy seminar) Newcastle (political theory seminar), Brighton (Brighton Philosophy Society), Glasgow (British Political Studies Association), Odense, Denmark (Man and Nature conference), Oxford (Nuffield College political theory seminar), and Wageningen, Holland. I would like to thank Finn Arler, Volkert Beekman, Bob Brecher, Simon Caney, Jerry Cohen, Tim Gray, Cecile Fabre, Alan Holland, John Horton, Mat Humphrey, Attracta Ingram, Michael Jacobs, Jozef Keulartz, Michiel Korthals, Will Kymlicka, David Merril, David Rothenberg, Ingeborg Svennevig, Robert van der Veen, Hillel Steiner, David Wongrow, and Jo Wolff for all their comments and suggestions, and for taking my half-baked ideas seriously. I don't know where I would have been without them. (Actually I do know, but I don't want to know.)

Many thanks also to Ruth Freedman for her help and patience and for all my friends who encouraged me to write and with whom I occasionally discussed some of my ideas. In addition, my warmest thanks to Cafe CoCo and the Jericho cafe, both in Oxford, for introducing such good and strong espresso to the Oxford scene. I believe some of my ideas came to me while sitting there. Who says you can't eat and drink well in Britain? Also, many thanks to Frei Zinger, in whose music I found comfort whenever I thought my writing was not going well, and to Didi and Dov, Sarah and Mick, Ken and Fran, and Ester and David for their warm hospitality.

Last but not least, I thank my beloved wife Yifat and children Daniel, Hillel, and Shiri, who have been so patient with me over the four years I have devoted to this book. Whether this was worthwhile I leave to you, the reader, to decide.

In writing the book, I have adapted some passages from the following articles, and I would like to thank the publishers for allowing me to do so.

Parts of Chapter 3 appeared in A. de-Shalit, 'Is liberalism environment friendly?' in *Social Theory and Practice*, 21 (1995), 288–292 and 295–301, and are reprinted with kind permission from the journal.

Parts of Chapter 5 appeared in A. de-Shalit, 'On behalf of the participation of the people', in *Res Publica*, 3 (1997), 62–65 and 70–74, and are reprinted with kind permission from Kluwer Academic Publishers.

AVNER DE-SHALIT

Jerusalem
Summer 1999

CONTENTS

FIGURES

Introduction

> The challenge for a green political theory is to avoid the fallacies of ecologism without lapsing back into the complacencies which are attendant on a reformist environmentalism.
>
> Tim Hayward, *Ecological Thought*

I believe that environmental philosophy has had little—or too little—impact on policy. This is not to say that there is any lack of environmental policies or politics in our world. On the contrary, the environment has become one of the key issues in world politics—and not only in the Western world. However, environmental philosophy, the philosophy that sets out to justify environment-friendly policies, and to revolutionize the way people think about the environment and themselves, has not been incorporated into environmental policies—yet. Governments and parliaments, local municipalities and politicians rarely, if ever, use the ideas and theories of environmental philosophy to justify their policies, even when their policies are environment-friendly.[1] Moreover, we often hear environmental *activists* complaining about a communication gap between themselves and environmental *philosophers and theorists*. What is this gap, and who is responsible for it?

The gap is twofold. First, the language and arguments used by most environmental philosophers are not the same as those used by politicians and governments to justify their policies. Secondly, the issues discussed by environmental philosophers are not those that cause environmental activists distress. Consequently, the arguments propounded by environmental philosophers are irrelevant to the debates the activists are engaged in.[2]

---

[1] Of course I do not deny that in some cases arguments about intrinsic value have been used to justify public policy; for example, they are sometimes used in Australia and New Zealand. (The phrase 'intrinsic value' appears in the Conservation Act 1987 in New Zealand.) But these are exceptions. More often, in particular outside these countries and Germany, the arguments used do not emerge from environmental philosophy.

[2] I personally have met many activists in several countries, and most of them have complained about this. In 1994 I participated in an international gathering of NGO activists representing over thirty countries from five continents, and most regarded arguments put forward by mainstream environmental philosophers as too out of touch with the 'philosophical needs' of environmental activists.

Notice, however, that the communication gap is not necessarily reflected in the policy recommendations themselves. Politicians and governments have adopted policies that environmental philosophers would find easy to accept, and activists' goals are almost identical with those of the environmental philosophers: namely, to change public and governments attitudes and help save our planet. Of course, different people have different ideas as to how to achieve this, and what exactly should be done, but in general, environmental activists and environmental philosophers agree on the goals. What they cannot agree on, however, is the cause of the problems, which many environmental philosophers believe is the result of a misguided moral belief regarding the superior place of humans in the world ('human chauvinism', 'anthropocentrism'). Similarly, when we look at the politicians and the governments, we see that the gap lies in the justification or rationale applied to (environment-friendly) policies. In other words, environmental philosophers, activists and environment-friendly politicians might agree on a particular policy (e.g., conservation of a forest, cleaner energy-use, etc.), but would disagree on how to justify this to the general public. While philosophers speak of the moral status of the environment, politicians relate to the needs/rights of future generations of humans, or to contemporary human beings and their well-being.

So it seems that, while the gap is twofold, it has a single source. The problem is that philosophers on the one hand, and activists and governments on the other, in fact address different audiences. Activists and governments must persuade the general public, which contains two very difficult groups to persuade. The first is those who have strong interests in development—even if development is not sustainable and destroys the structure that forms the basis for the development. The second group comprises those with anti-progressive, or very conservative, views who are therefore unlikely to be convinced easily of the need for novel, radical, or even revolutionary environmental policies. Therefore the example raised in the first chapter represents the views of those who do not believe that members of other nations or ethnic groups should be respected. We ask the question, How can these people be persuaded to respect non-human animals?[3]

Unlike politicians and activists, it is generally believed that the role of philosophers is not persuasion or the implementation of ideas. Thus, while politicians and activists are responsible for turning ideas into deeds, philo-

---

[3] There is broad empirical evidence that these two groups are the most difficult to persuade. Their positions are significantly different from those of environmentalists (Milbrath 1984: 86). In answer to the question, Do you think the government's actions in dealing with environmental problems have been adequate? on a scale ranging from 1 (inadequate) to 7 (adequate), business leaders in the USA awarded the government a score of 4.2, and business leaders in Germany marked their government with 4.1, whereas environmental activists in the USA awarded the actions of their government a score of 2.3 and in Germany 2.0. A number of sociologists have suggested that, since attitudes towards environmental policies are shaped along with other social attitudes, those with interests in development are less likely to support conservation or other environmental policies (Cotgrove 1982).

sophers are in charge of the 'truth'—or, to be more modest, the search for accuracy and clarity of mind. Indeed, if this is the way one looks at the role of the activists and politicians as opposed to that of the philosophers, there should in fact be two kinds of discourse:[4] the academic and the 'real life', or political.

If readers see philosophy this way, perhaps they should put this book aside (but gently, please), murmuring something about 'arrogant philosophers who think they can change the world'. But before doing so, consider what environmental philosophy is, or at least what it has always sought to be. It is applied philosophy.[5] Hence, the argumentation is inspired by problems that arise with the intention of solving them. Moreover, since the types of problem discussed are mostly public and policy-related, environmental philosophy is, ultimately, a *political* philosophy. We can say one thing about environmental philosophy: it is not simply an armchair exercise, nor is it a discipline of purely academic interest. The goal of environmental philosophers—interestingly, many of them are also activists—is to influence policies and change the world we live in. And quite a change this must be. The arsenal at their disposal contains words and sentences, theories and arguments, and they therefore need to be extremely sensitive to what happens to their words and theories and how they are met by their audience—not only their students and colleagues, but the general public as well. If we accept this description of philosophy and its relationship to the real world, then we can surely bridge the gap that separates the environmental philosophers from the environmental politicians and activists.

Many would agree with the above analysis of the distinction in attitudes between the philosophers and the activists and politicians. The question is, Who can we 'blame' for them and how can we bridge them? Perhaps many environmental theorists would be only too happy to blame the politicians, and even the activists, for failing to adopt the theories and argumentation proposed by the environmental philosophers: 'They are not radical enough', 'They are too lazy to explore things deeply enough'.[6] Perhaps the most common accusation would be: 'They dare not look in the eyes of their constituencies and tell them to change their outlook on morality, natural resources, the place of human beings in the world, etc.' Sometimes, as we listen to politicians, we may find ourselves agreeing that these accusations are not entirely groundless. Margaret Thatcher, for example, openly declared that she did not

[4] In fact, the reason I use the term 'discourse' rather than 'theory' is that I wish to examine the entire approach: 'theory' limits the debate to the university or the academic world. By 'discourse' I mean the way ideas and theories percolate down from the ranks of academia and 'professional' philosophy through to society, and to the way society utilizes this information. It is possible that by so doing we run the risk of being less accurate, but it is important to examine not only ideas, but their implications and applications.

[5] Or, some would claim, practical philosophy. Applied philosophy is when moral theories are applied to solving cases of moral dilemmas. Practical philosophy derives from the cases.

[6] For such frustrated attitudes and the motivation for writing about environmental policies, see Jacobs (1997*a*).

take the environment seriously when she spoke to the Scottish Conservative Party conference in 14 May 1982 on the Falklands campaign and remarked: 'It is exciting to have a real crisis on your hands, when you have spent half your political life dealing with humdrum issues like the environment' (Jay 1997: 361).

However, it would be wrong, if not dangerous, to blame the 'other'. From the prophets in biblical times to the French revolutionaries and the early Fabians, history is full of examples of theorists and philosophers who abandoned all hope of persuading others through deliberation, and became impatient and hence more radical in their ideas. This explains why the shift from humanistic to misanthropic attitudes has been rapid. Perhaps the 'easiest' way to solve a problem is to lose faith in a form of gradual change that can still remain respectful of humans. Such an attitude, I believe, only brings about a new series of problems encompassing dictatorship, totalitarianism, and lack of personal freedom. In this book I seek to maintain the philosophical impetus, not to point the finger at the politicians or the activists. Rather, I wish to examine ourselves—the philosophers who engage in discussing the environment—to discover how we might construct a theory that is much more accessible to the activists and the general public (without relinquishing any of our goals), and which can be harnessed to the aims of political philosophy.

Here, the counter-argument would go something like this: 'OK, so the argumentation supplied by environmental philosophers is so removed from that used by activists and governments. So what? The only outcome of this is that more arguments, or, if you like, a pluralistic set of arguments, will emerge. Some arguments are relevant to academia alone; others can be used in politics. Thus, for example, in the university we could maintain an ecocentric environmental philosophy,[7] whereas in politics anthropocentric[8] arguments would dominate.' In response to this, it could be argued that plurality of argument is indeed welcome. Moreover, as we saw earlier, the divergence between, say, ecocentric environmental philosophy and anthropocentric environmental philosophy is not so vast in terms of the *policies they recommend*. In fact, as John Barry argues, 'reformed naturalistic humanism' is capable of supporting a stewardship ethics just as well (J. Barry 1999: ch. 3). But my point is that saving the environment is not just a matter of theory: it is an urgent *political mission*. In a democratic system, however, one cannot expect policies to be decided without giving any thought to how these policies should be explained to the public, and thereby gain *legitimacy*. In other words, the *rationale* of a

---

[7] Ecocentrism is a current of thought in environmental philosophy that regards keeping the balance in ecosystems as a supreme moral obligation, from which many other obligations and moral codes of behaviour derive.

[8] Arguments that regard only human beings as moral agents and clients, or that deny that animals or even trees have a moral status similar to that of human beings.

policy is an increasingly important, if not inseparable, part of the policy; in particular, the openness and transparency of the democratic regime makes the rationale a crucial aspect of the policy. A policy whose rationale is not open to the public, or one that is believed to be arrived at through a process not open to the public, is considered a-democratic (cf. Ezrahi 1990). Consequently, a policy's legitimacy is owed not only to its effectiveness, but also to the degree of moral persuasion and conviction it generates within the public arena. So, when constructing environmental policies in democratic regimes, there is a need for a theory that can be used not only by academics, but also by politicians and activists. Hence the first question in this book is, Why has the major part of environmental philosophy failed to penetrate environmental policy and serve as its rationale?

The first part of this book, then, discusses this question and offers two explanations in response. These explanations are based on the premiss that environmental ethics and political theory should be differentiated and well defined so that later on they may join hands, rather than that they should be united in a single theory. It is assumed that they answer two questions. Environmental ethics is about the moral grounds for an environment-friendly attitude. Political theory with regard to the environment relates to the institutions needed to implement and support environmental policies. Thus, the failure to distinguish properly between environmental ethics and political theory underlies the failure of the major part of environmental philosophy to penetrate environmental policy and provide its rationale.

In Chapter 1 it is claimed that in a way environmental philosophers have moved too rapidly away from anthropocentrism—mainstream ethical discourses—towards biocentrism and ecocentrism.[9] My argument is that the public on the whole is not ready for this, and therefore many activists and potential supporters of the environmental movement become alienated from the philosophical discourse on the environment. In addition, I suggest that the reason for the gap between on the one hand environmental philosophers and on the other activists and politicians is that environmental philosophers have applied the wrong approach to political philosophy. I claim that all moral reasoning involves a process of reflective equilibrium between intuitions and theory. I distinguish between 'private', 'contextual', and 'public' modes of reflective equilibrium, arguing that environmental philosophers use either the first or second mode of reasoning, whereas political philosophy requires the third: the public mode of reflective equilibrium. The latter differs from the other two models in that it weighs both the intuitions and the theories put forward by activists and the general public (and not just those

---

[9] On ecocentrism, see fn 7. Biocentrism also rejects the idea that humans are the only moral clients, but its emphasis is on individual objects—animals or even trees, etc.—rather than on ecosystems. It is often claimed that the individual animals, for example, have intrinsic value. I discuss the theory of intrinsic value in Ch. 2.

of professional philosophers). The argument for this being so is that reasoning about the environment needs to include *political and democratic* philosophy. And yet, most of environmental philosophers' efforts so far have focused on such questions of *meta-ethics* as 'intrinsic value theories' and 'bio-centrism'. Environmental philosophers have been pushed in this direction out of a genuine desire to seek out the 'good' and the truth, in an effort to ascertain the moral grounds for an environment-friendly attitude. I suggest that environmental philosophers should not limit themselves to discussing the moral grounds for attitudes, or to trying to reveal the good and the truth, although these are important and fascinating questions. At least some of them should instead go beyond this and address the matter of the necessary institutions for implementing policies, and finally, and of no less importance, find a way to persuade others to act on behalf of the environment. In other words, while there is a place for meta-ethics, it should not be the only approach to philosophizing about the environment; it should not *replace* political philosophy.

I wish it to be clear that I am not suggesting either that truth is not important, or that truth is pragmatic, or that there is no such thing as truth. My view on the role of truth and the practice of environmental philosophy does not commit me to any rejection of truth. I believe that political philosophy implies truth-motivated, goal-oriented action. By 'goal-oriented' I do not mean that it is consequentialist, but rather that it should be aimed at 'getting somewhere'. It means hearing what people have to say and persuading them to do what is right. Persuading them, I argue, involves looking them in the eye, and talking about problems that interest them. Therefore the approach proposed here begins with the people and 'talks' to them. In this sense it is political, and in this sense environmental philosophy should include political philosophy. (Notice that 'environmental philosophy' encompasses more than 'environmental ethics'. It includes both environmental ethics, meta-ethics, political theory, and other methods of philosophical reasoning about the environment.)

In Chapter 2 I examine another explanation for the divergence between environmental philosophers on the one hand and environmental activists and the governments on the other. While in the first chapter it is argued that certain environmental philosophers have been overly preoccupied with the question of the moral grounds for an environment-friendly attitude, and that they seem to suggest that environmental ethics, or meta-ethics, can replace political theory, in Chapter 2 I argue that another group of environmental philosophers have also failed to distinguish between environmental ethics and political theory; this time they purport to advance a theory of the moral grounds for an environmental friendly attitude, while in fact presenting a political theory that does not necessarily address the needs of the environment. All this has brought about the kind of confusion that has been detrimental to the social status of environmental philosophy. The second chapter therefore begins with an analysis of the concept of 'the environment' and presents the claim that the environment comprises a system of ecosystems. Then, through an examination of 'Deep Ecology' and 'ecofeminism', I demonstrate how these two schools at the very least have misused the concept of 'environment'. I argue that their direction is in fact directed towards political goals that are not 'environmental' at all, and that they have thus 'conceptually exploited' the 'environment'. (This does not mean, incidentally, that I disagree with their messages. Ecofeminism is, I think, a very significant political theory of social relations and institutions; but it must be seen for what it is.) I then go on to analyse mainstream environmental ethics, particularly the concept of intrinsic value. I argue that this too has been overextended, and that it should be limited to intrinsic value in individuals rather than ecosystems. If my claim in these chapters bears up, then the reasons for environmental philosophy's lack of popularity among politicians and activists are (*a*) that it fails to distinguish between environmental ethics and political theory, and that it identified goals that do not necessarily appeal to environmentalists; and (*b*) that it has overextended the use of its main concepts and caused confusion and vagueness. Hence environmental philosophy has rarely been harnessed as a persuasive tool in the political debate against developers, vivisectionists, or those who lack sympathy towards the environment.[10]

Part I of this book then is mostly critical. Part II however is far more optimistic. The question pertaining to Part II is, What sort of theory should and can we use to persuade others of the importance of environment-friendly *policies*? I suggest that the answer lies not in a meta-ethical theory, but in a political theory related to the institutions that administer public life. But this then means we are left with the question of which institutions, and therefore which political theory, hold more promise in terms of environmental protection. Chapter 3 therefore asks in what sense liberalism is environment-friendly, and in what sense it is not. My reason for addressing liberalism first is that it is the most important and influential theory and discourse in the democratic world. It has been suggested that liberalism has been exceptionally effective in eliminating *environmental illiteracy* and raising *environmental awareness*. Nevertheless, I argue that liberalism is inadequate when it comes to fostering

---

[10] At this point it could have been argued that I have missed the whole point: it is not that philosophers are miles removed from what is needed in practice, but rather that we don't need philosophy at all. But this is far from what I would like to offer. Kate Rawles (1998) puts forward a beautiful argument as to why environmental philosophy is so important. She quotes Tolstoy, who thought that the greatest threat to life was habit, because it made everything seem banal, dull, and not important. He thought that the remedy was literature, because by being imaginative and provocative it could restore our lives to use. Kate Rawles thinks that a similar point may be made about ideas. So environmental philosophy has a role: to restore lost sight. Philosophy can contribute to the environmental movement by clarifying concepts that seem banal owing to ill use, by distinguishing right from wrong, by analysing values, and so on.

environmental consciousness.[11] Although my argument is primarily theoretical, I support it with an examination of the empirical evidence.

Chapter 4 takes up the conclusions of Chapter 3. Its starting point is the assumption that, in order to achieve environmental consciousness, we need communitarian, rather than liberal, politics. But what kind of community are we talking about? Many environmental philosophers suggest this should be a multi-species community. I reject this notion of community, and therefore go on to analyse its alternative, the human community. I explain why the notion of the human community is relevant to the politics of conducting public and moral life, with regard to the environment. Following my suggestion that *public reflective equilibrium* is part of the solution, I examine the position assumed by the activists. It seems that many environmental activists prefer *local* conceptions of community. I offer a critical analysis of this position, showing why environmental activism should not seek to foster mainly the local community, what I call 'localism', but instead should strive for the rather more abstract notion of a community of what I call 'collective rational reflection'. This is not a geographical or ethnic community, but rather a moral and political one.

Thus, Chapter 5 continues with the search for a political theory that encompasses the institutions that rule our lives. The first that springs to mind is obviously democratic theory. However, unlike a number of recent works that have praised representative democracy as the optimal form of democracy for the environment (Dobson 1997; J. Barry 1999), I argue that, the more deliberative and participatory the democracy, the more democratic and environmentally friendly it will be. Furthermore, the importance ascribed to majority rule is questioned. It is claimed that majority rule is a derivative, rather than a fundamental, value in democracy. The implication of this with regard to environmental policies is analysed. Here again I examine the activists' position, this time siding with the common arguments in support of deliberative democracy.

But we need to take this even further, since even when institutions are organized democratically this does not guarantee protection for the environment—and we have empirical and theoretical evidence to support this fear. Chapter 6 therefore examines economic arrangements—private *v.* public ownership, decentralized and free market *v.* centralized and planned production, etc.—and asks which are optimal where the environment is concerned. I argue that democratic socialism is best for the environment, and that, despite current scepticism, it is a feasible and reasonable system, especially if we combine the

---

[11] The difference between the three are as follows. *Environmental literacy* is when one has a basic grasp of ecology, CO and its effects, the ozone layer, endangered species, and so on. *Environmental awareness* is when one accepts that cases such as water contamination, or the extinction of species, raise moral, as opposed to technological, dilemmas. *Environmental consciousness* refers to the acceptance of the fact that environmental matters create *political* issues that need to be solved politically. I elaborate on this in Chapter 3.

social goals of socialists with the environmental goals of environmentalists. Finally, in the summary I tie in moderate (and not local) communitarianism, democracy, and socialism to demonstrate how my theory may be used by activists and governments to justify environmental policies.

I wish to emphasize that my goal is not to condemn environmental ethics as irrelevant to solving the current environmental crisis. On the contrary: I believe that environmental ethics has an important role to play in raising environmental awareness. But, unlike my many colleagues who emphasize environmental ethics and meta-ethics, I would like to see the emphasis on the place of political theory, because, if we ask ourselves which institutions best serve the environment, and if we are interested in justifying environmental policies, then we ought to conclude that political theory should play a leading role in answering these questions.

Perhaps some of the disagreement between myself and many environmental philosophers stems from the fact that they arrive at environmental philosophy from the study of ethics and meta-ethics, whereas my starting point is the study of politics and political theory (de-Shalit 1995a). But by no means do I mean this to be an excuse for any dispute. It is my belief that the debate should, and indeed must, take place between opposing positions and theories. As Thomas Nagel wrote in his recent book, 'to reason is to think systematically in ways anyone looking over my shoulder ought to be able to recognise as correct' (Nagel 1997: 5). I too wish to persuade others, and not only to explain my position. In fact, part of my critique of mainstream environmental philosophy and Deep Ecology is that they appeal to intuitions only and are therefore unlikely to succeed in persuading anyone of anything. Even though I may seem critical of some of my fellow environmental philosophers, I would like to stress that my criticism is of the theory and not of the theorists. Personally, I feel more than fortunate to be part of this community of environmental philosophers, theorists, and activists.

PART I

Why Hasn't Environmental Philosophy Had an Impact on Policies?

1

The Social Role of the Philosopher and the Philosophical Role of Society

As mentioned in the introduction, one of the goals of this book is to modify the discourse of environmental philosophy. The main target is to shift it from meta-ethics to ethical and, even more importantly, political issues. However, we must begin with a (rather long) comment which may be seen as one of meta-ethics, but which I prefer to see as a question of the sociology of philosophy. I wish to discuss the social role of environmental philosophers. As the title of this chapter suggests, I believe that society also has a role in the philosophical discourse, and that indeed the two roles are, and should be, linked. These roles will be discussed in relation to a case study: the debate over animal rights. At first sight this debate may be seen as a counter-example to my claim, because the idea itself is controversial. But this case is chosen because it offers solid good substantiation for my views regarding the social role of the philosopher and the philosophical role of society, and in fact serves as a good example of how philosophers have missed the opportunity to impact on policy. Furthermore, the debate may well help us to remove the barriers between the environmental philosophers and the activists.

People in North America and all over Europe, and recently in particular in Britain, have become involved in demonstrating and petitioning and in public debate about how humans treat animals. However, while the general public has been concerned mainly with cruelty to animals (that is, with a certain human attitude), philosophers have turned their thoughts to the moral status of animals. In other words, while activists are shocked by, and protest against, the degree of human cruelty, the philosophers are engaged in a different issue; the result has been that their theories are of little use to those seeking to persuade policy-makers to change existing policies. For the present I mean to concentrate on animal rights, but, as I shall claim, the argument put forward here is applicable to environmental philosophy in general.

I shall begin by explaining why I believe the issue of animal rights to be part of the environmental philosophy discourse.[1] There are those who draw a

---

[1] For a strong argument in favour of a similar position with regard to animal liberation, see Jameison (1988): animal liberation arguments rely on a theory of value consistent with 'environmental commitments'.

distinction between animal welfarism and preservationism, on the grounds that animal rights is not immediately related to, or even contradicts, environmental ethics. My claim is that, while the distinction holds for philosophical argumentation, it is irrelevant to the political and pragmatic aims of those supporting environment-friendly policies. I then turn to a brief review of the animal rights debate, omitting the philosophical problematics of the argument in favour of animal rights. In fact, the philosophical arguments are not the core of my present argument: rather, I discuss the implications for the discourse on the environment of an argument that relates to animals in terms of their *rights*. My main claim runs counter to that advanced so far by those opposed to animal rights, who use philosophical arguments to show the inconsistency of the argument for animal rights. Personally, I think that, philosophically, animals can be considered as having (certain) rights. But my claim is that the concept of animal rights is so remote from the 'person in the street' that it is counterproductive, not only for those who wish to see a more respectful attitude to animals, e.g. animal welfarists, but to environmentalists in general. People in most societies around the world do not recognize that other people, especially those from different ethnic or national groups, have rights; some of them have not even internalized the idea that they themselves have rights. Discussing animal rights with such people leads them to think that animal rights advocates—and, they often infer from this, environmentalists in general—are nothing but lunatics. This is devastating news for environmental philosophers, who invariably seek to make an impact on policies.[2]

One could still claim that animal rights arguments are intended to have an impact on the elite only, and that philosophers should not care too much about the layperson, or the general public. My response would be to ask how one is to practise a philosophy whose goal is to influence policy. I distinguish between three models of philosophizing. The first, which I have called *private reflective equilibrium*, is mainly the approach to moral philosophy offered by John Rawls, Thomas Nagel, and, more recently, Norman Daniels. These three regard moral reasoning as a process that establishes a balance between the philosopher's intuitions and his or her theory. I have termed the second model *contextual reflective equilibrium*. This is essentially what Michael Walzer conceives of as the proper approach to political and moral philosophy. He weighs his theory *vis-à-vis* the public's (that is, the community's) intuitions as well. The third model, *public reflective equilibrium*, concerns the way I believe political philosophy should be practised and requires the philosopher to consider (critically) the intuitions and theories put forward by the public in general. I elaborate on these models below.

---

[2] Of course, some would immediately reply that if I fail to take the position of animal rights advocates I am nothing but a speciesist or racist. Besides restating that I personally agree with many recommendations of the animal welfarists, I think that this position is far-fetched. Different positions can be supported philosophically in different ways.

Environmental Philosophy and Animal Rights

I would like to discuss animal rights as a vehicle for my argument in this chapter, but first I need to dismiss the claim that the issue of animal rights does not form part of environmental philosophy. Opinions among contemporary philosophers vary. Some see these two issues as 'complementary rather than conflicting' (M.A. Warren 1992; Clark 1984). Others contend that they are two distinct issues, sometimes implying contradictory imperatives. Bryan Norton (1984), for instance, thinks that what is good for individual animals (hence their rights) is not necessarily good for the environment. Thus, there are questions of animal welfare and there are questions of preservation, biodiversity, balance of ecosystems, and so forth. The two sets of questions also give rise to differences in policy.

Consider, for example, the question of deer hunting (Rawles 1997).[3] Setting aside the value of traditionalism and the conservation of human culture, if the issue is the suffering caused by this practice (the animal rights' perspective), then no doubt this should be stopped. But if the issue is preserving balance in ecosystems (the preservationist's perspective), then in many cases deer hunting should be allowed in order to prevent overpopulation, which might in turn bring about the collapse of ecosystems. Also common among environmental philosophers is the argument that humans should not interfere with nature, because this is 'nature's way'. Such a claim may contradict the notion of caring for an animal's welfare or rights. Holmes Rolston (1994a: 111–12), for example, analyses cases in which humans witness an animal suffering in the wilderness, and yet their obligation is not to help the animal because the death of this animal is required by the ecosystem.

Indeed, part of the controversy between environmental ethicists and animal rights philosophers is due to the question of whether the object of defence should be ecosystems or individuals (hence animals). Tom Regan (1988: 361) thinks that those who defend the balance of systems do this by sacrificing the rights of individual animals, and he therefore allows himself to call them 'environmental fascists'. Accordingly, he does not accept that individual members of endangered species are more important than individual members of non-endangered species (Regan 1988: 359).[4]

---

[3] Readers may recall the public debate about hunting which took place in the UK in 1998.
[4] I find this particular assertion questionable. It is an ecological and statistical fact that, if individuals of endangered species are hurt, the chances of other individuals of the same species to stay alive, let alone reproduce, are slimmer, whereas the chances of individuals of a species that is in no danger to survive or reproduce are not dependent on the survival (or death or injury) of a number of other individuals of the same species. I can sympathize with Regan's tendency to protect individual animals; but ignoring the systematic elements of the environment makes him blind to this difference. It seems that even from the perspective of individuals—but taking into account the systematic nature of nature—the rights of individuals from endangered species seem to have priority, or at least some urgency, over the rights of

I do not mean to draw any conclusion or offer the last word on whether the animal rights debate is at all part of environmental philosophy. It seems to me that it is enough if we think of environmental philosophy not as the narrow definition may imply, e.g. as issues as presented in Leopold's *Land Ethics*, but rather as a pluralistic term, encompassing several schools of thought—Deep Ecology, ecofeminism, Political Ecology, Social Ecology, Preservationism, Animal Welfare, Organic Farming, and so forth. These issues all involve, to a greater or lesser degree, questions concerning the moral relationships between humans and non-humans (mostly animals), as well as questions of relationships between humans; thus it may be argued that the animal rights question *is* part of environmental philosophy. Moreover, at the end of the day, the distinction should not matter that much in practice. As Eugene Hargrove (1992: xxii) puts it so well, 'Even if environmental ethics and animal welfare ethics remain distant fields theoretically, in practice some areas will overlap.'

The Case for Animal Rights

So what is the argument in favour of animal rights, and why do I question its use? In the background is the claim that human beings tend to prevent animals from having the sort of life they should have, or that they mistreat animals, or fail to treat animals in the way they should be treated. There are four principal problems here. First, there is cruelty to domestic animals, e.g. when they are exploited as objects of amusement (cock fighting, blood sports), or in battery farming, all of which cause animals undue misery, stress, and pain. Second, there is the problem of animal experiments, both in the sciences (for teaching and research) and in industry (testing new drugs or perfumes, etc.). Third, there is the issue whereby animals in the wild are ignored when humans calculate the costs and benefits of their policies; for example, when a forest is uprooted in order to cultivate the land. It is claimed that not only does this cause pain, misery, hunger, and death to countless individual animals (a typical animal welfare argument), but that it could also lead to the extinction of species, some of which might affect entire ecosystems (typically argued by environmental activists). For example, the international pet trade can be regarded either as deplorable because of the pain and misery it causes the individual animal, wrenched from its natural habitat and put into a cage, or as a question of the potential harm to a species threatened with extinction.

individuals from other species—not because the ecosystem is affected, but because harming the rights of individual A harms the rights of individual B, whereas this is not the case with species that are not under threat. Notice, however, that this is *not* a claim in favour of ecosystems' rights or intrinsic value. I shall come back to this—and in fact shall reject ascribing value to ecosystems—in Chapter 2.

Finally, many animals that are merely 'innocent bystanders' (Carwardine 1990: 84)—i.e. are neither a source of food nor a source of amusement—are nevertheless harmed by virtue of living in habitats heavily polluted or destroyed by humans. Often such animals are harmed when other animals, with whom they share symbiotic existence, are captured or become extinct. Animal rights advocates argue that all this abuse of animal habitats should cease because animals have rights which many policies and human activities abuse or disregard.[5]

It goes without saying that, if one is seriously[6] to claim that animals are rights holders, one should argue that animals possess certain capabilities or have features that make them similar to humans and hence entitled to some sort of an ethical status. Such an argument is made by both animal rights philosophers (Regan 1988) and environmental philosophers (e.g. P. Taylor 1986). Contemporary philosophers vary in their views about this claim. Perhaps the first among contemporary philosophers to discuss animal rights was Joel Feinberg (1974), who thinks that only entities capable of having interests can have rights (de-Shalit 1995a: ch. 5).

Among contemporary opponents of animal rights, one should mention the article by Francis and Norman (1978), who modify Descartes' claim that animals are nothing but machines, claiming that animals are incapable of reasoning, not to mention forming institutions such as the family (which is, one must immediately reply, not quite true: swans, for example, live in couples and form families.) Other arguments are that animals do not have language, hence cannot put forward a demand for rights or express their interests (to which Mary Midgley answers that language is not the only means by which expression and 'conceptual order' take place[7]), or that they cannot have interests because they have no sense of the future. At this point there seems to be an empirical debate: Regan, for example, answers that many mammals not only have a sense of the future, but also have memory, desires, beliefs and intentions (for other considerations see Radner and Radner 1996).

A more specific argument in favour of animal rights is what may be called the 'inconsistency claim':

1. Treating animals as lacking of rights is based on the empirical assumption that they are not (or are less) sentient than human beings and/or that they lack a capacity to experience well-being as human beings do.

---

[5] In addition, a different type of argument—one that perhaps demands further clarification by animal rights advocates—is often raised. Here the issue is not so much the ill treatment of animals, but the failure to consider their needs: the latter would be an equivalent of *welfare* rights among human societies.

[6] Tim Hayward (1994; 151) distinguishes between a loose sense of animal rights, 'meaning only that animals should somehow count in human deliberations' and a 'tighter connection with fundamental human rights'.

[7] Consider also the claim by Benton (1993: 47–8) that, although there are activities, e.g. reading, talking, that only humans do, this does not prove that animals do not communicate, but rather that humans communicate in a different way.

2. But there are humans (infants, severely senile persons) whose mental capacities are closer to those of animals than to the average human being.
3. Therefore, if it is not legitimate to use these persons for experiments, amusements, etc., even though they are much less sentient, it is not consistent to use animals for that matter (Regan 1988; Nozick 1974).

However, others may claim that this argument completely ignores the context of the natural world, which is a system in which species do kill and eat other species, while at the same time catering for the needs of their own offspring. Discussing animal matters outside the context of environmental philosophy may thus give rise to a biased and mistaken perspective.

In general, there are two types of argument against the idea of animal rights: on the one hand there are the philosophical arguments we have reviewed, and on the other, the political and pragmatic arguments. I do not intend to enter into a detailed account of the debate on animal rights, because my main focus in this chapter concerns the politics of using this sort of argument—or this mode of philosophy—in the public debate which seeks to change policies. In other words, my question is this: If the assertion that animals have rights is, philosophically speaking, coherent, consistent, and sound, does it follow that the issue of animals will, as a matter of course, enter the political agenda—just because the assertion is sound?

Prima facie, it seems that those who care for animals have good reason to discuss the morality of human–animal relationships in terms of rights, mainly because the issue of 'rights' is a heavy weapon that demands duties of another party. If, for example, one proves that Smith has a right, call it R, then one actually proves that Jones has a duty to respect R. But this is the Achilles' heel of the argument: that it places such powerful demands.

But before elaborating on this, I would like to distinguish between my argument and a more 'strictly' political one, namely that of Ted Benton (1993; 1996). According to Benton, animals are indeed mistreated, not because people have yet to be persuaded by one theory or another, but because capitalistic institutions are exploitative by nature, and therefore, until these institutions change, nothing else will change: animals, like humans, will continue to be exploited. I think that, even if present-day institutions are in need of change (I elaborate on this point in Chapters 5 and 6), the problem is not *merely* institutional. Changes in policies require readiness on the side of the general public. Hence a proper theory is needed in order to persuade people to change their attitudes and adopt new approaches accordingly. It is quite clear that the fight for public opinion has to be won against vivisectionists, developers, the interest of the capital, and so on. All these fully exploit their privileged access to decision-makers and to the media, and succeed in promoting their case against animal rights and against environmentalists rather forcefully. Therefore, in order to meet their challenge, a sound and pervasive argument must be used (Garner 1996*a*, *b*). This partly explains why, for many years, those seeking to protect animals have achieved more by dismissing the claim that humans benefit from such mistreatment (vivisection, animal trade, etc.) than by claiming that human mistreatment of animals represents an abuse of their rights (Garner 1993: 6–7).

So, while Benton emphasizes structural constraints, I would like to emphasize conscious blocks. My claim is simple: that the language of animal rights and the symbolism of using the concept of rights in association with animals, while millions of humans are exploited and tortured and their self-esteem, dignity, and rights are ignored and abused, inevitably leads to a double impact syndrome:

(*a*) Those who fight for human rights in their countries cannot comprehend how animal rights advocates could give equal weight to animals,[8] and consequently become alienated from the animal rights movement. Human rights campaigners often regard animal rights people as a bunch of snobs or else see them as detached (not to say egotistic) self-interested individuals who worry about the plight of dolphins but turn a blind eye to human misery.

(*b*) Those who have not yet accepted the idea that people outside their tribe/ethnic group/nation/political party have rights that limit what others may do to them will find the animal rights campaign weird to say the least, and will conclude that anything related to the environmental movement is marginal, over-radical, or even worse. Environmentalists can retort: 'Who cares about what these ghastly people think?' bearing in mind the ruling elites of totalitarian regimes. However, my reference to those who have not yet accepted the concept of human rights actually embraces most people in the contemporary world. This is a sad fact about humanity which philosophers need to confront.

Now, these opinions and attitudes—especially those adopted by human rights activists—may well be misguided and unjust for two reasons: (1) animal rights advocates may believe that their campaign not only does not contradict the campaign for extending human rights, but supports and sustains it; and (2) even if hostility towards animal rights campaigners is justified, it would be wrong to infer that 'all environmentalists are the same'. However, in practice this is how the public sees it. And the public has a point: animal rights campaigners have failed to form alliances with other (human) rights groups (Jasper 1996), which is a shame since our societies are founded on the simultaneous denial of human and animal rights in order to serve economic interests. If the case for animal rights is separated from that for human rights, then it would appear that what is wrong with our world is the denial of animal rights, as if

[8] Sometimes environmentalists are challenged for dealing with 'minor' problems (Brecher 1996: 77–8), but their answer is that more people die and suffer from environmentally caused problems and illnesses than from many other problems that are considered 'urgent' or 'important' because they are visible, e.g. traffic accidents, terrorism (de-Shalit 1997*a*: 123–37).

there were no such problem as the denial of human rights. This is the source of the general intuition among many people, viz. that animal rights are a luxury and, by extension, that environmentalism is either a luxury or a utopian dream.[9]

So animal rights philosophers have been missing the chance to find a way to many people's hearts. But why is this so crucial? I think it is crucial because it is the wrong way of practising political philosophy. To see why, let us recall a classical book by Max Weber (1968). In *Politics als Beruf*, Weber presented an important distinction between two approaches to moral reasoning. One is the 'ethics of conviction', which often follows deontology, or a set of rules of conduct; the other is the ethics of responsibility, according to which it would be irresponsible to act according to one's principles alone: rather, one should also consider what others will do as a result of one's actions. It seems to me that political philosophy has this approach in mind. Political philosophy should orient itself towards real-life problems, including the problem of public good and collective action, where people tend to react in certain undesirable ways to what others do. In such cases there must be a way of taking into account the effect that my actions have (we include here both what I claim to be doing and the reasons I give for doing it) on others' behaviour and actions. Political reasoning would then have two stages: first, a discussion of principles, but second, a consideration of their actual application and their effect on others' behaviour. However, many environmental philosophers, while ascribing rights to animals, ignore the way others may react. I believe that many people who might have been persuaded of the importance of treating animals fairly (using the argument of what cruelty can do to the human soul) will regard the notion of animal rights as so obscure or absurd that they dismiss as mad philosophers who suggest this idea, and scorn all such claims as nonsense.

Some may claim that I overestimate the criticism of the general public. But it seems to me that even activists and animal rights advocates are beginning to realize that the claim made on behalf of animal rights, while achieving more and more acceptance among philosophers, is still a curiosity as far as the media and the general public are concerned. Even in cases when activists and the general public do use the term 'animal rights' to describe their campaign,

---

[9] As an example of these reactions, consider this. In 1989 there was a campaign in the UK. People protested against a spring ceremony taking place in Spanish villages, during which clay pots in which pigeons were captured were hung high above the ground and teenagers competed in breaking the clay pots with stones. If the young man managed to hit the pot it often got broken and the pigeon was 'liberated', but not before it suffered and got wounded. During this campaign a philosopher appeared on television declaiming the abuse of these pigeons' rights. At the same time, however, blacks in South African were being humiliated, students in China jailed for speaking their mind, many women in certain Muslim countries were being circumcised, and Palestinians were being imprisoned for raising the national flag. For those concerned with these people's rights, the claim on behalf of these pigeons' rights seemed pathetic. Notice, again, that I am not claiming that these pigeons should not be protected and that this cruelty should not stop: but basing the claim on the pigeons' rights seemed only to alienate many people who could have supported the animal rights campaign.

they often do so metaphorically, to describe their opposition to cruelty to animals. This is why legislative bodies continuously pass laws marketed as protecting animals, but which in fact permit a wide range of ill treatment.[10] Thus, for example, Robert Garner admits that, even though in Britain animal rights has become a high profile issue, most of the time 'it simmers below the surface failing to emerge as a crucial vote decider at election times, regularly being ambushed by anthropocentric concerns usually of an economic nature' (Garner 1996a: xii; see also Ryder 1996: 166–94). Even in the area of animal experimentation, perhaps the area in which one would expect arguments of animal rights to be most appealing, because some of the experiments are so shocking, achievements are still very limited.

Political Philosophy: Public Reflective Equilibrium

One might still ask, What's wrong with claiming—philosophically—that animals have rights? Indeed, one can claim that animal rights arguments, perhaps philosophy in general, is first and foremost meant to have an impact on the elite—that is, other philosophers and maybe other scholars, intellectuals, and artists. Only later will the idea penetrate to the decision-makers, and later still to the general public. The public in general is important, but not *that* important, because it is not the public that has to be convinced, but the philosophers and decision-makers. I will therefore raise the question of how political philosophy, such as environmental philosophy, should be conducted. First, two clarifications are in order.

I am not dismissing the claim that philosophy in general is an elite practice, one less about convincing people and more about finding the truth or even about constructing aesthetic theories about the world. This could be argued. Those who see philosophy in this way might regard political, or applied, philosophy as inferior branches of philosophy. Others might think that philosophy is *only* about changing the world, and that everything else is a waste of time, a *petit bourgeois* preoccupation. I cannot devote too much space to debate either of these positions. Suffice it to say that I tend to find that there is room and need—both scientific and social need—for both: there is a time for 'pure' philosophy, and there is a time for 'political' philosophy. There is a time—and a need—to search for the truth, to be engaged in debates for the sake of the debate, and there is a time to change the world.[11] However, what is important,

---

[10] See Bahro (1986: 196–7). In Britain the laws did not prohibit any particular kind of procedure (see Garner 1993: 205–10). In Israel the parliament passed a law forbidding experiments to take place without the permission of a committee, but the committee consists of the scientists themselves . . .

[11] For the sake of analytical accuracy, I should add that empirically one may engage in political or applied philosophy and yet think that it has nothing to do with affecting

I think, is to remember that environmental philosophy grew out of a desperate need to supply sound philosophical, normative arguments against the continuation of several policies that were causing damage to the environment, putting people's lives at serious risks, ignoring the well-being of future generations, and harming other species. In that sense, at least, the need for environmental philosophy was a need for political philosophy.

Now some people distinguish between political, applied and practical philosophy. Some claim that environmental philosophy should be practical; others may call it 'pragmatism' (Light and Katz 1996). Practical philosophy is distinguished from applied philosophy with regard to the question of what comes first—the case or the theory. Political and applied philosophy usually start with the assumption that theories are there to be applied to cases; the theory is, so to speak, 'given'. The question is how to solve the case with the help of the theory. Practical philosophy begins with the case and seeks a proper theory to solve it. This distinction is sound. However, in this book I use the term 'political philosophy' to mean, in general, philosophy that is policy-oriented. I think that there is a strong need for a 'political' way of philosophizing about the environment, including humans relations with animals. Such philosophizing, while constructing the theory, will take into account two conditions: first, that the theory must relate to real life cases and, second, that the theory must relate to the existing deliberation about the case, hence to the actual arguments that have already been put forward. I think that animal rights philosophers have been meaning to supply not a theory that can actually be applied to both the case and the debate, as well as the reasoning, but a theory that is 'true' and logical. Thus, I shall now describe the way I believe environmental philosophy should be practised.

It is widely accepted that moral exploration involves a process of 'reflective equilibrium'. This concept is often attributed to John Rawls, who wrote about it in his *Theory of Justice* (Rawls 1973). Basically, reflective equilibrium means this: 'that we "test" various parts of our system of moral beliefs against other beliefs we hold, seeking coherence among the widest set of moral and non-moral beliefs' (Daniels 1996: 2). We find the coherence, which involves 'more than logical consistency' but also simplicity, by going backwards and forwards, continuously revising and modifying the theories and the intuitions. These revisions are very important: reflective equilibrium means that, if the theory is very appealing, in that it fully explains and justifies many intuitions, but at the same time it contradicts another intuition, it is often the case that we change the other intuition—the 'instinctive belief'—rather than modify the theory. Failing to do so would imply dogmatism.

policies. One then defines *political* philosophy as philosophy about politics. My position, however, is that the motivation to engage in political philosophy is to actually apply principles and theories to real-life cases, hence to bring forward the philosophical critique or suggestions for real life action (Light 1996: 2000). That is to say that political philosophy by definition means a branch of philosophy that includes considering the impact of theory on policy.

While searching the equilibrium between intuitions and principles and their theories, we also search for the balance between the personal and the impersonal views. Indeed, one of the main reasons that we need a process of reflective equilibrium is that at the end of the day none of us is super-human. We are limited in our analytical capabilities, and what limits us most in this practice is our psychology, or, in Thomas Nagel's words, the 'personal view' (Nagel 1991). When reflecting on morality one should aim at the impersonal, and yet one is limited because one tends to take a personal position, or examine things from a personal perspective, involving personal experiences and even subconsciousness. Some people claim (I am not sure I agree with this) that perhaps the ideal would be to capture the ultimate impersonal view and define it. But psychologically, and therefore in practice, this is difficult. Should this lead us to a desperate relativist view? Not at all. Several philosophers have already suggested the mechanism of reflective equilibrium, which aims to overcome, at least partially, these human psychological constraints. These philosophers differ, however, in their view as to whether it is possible fully to overcome these constraints. John Rawls, Thomas Nagel, and Norman Daniels are more or less positive about it; so is Michael Walzer, although his view is somewhat different. I shall modify Walzer's model to offer a third way.

Analysing the differences between these philosophers, it seems to me that the question is not only whether the constraints can, or even should, be overcome, but also whose intuitions and whose theories should be weighed against one another. The differences between the three models of reflective equilibrium are set out in Figure 1.1.

Model of reflective equilibrium	Institutions considered	Theories considered
Rawls (private reflective equilibrium)	The philosopher's	The philosopher's and other philosophers'
Walzer (contextual reflective equilibrium)	The philosopher's and community's intellectuals	The philosopher's
Environmental philosophy (public reflective	The philosopher's and the public's (in particular activists)	The philosopher's and public's; the philosopher engaged in and conducting the discourse

FIG. 1.1 Three models of reflective equilibrium

Let me start with Rawls's model. Here, the philosopher can sit in an armchair and reflect. The philosopher could be you or me or anybody else for that matter. The only condition is that she imagines herself in circumstances of perfect detachment. Philosophy, according to Rawls, is finding out (whether this is invention or discovery I leave aside) what God—or, if you like, an 'ideal' person—would have thought about the issue. It is, thus, what Nagel (1986) called 'a view from nowhere'.

Daniels, following Rawls, distinguishes between 'wide reflective equilibrium' and 'narrow reflective equilibrium':

The difference is that widening the process of reflective equilibrium occurs when we wish to clarify not only which values or norms we hold, but also why we hold them. It is thus necessary to put our principles and intuitions to the widest critical scrutiny, 'drawing on all the different moral and non moral beliefs and theories that . . . are relevant to our selection of principles. (Daniels 1996: 2 and ch. 2)

But however wide Rawls's method of reflective equilibrium is, it is still limited, in the sense of its being what I call 'private' reflective equilibrium. The philosopher sets herself aside, and contemplates her theory and her intuition, drawing mainly on logic (seeking consistency and simplicity), with the help, perhaps, of books and works written by colleagues. It is purely and strictly a 'professional' process, in which, not only do other people and their opinions not count, but, moreover, the more *detached* the process is, the more likely it is to succeed. The criterion for this success here is that finally the philosopher can offer a consistent and coherent theory, which ties in with the philosopher's declared intuitions. Sometimes these intuitions happen to be shared by many readers, but the point of the 'private' reflective equilibrium is not to convince the reader that a theory fits the *reader's* intuition, but rather to convince the reader that the philosopher has managed to write a very accurate theory, in which the principles of morality offered live in harmony with philosophical intuitions, which in themselves are reasonable. In other words, a successful theory meets the condition that, if the reader shares these intuitions, he is also likely to accept the moral principles, and consequently the theory. The reader does not have to agree with the philosopher, but simply to trust her.

I see three main difficulties in applying Rawls's private reflective equilibrium method to environmental philosophy. First, there is no guarantee that it is radical enough, from an environmental point of view. I shall say more about a theory being radical when I discuss Walzer's model, but here let me just raise this concern. Rawls's reflective equilibrium is a process in which we are to imagine decisions taken by one who transforms oneself from one's place to a placeless location; hence one voluntarily loses one's 'identity' (one's class, gender, social position, skills, physical characteristics, and so on) in order to reflect in a fair (i.e. not biased or partial) manner. But this dislocation, or placelessness, is one of the main reasons for the emergence of environmental problems. It is the physical and spiritualistic uprooting of humans from place—indeed, the very thought that they can easily and voluntarily uproot themselves—that make them indifferent to the natural and urban environments in which they live (Norton and Hannon 1997). So in order to be radical enough to solve these new problems, environmental problems, one has to position oneself, to be in place, to reflect from Earth—from here.

The second difficulty is that Rawls's reflective equilibrium is so private that the community ceases to exist. One must not know to which community one belongs. The theory thereby becomes universal. But this seems to me to stand in contrast with the needs of environmental philosophy as political philosophy: namely, that it should relate to the problems that characterize the community and the community's environment, especially if we accept that environmental problems are related to—and often derive from—social problems. On this difficulty too I shall elaborate when discussing Walzer's model below (see also Chapter 4).

The third problem is that Rawls's reflective equilibrium is a 'professional' process, one that detaches moral principles from ideas of the good that are held by the general public. But since environmentalism is such an idea of the good, it seems that the person practising reflective equilibrium is not allowed to consider genuine environmentalism in terms of moral and political principles. A biocentric outlook, for example, will not enter Rawls's reflective equilibrium if it is not the attitude held by the philosopher.

So let us move to the more promising, alternative, model of reflective equilibrium—what I would like to call 'contextual reflective equilibrium'—as suggested by Michael Walzer in three of his books (Walzer 1987, 1988, 1994). Walzer himself never claimed, as far as I know, that he was using a mechanism of 'contextual reflective equilibrium', as I call it here. But I think this is a proper reading of his suggestions regarding how to go about political philosophy.

Walzer argues that whenever we make a moral claim we actually make two claims simultaneously—or at least, so is the claim understood. First, we make a maximalist and thick claim. A claim is described as such when it is profound, detailed, precise, and its demand is far-reaching. A claim can be maximalist and thick if and when it relates to a shared background of understandings, values, and common experiences. And second, and embedded in the maximalist meaning, is the minimalist and thin claim. This is a claim that can be deduced from the maximalist one, though it relates to a much wider audience. It is therefore likely to be far less specific and detailed (since the wider the audience is, the less common the background it has). The moral claim people make, which is expressed in particularistic terms when it is thick, becomes more universal—but also much more vague and hence thin—when it is interpreted by people from other communities. It should be noted that, although the minimalist meaning is 'hastily constructed'(Walzer 1994: 18), it is not necessarily less important than the maximalist meaning. In fact, it is quite the contrary: the minimalist meaning of the moral claim is framed as principles about what we oppose, e.g. 'Don't be indifferent to the suffering of other people' (Walzer

1987: 8), and is therefore very important to us as red lines which should never be crossed; whereas the maximalist meaning of the moral claim defines what we want, and therefore usually involves compromise, complexity, and disagreement (Walzer 1994: 6).[12] However, this dualism, the universal and human on the one hand and the particular and social on the other, is an 'internal feature of every morality' (Walzer 1994: 4).

Social criticism, then, according to Walzer, is practised with relation to a particular community and its morality. Thus I call it a 'contextual' reflective equilibrium. The philosopher learns and examines the values of the society and theorizes about them. This process of learning is interpretative (Walzer 1987: 1–33) rather than inventive. The philosopher examines the behaviour and expressed views of the individuals who make up the community, and interprets them *vis-à-vis* what she thinks the community's values are. The philosopher does not invent morality. She holds up a mirror and shows her community what it really is. The mirror is a sort of critic because it consists of a 'profound social idealism' (Walzer 1994: 42). The philosopher reveals all the lies the society tells about itself to itself. This activity is 'reiterative' (Walzer 1994: 52–3) in the sense that the philosopher does not aim at putting forward the last word; rather, she regards her theory as a new input to the moral discourse, to be re-evaluated. 'The critics who aim to get things right aim at a rightness that is relative to their critical occasions. They want to produce a strong argument and a local political effect, but also . . . an object of reflection and debate'. pp. 52–3).

This 'reiterative' character of philosophy is one reason I find Walzer's 'contextual' reflective equilibrium far better suited to environmental philosophy than Rawls's 'private' reflective equilibrium. Philosophizing about the environment, perhaps all political philosophy, should be subject to the debates and opinions among the general public, because these people will use and apply the moral theory in actual cases, and because they know the actual (real-life) moral dilemmas.

Another reason for preferring this model of reflective equilibrium is that Walzer thinks that the interpretation of norms and codes of behaviour is 'governed as much by ideal as by practical considerations' (Walzer 1994: 4). It therefore seems to me that Walzer will accept *applied* (or political) environmental philosophy as legitimate much more easily than Rawls. Rawls thinks that philosophy should work on the level of abstract principles, and that the philosopher should offer guidelines only.[13] But, as I argue above, environmental philosophy is political and applied philosophy. Therefore Walzer's

---

[12] I shall come back to this point when I explain why, even if we accept Walzer's model of reflective equilibrium, we should move to the 'public reflective equilibrium' model.

[13] For this reason I find it surprising that several authors have tried to use Rawls's theory in environmental ethics; see Singer (1988).

model suits it better, the process of contextual reflective equilibrium being interpretative and practice-oriented.

However, it has long been argued against Walzer that the contextual perspective in moral reasoning leads to moral relativism. The danger is that we are left with a situation where each moral claim is understood differently in different cultural or moral contexts, and that philosophers can do nothing about it. 'What we do when we argue is to give an account of the actually existing morality', writes Walzer (1987: 21). This, he claims, is a built-in difficulty in the moral discourse, imposed on the moral discourse by limitations of language and human psychological constraints, or simply by historical developments of varied moral codes of behaviour. Walzer has nevertheless rejected the accusation of relativism on the grounds that relativism would mean that we first try to identify universal principles, and only later realize that we cannot use them, and hence move on to a system whereby each community lives according to its own moral codes. But, claims Walzer, this is not the case: first we have a thick and maximalist morality, which forms the foundational morality. 'Morality is thick from the beginning, culturally integrated, fully resonant', he writes (1994: 4). Subsequently, universal principles are deduced from this maximalist meaning. So Walzer does not reject universal (thin) morality. He only makes it clear that the two—the thick and the thin—exist side by side at one and the same time, and that the particular is the source of the universal.

This answer, though, gives rise to another difficulty. When Walzer writes about 'home' (as opposed to 'abroad')—home being the place within which thick moral discourses take place—he has in mind a single community, primarily a national one. But it is a sociological fact that we all belong to various communities simultaneously. How would this affect Walzer's theory? Consider this: when I argue against Occupation, my 'home' is Israel. It often happens that when I discuss my resentment of Occupation with foreigners, say British people, I mean something slightly different from what these British people may mean when they talk about Occupation. My connotations (hence my parameters) are the Israeli–Palestinian experience, where two nations have been quarrelling about the same piece of land, both claiming historical rights of ownership. The British with whom I discuss this may resent Occupation as much as I do, but they have in mind British control over India, or something of that sort, where one nation invades another's territory for reasons that are completely different from the Israeli–Palestinian case.[14] However, when I then move on to make a moral claim about, say, academic freedom, I am at 'home' with my British colleague—whereas I am not quite at home, unfortunately,

[14] So Walzer may have a point here. We both resent occupation, in a thin way—perhaps we can define a principle, relating to the injustice or exploitation that occupation involves. We also resent occupation in a thick way, contextual and local; but this may mean two different things for me and for a British person.

with many of my Israeli fellow citizens. And later, when I make a third moral claim about environmental values, my 'home' is the community of environmental philosophers, wherever they are, rather than that of Israelis or academics. So either we accept that each claim assumes a different 'home' and 'abroad', thereby making a thin, universal morality very complicated, or we end up finding ourselves in a very narrow community (e.g. the Israeli environmental-friendly academics in the example above), making a thick, maximalist morality almost meaningless, because it relates to such a narrow community, consisting of very few persons.

A related difficulty with Walzer's 'contextual reflective equilibrium' is that, since it is contextual, it may preclude radical criticism and change, for instance by not being open to external ideas (ideas originating from other communities). Walzer himself denies this. He claims that his works on interpretation and social criticism have been 'nothing if not critical' (1994: 41). But it seems to me that there are three ways to understand 'critical', and I shall now argue that Walzer's model of reflective equilibrium is critical according to only two understandings of the term.

The first understanding is that the community's principles are put under any, and as much, critical scrutiny possible. This, what Norman Daniels calls '*wide* reflective equilibrium' (Daniels 1996: 6, 22–6), is indeed undertaken by Walzer, especially when he delivers so many anthropological examples.

The second understanding is that a theory should entail raising new questions and offering radical changes as solutions to problems.[15] I think that in this sense Walzer has been radical indeed. It is rather surprising therefore that mainstream liberals accuse Walzer, a social democrat who proposes radical change in American conceptions of justice, and subscribes to very egalitarian policies, of not being radical enough. And yet, there may be doubt as to how critical such philosophizing can be, given the existence of a third understanding of what it is to be radical.

Consider environmental philosophy. Suppose the philosopher wants to criticize policies such as the destruction of rain forests, the extinction of animals, the contamination of soil. Since the philosopher should regard his role as holding a mirror to society and showing 'what it really is', he will probably seek to compare these deeds with, and weigh them against, other moral and metaphysical beliefs that the society holds. But in societies that rest on individualism and anthropocentrism, this mission may be too difficult. If the philosopher refers to, say, the Judeo-Christian belief of stewardship (man being 'nominated' by God as responsible for nature), developers could defend

---

[15] Notice that I do not mean that the changes should take the form of stepping outside the traditional ethics, such as is offered by many radical environmental philosophers who would like to change 'the whole system'. I think a theory can be radical enough without this. Indeed, as I claim in this chapter, sometimes being too radical in one's ethics to the point of stepping outside the common discourse may lead to one's not being able to be radical enough in politics (including being successful and achieving results).

their positions by referring to other metaphysical and basic moral beliefs. The environment is a 'resource', they will claim, and animals are inferior to human beings. Or they may also relate to the widely shared belief in 'the market'. The way we are with regard to environmental matters, they will claim, is not so distant from the way we want to be in general, or from our metaphysical beliefs.

Walzer answers this challenge. After giving several examples, he writes: 'Social criticism in maximalist terms can call into question, can even overturn, the moral maximum itself, by exposing its *internal tensions and contradictions*' (Walzer 1994: 47; emphasis added). Quite right. But herein lies the problem. It makes contextual reflective equilibrium radical enough, but uses the wrong criteria (for being radical) from the point of view of environmental philosophy. The criteria to which the philosopher is committed according to this approach are only coherency and consistency. The internal tensions and contradictions make the 'maximum itself' less appealing, particularly in the eyes of other philosophers or those who are able to follow these contradictions and who tend to think that if a theory contains logical tensions then something is wrong. I do not want to dismiss the importance and the radicalism of this. But a theory can be wrong or not radical enough in other terms. It can be wrong if the tension is not internal but external—when applied to real cases. A theory can be perfectly coherent and consistent, but not relevant! And it is here that the additional meaning to 'radically critical' comes in, a meaning that is highly important in political (hence in environmental) philosophy.

A theory in political philosophy should lack 'external tensions': it should relate to real cases and should be relevant to real life. To do this, it should also arise from the cases in question. The best way to achieve this would be to start with the activists and their dilemmas. Hence an environmental philosophy theory should derive from extended sources, i.e. not only from the laid-back philosopher or anthropological explorer, but from the general public as well. It is therefore a theory that reflects the actual philosophical needs of the *activist* seeking to convince by appealing to practical issues, and not necessarily the philosophical needs of the philosopher, who convinces others by appealing to consistency and simplicity (despite the fact that the more coherent, consistent, etc., the environmental theory is, besides being relevant, the better it is). Naturally, the philosopher should not take the value of the activists' claims for granted; their intuitions, arguments, claims, and theories should also be scrutinized.[16] However, the fact that they need to be critically examined does not affect the main point: that the activists' intuitions, claims, and theories ought to be the starting point for a philosophy aimed at policy

---

[16] For example, in de-Shalit (1995a) I analyse the popular claim in favour of considering the rights and needs of future generations, and although at the end I find that environmental policies could be based on claims for transgenerational justice, I think that the popular version of this thought is far from being consistent or coherent; see also the interesting discussion of how environmental organizations address the general public in Merchant (1992: 159–63).

change. As such, environmental philosophy theory is *radical in a third sense*, in that it derives from, and speaks to, those previously denied access to the formation of the morality of our institutions (since, at the time, only 'professional' philosophy counted), and in that it derives from issues previously marginalized by what has been considered the 'real' or 'important' issues on the moral agenda. (In the case before us, these would be growth, economical considerations, etc.)

This is a different sort of radical criticism, which, I am afraid, Walzer's model of contextual reflective equilibrium almost achieves, but not quite. Walzer does mention non-professional philosophers joining the social discourse regarding norms and values. When he writes about those who 'read the texts', he adds a footnote: 'I mean readers in the widest sense . . . members of what has been called the "interpretive community" ' (Walzer 1987: 30, fn. 21). But there is a difference here: for Walzer, these people are not necessarily the previously marginal parts of society—he has in mind poets, novelists, architects, and so forth (1994: 52)—whereas I suggest that everybody can be included. The role of the philosopher, then, is to be sensitive to arguments from activists and the general public, and to raise the discourse to a high level of excellence. The philosopher can do this by *refining* the argument put forward by activists and the public and then weighing it against the public's intuitions and other beliefs. Of course, a theory can originate in the philosopher's mind, but then it should be regarded as one theory among many that arise from the public. The philosopher is a member of that public.

Indeed, there are environmental movements in many countries. They vary (Jamison *et al.* 1990; Talshir 1998); but they all consist of very articulate individuals, and they all conduct lively and very interesting debates. In some countries these forums of debates are even financed and supported by public (state) money. It seems simply arbitrary to divide the discourse between professional philosophers (e.g. those paid by the university) and amateur ones. The division should be between well and badly constructed arguments. Moreover, not only are there many interesting intuitions and many good arguments made by the general public and the milieu of environmental activists, but also it is extremely important that professional philosophers bend their ears to the voices of those who are active; the latter know the real philosophical problems emerging from the political and social debate. It is only by this interaction and interchange of intuitions and theories that environmental philosophy is able to make any impact on politics. It is only when the philosopher realizes that she is 'professional' not by having 'better' intuitions, but rather by having the skills and the means (including time), to devote herself to a profound reflection—i.e. the formation of a proper theory—about the intuition. Only then will philosophers have an impact on policies—once they have taken the intuitions and theories current in societies seriously. I call this third model of political philosophy 'public reflective equilibrium'. I shall first characterize this model and then argue why it best suits environmental philosophy.

The process of public reflective equilibrium starts from within: with the philosopher inside her community. The philosopher then studies the intuitions and theories that exist within the given society and analyses 'popular' theories with a view to *refining* them. The theories and intuitions are then subject to various critical scrutinies, including some 'imported' from other communities.[17] After this comes the search for an equilibrium between the intuitions, principles, or theories, all scrutinized critically. Another difference from the other models is that the critique addresses not only internal criteria—consistency, coherency, simplicity—but also the external criteria—whether the theory explains what must be done, whether it relates to actual problems, and whether the intuitions tie in with other, moral and metaphysical, beliefs about policies.

At this point it should be clarified that the philosopher practising the public reflective equilibrium should not offer her services to just every activist or group. For example, she may refuse to refer to, and help by criticizing, fascist groups, and rightly so. This may suggest that there is a 'preliminary' stage in the public reflective equilibrium, and that this stage involves a mechanism of private reflective equilibrium, whereby the philosopher analyses the theories at stake according to her own theory and intuitions. This is true. However, it does not imply that public reflective equilibrium is impossible. All it indicates is that a preliminary stage of filtering is inevitable, as a means of selecting which theories and intuitions are reasonable and which ones are not. The point, however, is that following this stage the philosopher applies the mechanism of public reflective equilibrium to a large variety of what she may now call 'reasonable' theories. Even now, it is important to remember, the philosopher does not step outside the normative arena: she may still criticize these theories and intuitions.

Public Reflective Equilibrium and Environmental Philosophy

Now that we have seen the process of public reflective equilibrium, the question arises: Why is public reflective equilibrium a better way of philosophizing with regard to environmental policies? I argue that it is not relativist: it is successful means of constructing a meaningful thin theory and at the same time a feasible thick theory; and it is radical enough for environmental policies. For

---

[17] Some people think that this is impossible, but I must ask readers *not* to come to hasty conclusions. I elaborate on this in Ch. 4.

these reasons this model is preferable to those of Rawls and Walzer. In addition, I argue, it is practice-oriented and at the same time it is not intolerant. Let us examine all these claims.

The public reflective equilibrium is not relativist because, although it relates to all arguments raised and takes them, at least initially, as being of equal moral worth, it does aim at forming a universal principle. Indeed, this universal principle is not an abstract derivation from an exercise in moral reasoning. It is a principle that in fact exists, even if it is only latent in the arguments people use. It derives from an analysis of the many deliberations occurring in real life with real human beings. By stepping outside the academic community, to include the discourse taking place within society in large, we can arrive at the real, universal, common principles that guide, and should guide, our environmental policies. By making the borders of the discourse even more flexible. we can reach a more authentic universal principle. At the same time, by examining activists' theories *critically*, comparing them with other activists' and philosophers' theories, we do not fall into the trap of relativism: acceptance of every theory as a certain community's theory.

This is also why this model of reflective equilibrium can achieve a meaningful thin principle. But it is also likely to achieve feasible thick principles. The reason is this: when we look for thick principles, we look for 'our' principles ('our' in a narrower, but stronger, sense). However, principles cannot be ours before we have persuaded others among ourselves. We cannot persuade before we engage in the debate, both because in order to persuade one literally needs to meet the other, but also because in order to persuade one must be aware of the arguments raised against one's position, so that they may be refuted. This is precisely what occurs in the case of public reflective equilibrium; the philosopher and the public in general all search for the widest possible range of intuitions, arguments, and theories. There is a greater chance of the philosopher encountering the range of arguments raised, which obviously increases the likelihood that the philosopher will not miss any challenge, but rather will meet these challenges and perhaps be able to persuade (or be persuaded). Thus, the philosopher becomes engaged in the widest possible community, and may then construct a meaningful thick morality.

Public reflective equilibrium also takes into account the positions of those previously excluded from the collective formation of morality. It regards public deliberation as the point of departure prior to the philosopher's input, and sees it as being of value. It is of value both because important arguments are raised and discussed and because the deliberation itself is of value. Admittedly, the deliberation is often confused, full of self-contradiction and rhetoric, and not terribly articulate. But so long as it is democratic (and non-democratic elements are avoided by certain institutional or legal arrangements), it is of value (see Chapter 5 below). Viewed this way, public reflective equilibrium is more radical than the private and contextual models of reflective equilibrium.

In addition, environmental philosophy is political philosophy, and in *this* sphere of philosophy reflective equilibrium should include not only weighing intuitions or theories, but also examining the practicality of the theory as well, because it is meant to be applied. But how can we weigh and relate to practicalities in the context of philosophical deliberation? It seems to me that the best way would be to rely on public and individual experiences when applying different philosophical theories to actual cases. It is therefore necessary to relate to the theories and intuitions of individuals who are, and have been, active in environmental matters. It is the philosopher's task to reflect upon the conclusions they derive from their experiences. The philosopher thus should analyse the moral codes and imperatives latent in the practicalities and actual deeds of environmental activists, as well as in the theories they develop. The next step should be comparing these with (the perhaps more sophisticated) theories put forward by environmental philosophers, and with intuitions and theories that we as a society have about other moral matters. The philosopher will then construct a theory, which will be taken on trial by the activists, as a process of weighing the principles against their intuitions and their theories. And so on.

Finally, reflective equilibrium with regard to environmental matters must be 'public' because, when promoting such drastic changes in a way of life, in public behaviour and moral attitudes—as indeed environmental philosophy should imply—one must be careful not to appear, and even more careful not to become, intolerant, impatient, too authoritative, and totalitarian. Now, my claim is that the process of public reflective equilibrium is far more tolerant towards the public than most animal rights theorists and environmental philosophers, who do not use the public reflective equilibrium mechanism.

As for animal rights theorists, my claim seems obvious now that I have discussed their theories. Many of them ignore the public's attitudes to 'rights'— not only animal rights but also human rights. However, I also wish to stress that a similar critique is true with regard to environmental philosophers in general. I think that we are allowed to tell somebody that his morality is wrong (or that there is something wrong with his personality) only after he has gone through a process of reflective equilibrium, i.e. after he has been made aware of the principles and theories we think are right, and has weighed them against his previous intuitions, and has not, apparently, accepted the principles that seem right, or moral, to us. The claim concerning this person would then be something along these lines: 'You are guided by personal views which ignore the impersonal', or 'You are guided by mistaken intuitions without recognizing their falsity when you are shown the theory that proves you wrong.' But most environmental philosophers, mainly those who rely on the notion of 'intrinsic value', accuse people of immoral judgements simply on the basis of their lack of an intuition (regarding the 'intrinsic value'). Arne Naess says that everybody will eventually achieve this intuition if they experience the same experiences that he experienced in his mountain hut (Naess 1989: 1–23). He even calls his theory, which is based on this experience, 'ecosophy', to distinguish it from philosophy. Holmes Rolston argues that if you walk in the mountains and see the woods you will understand the idea of intrinsic value. Fine. But can we accuse those who haven't done so, or who have done so but are still not 'enlightened', of being immoral? If we do not use reasoning to explain, how can we blame? We cannot blame them, not only because it is not fair, but also because intuitions might be misleading. Consider the following evidence.

In the summer of 1994 I was walking with my wife and children in Wales, with which, coming from another continent, I was not very familiar. After travelling for a long time in south England, where all land is cultivated, I was very pleased and surprised to come across a completely wild, untouched area. It was clear that our children sensed something—although at that time they were really too young to think rationally or theorize about anything. But the beauty of the landscape was incredible. We suddenly found ourselves in the middle of nowhere, facing bare mountains; below us was a magnificent lake. The combination of the rocky and bare mountains, the deep blue water, and the huge trees surrounding the lake, the cry of the birds above us—all summed up to sheer happiness, a sense of liberty; and, as I say, even the children could sense it. When we took a break I talked enthusiastically about intrinsic value in nature, about the beauty of the virgin, untouched, wild lake, about Naess's book, and I finished by asserting that all one has to do is 'see this lake and feel it in one's guts'. I remember that my wife was a bit more sceptical, but this, I thought, was just because she had not been aware of these works of Naess, Rolston, and other environmental philosophers, who based their theories on intuitions, and whom I considered to be the founding fathers of environmental ethics. It was not, I thought, because she could not sense this intrinsic value, or that she would not distinguish between wilderness and cultivated land. We continued walking, with me praising wilderness, and talking about how it was the lake itself that spoke to my mind, and how I now realized what I should have realized a long time ago.

What a great disappointment it was when after a short walk we saw, at the bottom of the valley, where the 'lake' ends, a huge dam, and a group of Japanese tourists taking photos of the fantastic, incredible, dam. It was not a natural lake, there was no wilderness—just technology and man-made objects.

This story—I have not invented it—points to the possibility that intuitions can mislead. The story-teller thinks about the intrinsic value of nature. He suggests to his family that, now that they 'sense' it, there is no need for a theory. Intuition, he believes, has been sufficient to prove this. Unfortunately, while thinking that he was sensing nature at its best, he was actually facing technology at its best. Thus, it was misguided for him to infer from what he saw and felt a generalization about value in nature. In other words, his intuition had misled him.

Now it is true that, if one has many experiences, the intuition may be more 'correct'; however, to reach this overall intuition, one actually needs a theory to help distinguish between intuitions that are/might be/have been misleading, and those upon which one can rely. This is especially so if one blames the other for not sharing the same intuitions. In other words, we must allow the process of reflective equilibrium to occur. Indeed, the public reflective equilibrium model is more cautious with regard to, and less intolerant towards, the general public. The reason for this is that this model is never satisfied with limited intuitions: it prefers considering as many intuitions as possible (that is, including those intuitions held by the general public), and weighing them against theories. It therefore treats others' intuitions with respect.

To conclude, the model of public reflective equilibrium differs from the previous two in several aspects. First, for Walzer and Rawls and Nagel, social criticism takes place in tranquillity. Nagel even goes as far as to compare a sort of 'objective', ideal, philosophizing as a 'view from nowhere'. Rawls imagines reflective equilibrium as a process involving detachment which reaches the stage of voluntary 'ignorance' concerning one's roots, belonging, relationships, social ties, and political standpoint. A good theory, contends Rawls, is one that is neutral. But this position of tranquillity is also shared by Walzer. When he compares self-criticism with social criticism, he writes: 'Self-criticism for the philosopher is much like social criticism [for the philosopher]: it is a kind of reflection in tranquillity, a scrutiny of the self *sub specie aeternitatis*. I step back, detach myself from my self . . .' (Walzer 1994: 89). Even if it is from within, as Walzer claims, social criticism still arises by one's stepping back, by allowing oneself a perspective drawn from the rational, without too emotional and active an involvement.

Contrary to the positions adopted by Rawls and Walzer, the model of public reflective equilibrium requires a philosopher who is deeply involved and engaged, who not only theorizes the norms of society, but also takes the theories in the common discourse seriously. She must be sensitive to the arguments, pick those that are well defined, and analyse them as part of her social criticism. She will regard the act of criticism as an exchange between herself, activists, and the general public, rather than primarily with academics or philosophers. She will regard her role as empowering the people with arguments and words. This is why the chapter's title refers to 'the social role of the philosopher'. However, society also has a key role to play in the philosophical discourse: it must supply the initial argumentation, and then reflect on the philosopher's ideas—just as the philosopher reflects on ideas held and expressed—either in words (theory) or in action (practice), by the rest of society. Thus, while in the first two models society remains outside the philosophical discourse, in this model it is inside it; and, while in the first two models the philosopher is outside society, in this model the philosopher is part of society. (Hence 'the philosophical role of society' in the title.) The only difference between the philosopher and the rest of the community is that the philosopher leads the discourse, in the sense that she is committed to certain standards.

Before continuing, I would like point out a possible challenge to my argument so far. I have claimed that environmental philosophers should decide how to persuade the public of the need for environmental policies. It could, however, be argued that many of these philosophers are convinced that animals have rights, or that there is intrinsic value in nature (I discuss this idea in depth in the next chapter), and they may feel they have to discuss this, as a mission. They don't want to give up persuading people about animal rights or intrinsic value, and they don't want to 'sell out' just in order to persuade. It seems (the argument would continue) that I might expect these philosophers to suppress their ideas and feelings. However, philosophers should be loyal to their ideas and thoughts as well: they should be authentic; their role is not merely to persuade for the sake of forming a majority of well-informed citizens.

I need of course to emphasize that this is not what I expect philosophers to do. Indeed, I think that a place does exist for environmental ethics and meta-ethics and that there is also a time to discuss issues bearing no relation to policies. However, environmental philosophers cannot escape the need to engage in real-life public deliberation because what they discuss is not wholly 'academic'.[18] The issues at stake are crucial both to human beings and their welfare, and to ecosystems and the state of the environment. The ecological crisis is not a question that can be discussed in tranquillity, and one cannot experiment with thinking about it for too long. There is a strong and urgent need for some thoughts and theories that are oriented towards institutions and policies. So, while accepting that environmental ethics and meta-ethics reflect sincere and authentic concerns, and that these concerns should be voiced, as an important part of this debate, I would stress that these cannot *replace* political theory concerning the environment. Such theory is vital for obvious reasons.

---

[18] I often wonder why the term 'academic' stands for ideas and theories that are not relevant to real-life problems.

2

Where Philosophy Meets Politics: The Concept of the Environment

The previous chapter analysed the way in which several environmental philosophers have neglected political theory with regard to the environment. They seem to argue that environmental ethics is sufficient. I suggest that part of the reason for this is that these scholars fail to distinguish between environmental ethics (questions about the moral grounds for environmental attitudes) and political theory (questions about institutions and environmental policies). However, other environmental philosophers have also failed to distinguish between the two, though they sometimes claim to be addressing environmental ethics, whereas in fact they are engaged in political—or psychological—theorizing. The problem here is that their political theory is not necessarily related either to environmental policies or to the institutions that protect the environment: rather, they are concerned with psychological and cultural changes, some of which are meant to replace politics altogether. It is to these schools of thought that I now wish to turn.

Introduction

It is often claimed that we humans abuse the environment. But what does this actually mean? We may be referring to one or more of the following: depletion of resources, extinction of species, use of animals for scientific experiments (vivisection), pollution of rivers, the air, the soil. Scientists will refer to the 'environment' as a *system of ecosystems*, and will charge our interference in the world's ecosystems as being both too great and too dangerous. Not surprisingly, this is the view of both Green activists (Porritt 1984: 4) and environmental philosophers (Brennan 1988; Rolston 1994a: 77–82; Callicott 1986: 308). Philosophers often add that treating an object as if it were a mere instrument is at least one, if not the main, component of abuse.

Now, if we accept that the environment is a system of ecosystems, it ceases to be a single object—as, say, in the case of a tree, a person or a book—and becomes instead a matter of relationships. Some may prefer to call it a 'community', while others describe it as a 'system'. Whatever the term, all agree that the 'environment' involves relationships. But to return to what the philosophers mean when they say that we abuse the environment: how can one abuse a relationship? Does it make sense to claim that 'relationships' are treated instrumentally and that this treatment is wrong because it is *instrumental*? Well, perhaps it could be argued that not only objects can be the subject of abuse. For example, trust can be abused. But in fact, when we speak of 'trust being abused', we really mean that a certain person's trust has been abused, i.e. that the person who trusted has been abused. In that case, we may wonder when it makes sense to claim that the 'environment' is being abused, or treated merely as an instrument. One of the contentions in this chapter is that such a claim may be made only when we relate to the individuals living in the environment rather than to the environment as a whole. However, many environmental philosophers have in mind the environment as a whole when they talk about 'value', or when they protest about humans treating the environment instrumentally. I suspect that some of the arguments may be misguided and that this has affected the tendency among the general public to dismiss arguments put forward by environmental philosophy with regard to policy-related discourse.

I will return to this claim towards the second half of this chapter. But first I wish to examine a further, related, claim: namely, that there is another way of treating something instrumentally, i.e. when one uses a new interpretation of a concept that is different from the conventional one in order to re-interpret the normative significance of another object or concept—for example when we claim to be talking about one thing but are in fact talking about another. I call this attitude *conceptual instrumentalism*.

This is therefore the first issue raised in this chapter. I argue that many environmental philosophers have done just this; i.e., they use the *concept* of the 'environment' in a political and instrumental manner, in order to talk about something else, and thereby to evoke certain political (not necessarily 'ecological') attitudes. I reach this conclusion after examining the ramifications of an understanding of the concept of the environment as a system of ecosystems or relationships. Again, because environmental philosophers have taken this position, and directed their views towarda certain political—*but not necessarily environmental*—goals, while claiming to discuss environmental philosophy, their theories have lacked relevance in terms of the argumentation put forward in the political, real-life, debate on the environment.[1]

---

[1] Let me just remind readers that I do not oppose political theory in the context of the environment: on the contrary. However, mixing environmental ethics with political theory and pretending to discuss the environment while discussing other goals (e.g. psychological changes) confuses the general public and limits the credibility of environmental philosophy.

So, in what follows I will explain the notion of 'conceptual instrumentalism', and argue that the 'environment' is indeed a description of relationships and that we cannot therefore conceive of it objectively, but only through interpretation and language, which in this case is political.[2] I further claim that several currents of thought in environmental philosophy are to be blamed for conceptual instrumentalism, since they use the 'environment' to promote political ideas related to non-environmental issues.[3] Next, I discuss the implications of the claim that the environment is a description of relationships in mainstream environmental philosophy and return to the argument that environmental philosophy ought to be considering objects within the environment, rather than the environment as a whole. Finally, I conclude on a more optimistic note and maintain that we should not jump to the hasty conclusion that environmental philosophy lacks validity and relevance. Nevertheless, I feel that there is a price to be paid: namely, that we must learn to distinguish between environmental ethics and meta-ethics on the one hand, and the political theory regarding the institutions most likely to protect the environment on the other.[4]

Economic and Conceptual Instrumentalism

Economic instrumentalism is of course a widely recognized concept, and I will not be discussing it here in any detail. It often stands for a situation in which the valuer seeks exclusively economic objectives, or, where the object valued is treated as a means to economic benefit for the valuer. Examples of this phenomenon are the evaluation of African elephants solely in terms of the income they generate in the ivory trade, the rapid development of historically important or aesthetic urban centres with the construction of huge complexes in their place, the idea that we may evaluate the lives of seals in economic terms (e.g. the value of their lives equals the price of their fur), and so on.

---

[2] This is not to say that some of the elements in the environment, i.e. individuals and species, do not have objective existence or that they are not real (see Rolston's answer to this claim: 1994b: 22). Rather, I argue that the true meaning of the term is different from that often ascribed to it.

[3] I mainly discuss Deep Ecology and ecofeminism. I do not discuss all currents of thought in environmental philosophy, because my point is not to evaluate which is more coherent or consistent and so forth, but rather to exemplify my claim.

[4] In fact, I wish to postulate something that is not far from Andrew Light's argument (1994a: 3) with regard to the concept of 'wilderness'. He claims that 'wilderness is a term whose reference is historically dependent on the social context in which it is used, and may be too culturally loaded to represent anything of foundational moral significance . . .' (see also Light 1994b: 140). He therefore draws a conclusion that theorists should avoid 'appealing to wilderness in the foundation of an environmental ethic'. My line of argument is parallel with regard to the concept of the 'environment', but I later suggest theoretical conclusions that are, I think, more far-reaching.

While the above examples probably sound familiar to those interested in environmental matters, the notion of conceptual instrumentalism may be novel.

Outside the environmental arena, we find that conceptual instrumentalism is, in fact, quite common in the world of politics. For example, when George Bush accused his presidential opponent, Michael Dukakis, of being a 'liberal' during the 1988 campaign, what he meant to say was: 'softie'—weak, unstable, hesitant, ambiguous, etc. But we all know that this does not describe liberalism.[5] Bush may have referred to 'liberalism', but in fact he was out to say something about Dukakis. In his use of the term, he disregarded its definition, and distorted its meaning to say something quite different about a specific individual. He did this by capitalizing on a certain amount of confusion and misunderstanding on the part of his audience. Another example would be Tony Blair's assertion that he is a 'socialist' while presenting an agenda that is the closest the British Labour Party has ever come to a Conservative manifesto. It may be argued that he uses the term 'socialism' in order to put forward non-socialist ideas while at the same time speaking to those who regard themselves as socialists.

However this is a book about environmental philosophy, and my next example therefore relates to the environment (de-Shalit 1995*b*). In the short history of the Zionist movement there have already been three interpretations of the concept of the 'environment', two of which at least have been entirely political. The attitude of the first Jewish immigrants to Palestine to their new environment was one of anxiety. Coming from Europe, they found a new world that seemed to them totally alien. Thus they regarded the sandy dunes, the desert and the swamps as a threat to their survival. The leadership chose the route of romanticizing the environment and the immigrants' relationship to it. They claimed that the reunion of Jewish soil with the Jewish soul would serve to emancipate the Jews from their bourgeois character. However, when this strategy failed, it was followed by a second interpretation, whereby the new environment was to be 'conquered' to make it more tame and human-friendly. The environment, which hitherto had been described in political speeches and school textbooks as 'nothingness', 'emptiness', 'loneliness' 'desolation', 'ruin', and 'dreariness', thus became an object to be 'conquered', 'suppressed', 'made to flourish', and 'civilized'. These interpretations, in which the environment played the role of 'emancipating' the Jews, 'abolishing their alienation', or binding (in the political sense of the concept) the Jews to their new land, in fact treated the environment instrumentally. In other words, Zionism adopted different interpretations of the environment in order to cre-

---

[5] Notice I do not claim that we all agree on what liberalism is. Rather, I maintain the more modest claim that we know what it is not.

ate a new type of Jew, or to prove that Zionism was right. In so doing, it constantly redefined the environment.[6]

This example is given not as a critique of Zionism, but in order to raise the question of whether it is at all possible to think of the environment in a non-political manner. It seems that something happens to the concept of the 'environment' once one moves from the scientific to the social discourse. (As explained in Chapter 1, we should consider the philosophical discourse to be part of the social.) Instead of being an object that is scientifically observed, the environment becomes an object of political discussion. This leads to the subordination of the environment to political preoccupations, and to the abandonment of an objective and neutral conception of the environment. Consider, for example, the concept of 'the British minister for the environment', or even 'the British environment', as if the environment has artificial borders. At the end of the day, what is 'British' about this environment?[7]

What I have just been describing may seem inevitable; when we humans come to enjoy, or treat, or even conserve, the environment we discuss it as a public good, and hence by definition it becomes a political object. But is the phenomenon of conceptual instrumentalism restricted to the general public, rather than common to everybody, including environmental philosophers? I doubt this, though we would expect it to be the case. Before continuing, however, I would like to distinguish myself from the current post-modern approach to environmental philosophy, according to which the 'world' is 'constituted' by diverse cultures, and therefore it is epistempologically impossible for humans to have non-instrumental knowledge of the environment: humans know nature through socially constructed science. As argued below, I think that objects in the environment have an objective existence, and that there should be an objective understanding of the 'environment'. This thinking however is absent from most of the current philosophical works on the environment, for reasons I explore below.

The Environment and Language

It is widely believed that the 'true' (or most neutral) notion of the 'environment' is the one held by scientists. Some people question this. In a brilliant article, Shrader-Frechette and McCoy (1994) argue that so-called 'scientific' notions of the environment presuppose certain normative commitments, and

[6] The third interpretation is a more scientifically based environmentalism. On the definition of this attitude, see de-Shalit (1996).

[7] Notice that 'British' may be constituted partly by this environment, but the environment is not constituted by the political and/or cultural term 'British'. See also Dryzek (1997: 3–6) for a discussion of how concepts related to the environment have changed in the past 30 years.

that 'environmental *values* can, and do, contribute to ecological hypotheses'; environmental values influence the practice of the science of ecology. John O'Neill (1998*a*) also doubts whether there is any 'true' (in the sense of neutral) notion of the environment. He claims that the 'environment' is pre-scientific, pre-theoretical; therefore one might not expect science to offer a privileged characterization of the 'environment'. O'Neill goes on to claim that he does not question the objectivity of science, nor does he deny realism about science; but, while he concedes that there are some concepts, e.g. those used to refer to natural objects, such as water or copper, that science does establish a privileged definition for, the environment does not fall into this conceptual category. He contends that any talk of 'environments' is inevitably elliptical: it is always possible to ask 'whose environment?' or 'the environment of which individual or community?'[8]

And yet, it seems to me that we can still try to point to the core of the scientific, non-normative notion of the environment, especially if we relate to the difference between biology and ecology. The difference basically is that the former describes objects in nature without reference to other objects to which they are related, whereas the latter describes and analyses relationships, rather than objects. This characteristic of the environment is crucial to an understanding of the concept of the 'environment'. Indeed, if we look at the dictionary, 'environment' is defined as 'conditions' (*Oxford Dictionary of Current English*), or as 'the aggregate of surrounding things, conditions, or influences, especially as affecting the existence or development of someone or something' (*Random House Dictionary*). In textbooks, ecologists define their science as 'the research of the forms of balance in nature' (Arthur 1990: 39, 226; Williams 1964). And notice that 'balance in nature' is not the same as 'nature'. The 'balance' here is defined in terms of persistence (existence over a long period of time), stability (ability to return to a regular pattern of existence after a change caused by a disturbance or interference), and robustness (continuous stability). As for ecology, it is a science that seeks to understand the process within the biosphere. Hence an ecological theory is a theory about the nature of this process. Now, processes, influences, and conditions, or forms of balance, are not objects; rather, they describe relationships. (Notice, again, that I do not claim that they do not exist objectively: my claim is much more modest, namely that they are not objects, as, for instance, a tree is.)

Thus, the environment is scientifically characterized as relationships. But what about the social description of these relationships? Can we assume that relationships may be described objectively, and hence that there is an object-

---

[8] However, I think that the same can be said about concepts such as the 'state'. One could ask 'whose state?' etc., and yet this should not imply that science cannot and should not supply an objective definition of the 'state'. Admittedly, when the concept of the 'state' is used within an ideological discourse, it will be a biased use of the term. But this, of course, ties in with what I would like to claim about the 'environment'.

ive understanding of what we mean when we say the 'environment'? (Notice that by objective, I mean neutral and unbiased. Of course, I ask this question not in the ontological, but rather in the political sense.) We define it, I have argued, as relationships within and between ecosystems. This is indeed object-ive and neutral. But what happens in the *social* discourse when we describe the environment? I would like to argue that when the environment is discussed in the social discourse it is not described objectively. This might be due to two reasons:

1. it may be that no set of relationships can be described objectively in the social discourse; this may or may not be true, but even if it is false,
2. it may be that there is something about the notion of the 'environment' which makes it impossible to describe objectively.

Let us first examine relationships in general. This in itself is a controversial goal, since it has been argued that the insider—whose relationship is described—cannot describe it objectively if she remains an insider, i.e. does not take the view of an outsider. Furthermore, the question has been raised as to whether it is possible for an outsider to characterize relationships object-ively. Those who doubt it claim that it is impossible to be an outsider when it comes to relationships. The point is that one cannot describe a certain rela-tionship (X) without having a certain other relationship (Y) with one or more of the parties in the described relationship X. The relationship Y does not need to be continuous: it is enough that, at the moment of describing, the outsider calls this or that party PP rather than ZZ (assuming that both ZZ and PP are proper names for this party; e.g., I am known as Dr de-Shalit *or* Avner). But if this is true, then to some extent one automatically becomes an insider, in the sense that one has a view—indeed, a relation—to the described party, and therefore is unable to describe the relationship in an objective and unbiased manner.

Here is an example: suppose I wish to describe my wife's relationships with her parents. It is obvious that I see my wife in a certain way (my; wife), and I have a certain interest in these relationships. This is also true, I believe, with regard to more complex matters. If I wanted to describe the relationship between the Scots and the English, I could not detach myself from my own relationship with the English. This is often because one has a certain relation-ship, ranging from ethnic to ideological, with at least one element in the sys-tem of relationships one is describing. But even if we do not have such relationships Y, we are unable to describe the relationship X objectively. This is because the language used to describe the particular relationship determines the content of our interpretation. Do I describe the relationship between James and his wife Anne, or between James and his spouse, or between Anne and her spouse, or between Anne and her husband? or perhaps her partner, or friend? In general, it is claimed, relationships cannot be described without one's personal, subjective outlook being revealed through the words chosen to describe the relationships.[9]

At this point, this argument may be challenged by drawing a distinction between social and natural relationships. Thus, it could be claimed, the relationships between a deer, the grass it eats, and the nearby lake can be described both neutrally and objectively. Moreover, physical phenomena such as magnetic fields may also be defined as relationships and described objectively. So, in response, the claim that relationships cannot be described objectively should be modified by adding that this claim refers to relationships between moral agents. This then rules out relationships such as magnetic fields. But more important is the general claim about natural relationships. Here I wish to re-emphasize that this claim is *not* the post-modern one whereby everything is political and subjective. It does not claim that relationships are always political, nor does it claim that relationships can never be described or stated objectively: rather, it offers an empirical observation concerning the limits of the social discourse. When we apply this claim to our context, we could agree that scientists have a neutral and objective model of the relationships within the environment (at least they should have one, if we accept the above thesis of Shrader-Frechette), but at the same time we could argue that, once the term 'environment' moves from the scientific to the social discourse, its understanding becomes subject to the values, emotions, and political goals attached to that discourse. These values, feelings, and goals are part of the context within which this discourse takes place.[10]

Thus, when one says 'this is a lion and that is an antelope', one assumes we all know what each is, and that there is an objective understanding of this statement. When a scientist states that the relationships between them is such that the lion chases the antelope and eats it, this too is neutral. But, once this statement is made within a social and philosophical discourse, it assumes other meanings related to certain ethical or political goals. Consider the sentence above in the context of a Walt Disney or National Geographic film. Or think of this: would the person describing these relationships wish us to do something about it because, for example, antelopes are becoming an endangered species, or does he mean that we should not interfere because this is nature, and humans are best kept out of it? Or does this person want us to stay out of it because this way we can overcome our speciesist attitudes?

Notice that the move from the objective to the non-objective is not related to the person who talks; a philosopher is capable of being objective in many circumstances, just like the scientist. Instead, it has to do with the concept of

---

[9] Readers may think this is an argument in favour of political correctness (PC), but it is not. It only describes the difficulty, without claiming that PC is the answer.

[10] A good example might be the question of why and how we decide upon the preservation of certain species or individual animals. Why, for example, do governments and environmentalists pay so much money to save dolphins rather than certain snakes and frogs whose extinction is far more crucial for ecosystems?

the environment as a set of relationships and the use of this concept within a specific discourse. The word 'lion' describes an object that can be defined objectively; the relationships between the lion and the antelope can be defined objectively within the scientific discourse, but not within the social discourse. It is the context of language and discourse that affect the objectivity of the meaning.

One might still challenge this line of argument, claiming that there *are* cases in which the observer is not an insider. Well, perhaps this is so. But then, in the case of the environment, there is something about this particular concept that makes it difficult to describe it objectively: namely, that we are all inside it. You and I discuss the environment, but we are also part of it. And if we are insiders, can we describe it objectively? So if the person describing the environment is part of the environment, and if, as Rolston claims, this person's organs are 'natural', and hence also part of the environment (Rolston 1988: 244),[11] then it follows that the environmental philosophers' claim to be objective about nature (their capacity to get outside of their self-interested reference frames), and their argument that they respect nature because they regard it objectively and without instrumental intentions (perhaps even neutrally), is at least questionable. (I do not question the fact that they respect nature, but rather that this is because they can be objective.) In that respect, the environment is a *contested concept*, just like other concepts in moral and political philosophy, e.g. liberty, justice, and so forth.

Political Uses of the 'Environment' among Environmentalists

Accordingly, the description of relationships, and hence the use of the term 'environment', besides not being objective or neutral, is often biased, ideological, or political. Notice that my claim is not against discussing environmental matters politically. On the contrary: this is highly necessary. Rather, I claim that the concept itself—the 'environment'—has become political. It is thus subject to political goals that are not necessarily related to the environment. Moreover, while pretending to discuss environmental ethics, many philosophers have been discussing non-environmental goals.

The amazing thing is that the politicization of the concept of the environment is legitimized by well-meaning environmental philosophers, who seem to misunderstand the consequences of their action. For example, they use the term 'ecology' to describe political attitudes (e.g. 'deep' ecology). In fact, they

[11] This actually means that, unlike the general case of relationships, where there are both insiders and outsiders to describe them, in the case of the environment there are only insiders, which makes objective description impossible.

are taking a 'scientific' term that belongs to one discourse and using it in another, without reference to the original ('scientific') meaning. For these scholars, nature and the environment are not a genuine 'telos' in the Aristotelian sense. Without being aware of it, they conceive of the 'environment' politically even when denying it. For example, following Deep Ecology, Andrew Dobson says we can learn from nature how to improve our human existence:

There is a strong sense in which the natural world is taken as a model for the human world . . . Many of ecologism's prescriptions for political and social arrangements are derived from a particular view of how nature 'is'. . . . The principal features of the natural world and the political and social conclusions or prescriptions that can be drawn from them are: diversity—toleration, stability and democracy; interdependence—equality; longevity—tradition; nature as 'female'—a particular conception of feminism.[12] (Dobson 1990: 24)

This is, in fact, a new conception of society and politics arrived at through a new understanding of the environment. The environment, of course, cannot teach us moral or political goodness, because it is amoral and apolitical. Nature is natural and politics is artificial. (I elaborate on this in Chapter 4.)

But Dobson (if he affirms this view) is clearly not alone. There are currents of thought among environmental philosophers which consistently use conceptual instrumentalism. I would like here to discuss two examples: Deep Ecology and ecofeminism. (Once again, I must emphasize that these are discussed as examples to my claim. The following does not intend to be a full analysis of these schools of thought.) With regard to ecofeminism, I believe I have a novel argument to put forward; as for Deep Ecology, which I have already touched on, I am widening a critique put forward by Andrew Light (1992; 1995). However, I do this not out of criticism for these theories, but rather as an illustration of my argument and my critique of the use of the term 'environment' in environmental philosophy.

'Deep Ecologists' put forward a theory that stands on two pillars: the first is their idea that human beings should stay out of the game when it is a matter of stability in nature—where a stable ecosystem is a system that is hardly

---

[12] This recalls the words of the famous English poet, William Wordsworth, who in 1795 wrote: 'One impulse from a vernal wood/ Can teach you more of man/ Of moral evil and of moral good/ Than all the sages can' (from *Lyrical Ballads*). To be precise, it is not clear whether Dobson puts forward his own ideas in this case or simply describes others' attitudes.

[13] Stability and changelessness are not always explicit but rather are implicit in their works. For example, Devall and Sessions (1985:145) talk about 'letting the river live', and assert that they 'envision humans living harmoniously in a world environment which is left natural' (p. 172). All Deep Ecologists relate to Leopold's phrase: 'A thing is right when it tends to preserve the integrity, stability and beauty of the biotic community'. Fox (1995) quotes James Hefferman: 'A thing is right when it tends to preserve the characteristic diversity and stability of an ecosystem'. Hefferman (1982) went on to claim that the stability of an ecosystem is an intrinsic value.

changed—and the other is their belief that if we act in this way we shall achieve a 'new self'.[13]

While these two ideas are interconnected,[14] the goal is not a different environment, but rather a change in 'life quality' (Naess and Sessions 1984), coupled with personal growth and improvement (Devall and Sessions 1985). Thus Naess's first principle of Deep Ecology rejects the concept of man-in-the-environment in favour of a relational image (Naess 1973: 95). But this is only a basis for a new conception of the subject, or the person. He uses the concept of the environment in order to put forward a different conception of the 'self', which is regarded as part of a total holism and the integration of all with all. Indeed, the idea of the extension of self to a self whose self-realization is part of an ecological whole—or, in Naess's words, the extension of the 'social self' to concepts of the 'ecological self' (Naess 1989)—is regarded by Deep Ecologists as one of their main contributions to philosophy.

But let us return to the initial postulate and the demand for a stable environment. A stable environment is, in fact, a stable system of ecosystems. But a stable ecosystem is not a system that does not change at all. The conception that an ecological system is stable when it does not change (as Deep Ecology implies) is a political, not a scientific, one. Indeed, it contradicts the scientific notion that an ecological system is stable when it is capable of regaining its equilibrium following any deviation. So, not every change is anti-environmental: only changes that alter the balance irreversibly should be considered immoral from the point of view of environmental philosophy. Thus, Deep Ecologists use the concept of a stable ecosystem instrumentally, revising its conventional (and, I would add, only reasonable) meaning.[15] Their theory is, therefore, a very original and important political (or psychological) theory, but not necessarily a genuine environmental one.

In fact, Deep Ecologists themselves declare that they are not interested in a value theory (axiology) or in a new moral theory. Theirs is an eco-sophy, not a philosophy. It is based on intuition and is subjective,[16] not 'rational' in the usual meaning of the term. When Henryk Skolimowsky compares eco-philosophy with what he calls 'present philosophy', he claims that, while present philosophy is spiritually dead, eco-philosophy is spiritually alive; that,

[14] As for possible connections with socialism, see Gottlieb (1995) and Eckersley (1995*a*).

[15] At this point, it is worth mentioning that the instrumental use of the term 'environment' and related terms by Deep Ecologists is even more extensive: they also re-interpret the concept of 'bio', as Richard Sylvan and David Bennet (1994; 99) argue. Naess and Sessions acknowledge that they use the term 'bio' in 'a more comprehensive, non-technical way to refer also to what biologists classify as "non-living"; rivers, landscapes, ecosystems'. Thus, 'bio' is used to mean both the living and the non-living, whereas it should stand for 'of life', 'of living organisms' (e.g. *Oxford Dictionary*). But of course, when one relates to rivers as 'bio' one breathes life into the river. It is thereafter so easy to claim that we have to respect the rivers: they are alive, after all.

[16] As David Rothenberg writes in the introduction to the book, 'The name [of this philosophy, eco-sophy-T] is said to represent [Naess's] mountain hut Tvergastein ('cross the stones') but it is its personal nature that is most important' (Naess 1989: 4).

while present philosophy is intolerant to trans-physical phenomena, eco-philosophy tolerates them (this represents a new and broader conception of the self); and that, while present philosophy is politically indifferent, eco-philosophy is politically aware (Skolimowsky 1992: 40–1). Warwick Fox, in his own defence of Deep Ecology, claims that the main concern of Deep Ecology is 'to express the *characteristic attitudes* which will be adopted by those who go along with the metaphysical teaching' of Deep Ecology (Attfield 1994: 120; see also Fox 1986, and Fox 1995: chs. 7 and 8 and app. B). Fox thinks that this teaching is metaphysical, but I am of the opinion, and I hope that my argument below proves this, that this is a *political* theory, which aims to change politics or, in its radical version, to replace current politics with *the theory of the new self*. Notice that I am not making a claim against metaphysics in general. Notice, also, that in the previous chapter I argued in favour of political theorizing on the subject of the environment. However, the argument here is twofold: first, that Deep Ecology seeks to replace politics with psychology; and second, and more relevant to this chapter, that Deep Ecology pretends to be a theory about the environment, but this is not necessary so. Consider the following paragraph in which Attfield (who is not a Deep Ecologist) summarizes the approach of Fox, one of the most interesting Deep Ecology philosophers :

The central tenets [of Deep Ecology] include . . . denying various classical dualisms . . . an enlarged conception of the *self*, such that the world is seen as part of the *self*; and an emphasis on *self*-realization, granted this enlarged conception of the *self*, such that any diminution of natural entities becomes a diminution of one*self*, and such that *self*-love comes to involve care for the world as for one*self*. (Attfield 1994: 121; emphasis added)

Is this a theory about the environment, or about the self? Does this reflect any sense of care for other species, or does it in fact discuss ourselves, allocating care for other species a merely instrumental role? Is it concerned with the environment, or does it represent an attitude that uses the concept of the environment in order to put forward a new conception of the self? Does it aim at the liberation of the environment or at the salvation of human kind?

Now, you could say that the Deep Ecologists are well-meaning individuals who do not want to use the environment instrumentally. I agree. But the point here is that in their approach, and in their attitude to the environment, there is a built-in tendency to subordinate the concept (not the components or the objects, e.g. the bee, the elephant, etc.) to other goals. The language, at any rate, indicates that the main target is a new self.

The idea of a new self has also been suggested by Rudolf Bahro, the leading German environmental theorist and Green Party member, who later taught philosophy at the Humbolt University in Berlin. The target for Bahro is not merely an environment-friendly world, but rather the abolition of the existing order, a 'world transformation', a 'new collective psyche', a 'spiritual renaissance', the 'rise of a new consciousness' and 'spiritualism'—emancipation from the logic of 'self-extermination' (Bahro 1994: 4, 14). He speaks of the need to change the 'basic psychological structure of Western humanity'; as he puts it at the start of his recent book, we should aim not at 'ecologising the boat [in which we live]' but at building 'new lifeboats' (Bahro 1994: 1). It seems that the goal here is the abolition of bourgeois democracy.[17] The *means*—to become green.

This is a 'politics of salvation' rather than of the environment, though the first step towards realizing this politics is by acknowledging the interconnect-edness of humans and nature. In Bahro's description of the new world, little is said about the condition of trees, rivers, animals, etc. A great deal however is said about the 'new spiritual authority . . . the invisible church, [which] will depend on the amount of inner space freed up from ego-control and waiting for restructuring' (Bahro 1994: 229–30). Under the title 'Overcoming Ecological Crisis', Bahro writes about 'transcending oneself' (1994: 250–65). We can thus say that, like many other Deep Ecologists, Bahro uses the concept of the environment instrumentally. The ecological crisis is another name for the psychological one, and as such relates to the environment instrumentally. Bahro sees the environment as a reflection of our consciousness: the damaged environment is the reflection of our current logic of 'self-exterminism'; the new environment will reflect the new psyche and our emancipated soul.[18]

One may ask: so what? Does it matter that Deep Ecology uses the term 'environment' differently from science? My answer is: it may not matter, as long as we recognize that this is indeed the case, that Deep Ecology is a polit-ical (or psychological) theory whose goals do not always seek to reform our attitudes about the environment, but rather seek to replace politics by a non-political system. If, however, Deep Ecology claims to respect the environment and treat it 'as it is', then this claim may be deceptive because environmental attitudes become a means of changing the 'system'. Their theory, then, is not about the moral grounds for respecting the environment, but about non-envi-ronmental goals.[19] If we understand this, it is clear at least why Deep Ecology has rarely, if at all, served as a rationale for environmental policies. The gen-eral public, including activists, may have sensed that, when they want to jus-tify recycling or the treatment of sewage, talks about the new psyche will not

[17] Bahro speaks openly against parliamentarism (1986: 156, 230), and states that the pol-itics he has in mind is 'not a question of democratic decision, but of natural necessity' (1994: 22).

[18] Indeed, Bahro actually admits the instrumental way in which he regards the environ-ment when he declares: 'There could scarcely be a harder test for our capacity for conscious-ness than the ecological crisis' (1994: 261). Just as Marx thought that, the more the industrial world causes social and economic tensions, the greater are the chances for a revolution, Bahro thinks that, the more the industrial world causes ecological disaster, the greater are the chances for psychological transformation, and so, ironically, the better it is.

[19] The reader may get the impression that I see a dichotomy between environmental and social goals. On the contrary: I think that many social goals tie in with environmental ones. However, in this section I analyse the instrumental use of the 'environment' in order to put forward social goals not necessarily linked to protecting the environment.

do. The deeper problem, I fear, is that, since Deep Ecology is rather dominant in environmental philosophy, many people in the general public conclude that 'this is environmental philosophy' and therefore that 'arguments taken from environmental philosophy in general will not suffice in real cases'.

The other current of thought I would like to examine as a general political theory rather than an environmental ethics is ecofeminism. (I wish to emphasize again that this is not a critique of ecofeminism, let alone of feminism, but rather an example of my argument. Actually, ecofeminism is much more diverse than the principles described here would indicate. As Karen Warren (1994: 1) writes, ecological feminism is an 'umbrella term'. And Ariel Salleh argues in her recent book (1997) that all 'ecofeminism' theories are political, and about politics.)

To begin with, ecofeminists claim that nature is female, pointing to ancient cultures which had a goddess of nature, the 'nurturing mother' (see Merchant 1995, though she discusses this as a metaphor). But, bearing in mind that the environment is a matter of relationships, does this claim have any meaning, apart from the assertion that certain relationships are female? And does this make any sense? 'Female' is an adjective that cannot be attached to relationships; the environment, then, can be neither female nor male.[20] So why do ecofeminists present this argument? The answer is that they would like us to rethink the relationships between the sexes through a reinterpretation of the environment. So it may be argued that these ecofeminists have a non-environmental motivation for discussing the environment. Again, this is legitimate and highly important, but at the same time, it must be recognized and acknowledged.

In order to make myself clear, let me emphasize that ecofeminism, as well as feminism, is an important and valid political theory. As such , it can also carry implications for environmental policies. For example, it may be true that the domination of women by men has been 'replaced', so to speak, by the human control of nature.[21] However, this is different from claiming that these attitudes of domination are basically the same and that therefore abolishing one will immediately abolish the other.

Val Plumwood's attack on Paul Taylor's *Respect for Nature* is a good example of the way several ecofeminists treat the environment. For Plumwood, it is another opportunity to expose the prejudiced, biased character of male-dominated ethics (and, I agree, it is more than reasonable to claim that ethics has traditionally been male-dominated and biased), and to offer a radical feminist theory concerning the place of women in the world. But the place given

---

[20] In fact, in languages where there must be some reference to gender, even though it may lack a gender meaning, the environment can be both. In Hebrew, for example, environment, soil, land, and the 'creation' (another name for nature) are female, whereas nature, landscape, and Earth are male. But all these nouns and their adjectives lack a real gender significance.

[21] I take it that this is part of the argument of Val Plumwood in her very interesting article (1988).

to the environment in her theory is only minor and instrumental (Plumwood 1991: 11). Plumwood complains that Taylor's 'respect for others' is not genuine, since he treats care (a concept described by many feminists, with good reason, as having been neglected in morality, politics, and *political* philosophy) as 'desire', and therefore as irrelevant to morality.

From this, Plumwood moves on to a criticism of male-dominated morality. The latter, she argues, treats 'feminine' emotions as essentially unreliable, untrustworthy, and hence morally irrelevant. Therefore a distinction is drawn between personal and particular values (mostly feminine) versus universality and impartiality. From here, the road leads us to a critique of Kantian ethics as chauvinistic.

Thus, ecofeminists see a connection between an instrumental attitude towards the environment (the view that the value of the environment lies in its usefulness to a 'privileged group', i.e. human beings), and instrumentalism towards women (the view that their value lies in their usefulness to a 'privileged group', i.e. men). Thus, they conceive of both the environment and women as passive within male attitudes (Plumwood 1991: 17). They may be right, but this is irrelevant to the present discussion because several ecofeminists are themselves instrumental towards the environment, when they use the concept to reveal the political injustice perpetrated on women, and the philosophical poverty of the 'self-interested individual presupposed in market theory':

The interests of such an individual . . . are defined as essentially independent of or disconnected from those of other people, and his or her transaction with the world at large consist of various attempts to get satisfaction for these predetermined private interests. Others are a 'resource', and the interests of others connect with the interests of such autonomous selves only accidentally or contingently. (Plumwood 1991)

At the same time, it is argued, this kind of instrumentalism is absent from feminist theory:

People do have interests that make essential and not merely accidental or contingent reference to those of others; for example when a mother wishes for her child's recovery, the child's flourishing is an essential part of her flourishing. (Chodorow 1979)

I am most sympathetic to this theory. But didn't we lose sight of the environment somewhere?

One might argue that I have misinterpreted ecofeminism, which is, in fact, a theory of moral relations with nature. But, while protesting against misinterpretations of ecofeminism, the ecofeminist Deborah Slicer recently argued that Fox and others who challenge ecofeminism have reduced ecofeminism to an environmental theory, which, she argues, is wrong: 'In our best forms [ecofeminists] examine the interconnected and mutually reinforcing oppression of women and nature in patriarchy . . . [and we construct] new versions of self' (Slicer 1995: 154).

Now, it may further be argued against me that the two—a change in the attitude of men to women, and a change in the attitude of human beings to nature—must go hand in hand. Ecofeminists therefore emphasize this connection and the need to change both modes of behaviour. This I agree with. I have even reasoned this way myself on the basis of empirical research (deShalit 1994*a*). But this is not the main point here. The point is that we must be aware of what takes place in the name of 'environmental' philosophy: namely, that we are being offered a feminist philosophy about the politics of gender relations. Now, morally or politically speaking, this may be positive – it can demonstrate how environmental philosophy can collaborate with other radical ideologies and theories (Sandilas 1995)—but we must realize that this is indeed what is happening. We must realize that often when people, including environmental philosophers, discuss the environment, they have in mind a political concept that already involves non-environmental political goals.

So what do many Deep Ecologists, ecofeminists, and others have in common? The fact is that these philosophers have political goals that are not necessarily related to pollution, sewage, radioactive radiation, waste disposal, the extinction of wild animals, or the keeping of balance in ecosystems. They are looking to say something about politics—from the definition of the self to the system of order (e.g. the chauvinistic male hierarchy). They cannot emancipate the environment, because relationships, being a matter of interpretation and language, cannot be 'emancipated'. The self, on the other hand, may be emancipated via a new interpretation of the environment. The working class and all citizens can be emancipated through a new interpretation of the environment. Women and, finally, everyone can be emancipated through a new understanding of the environment.[22]

Should We Dispense with Environmental Philosophy?

So far, my argument has been limited to the two examples discussed above, i.e. Deep Ecology and ecofeminism, two representatives of what Light refers to as 'environmental ontologists', i.e. those who base their theories on the 'inseparable ontological roots of humans and non-human nature' (Light 1995). However, I have also stated that I am not after a critique of their theories:

---

[22] I want to emphasize again that my argument is not against these theorists engaging in political theory; rather, my argument is that theorists should make it clear when they are discussing political (and not necessarily related to the environment) matters, and that they should refrain from using the 'environment' as a tool in these theories.

rather, an illustration of my argument concerning the 'environment' and its description through language. But if there is a problem here, what does it imply? Should all the environmental philosophers go back to their universities and suggest that their deans and rectors close their departments down? Should all environmental philosophers become political theorists? The answer, of course, is 'no'. Not all environmental philosophers have non-environmental political motives, and environmental ethics as an independent field of research is highly important. The reason Deep Ecology and ecofeminism fall into the trap of conceptual instrumentalism with greater ease is that they refer extensively to relations and relationships. The way to avoid making the environment *subservient to* other political goals is to avoid relating to it as a whole, i.e. to its relational aspect, and rather to relate to the individuals within the environment. This may be difficult because, as we have seen, the environment is a system of ecosystems, and as such, involves relationships. The issue, then, is how not to overemphasize the relational aspect. Deep Ecology and ecofeminism cannot do this because the essence of their theories rests on the relationships. This leads us to the question of whether mainstream environmentalism itself can avoid conceptual instrumentalism. Any mainstream environmental philosopher could come to me and say: 'OK, but does your argument have any bearing on us? Is it wrong or instrumental to maintain that, for instance, there is an intrinsic value in nature?' My answer to this would be as follows.

First, that I propose using the term 'environment' very cautiously; I believe that we should be aware of our conception of the 'environment', and that we should recognize our tendency to use it as a political idea, especially when trying to promote social change. Secondly, I would like to examine the implications of my argument in terms of the theory of intrinsic value.

Let me begin by elaborating on the point that we should be more careful when using the term 'environment'. This is no light request. It relates to the is–ought fallacy and to a tendency among several environmental philosophers to derive the 'ought' (moral and political behaviour) from the 'is' (the 'environment'). When discussing the ethics of relationships between human beings, philosophers are careful not to derive the 'ought' from the 'is', because the existing relationship (the 'is') already reflects a certain morality. Hence, philosophers should do more than simply justify our ways by clinging to the practice of a certain, already existing morality, on the grounds that we should follow it simply because it exists. *A minori ad majus*, they have to do more than describe and explain what happens. They have to supply normative justifications for (or against) it. But environmentalists may say that, with regard to environmental ethics, the 'is' (a certain model of the world, or of the environment) is not created by human beings but is given. It is not first constructed by humans, but is discovered. So it does not already reflect a certain morality. It may therefore be claimed that *environmental* philosophers do not have to be so careful with the is–ought distinction. Thus, Rolston (1988: 232), for example, argues against the dichotomy between facts and values in environmental matters.

Nevertheless, if I am right so far, then the environment model currently used by philosophers is *not* a natural given, nor is it neutral and non-political; hence the model—although not the environment itself—is constructed as opposed to discovered, and is often politically oriented. This is not to say that there may not be a neutral and non-political model of the environment in the scientific discourse, but it seems that often, in the social discourse, we do not have an objective model for the 'environment': rather, we have a number of different political models. Often people relate to the environment as a concept that is subordinate to other (non-environmental) political goals they hold. I therefore think that we should be careful not to assume, or take as given, that the model of the environment used by philosophers in the social discourse is a scientific, 'true' description. And if this is the case, then philosophers should indeed be very careful not to derive the 'ought' from the 'is', and not to derive social codes of behaviour from 'the way the environment is'. Notice, however, that my claim is twofold: first, that environmental philosophers should be careful not to derive the 'ought' from the 'is' in general; but also that they should be careful not to move from a particular and biased 'is' (which, because it is particular and biased, has its own 'oughts' within it), to the 'oughts' that follow from it.

Secondly, I wish to make a bolder claim: namely, that my previous arguments carry implications for some theories of intrinsic value. The notion of intrinsic value means, in very broad terms, that an object can have a value that is both (or either) not instrumental to any other person, and exists objectively. The theory of intrinsic value—again, in very broad terms—is that humans cannot treat the environment merely as an instrument (e.g. by regarding everything in the environment as a 'resource') because many objects in the environment (or, indeed, the environment itself) have 'intrinsic value'. When we humans face objects that possess this intrinsic value, we disregard this value if we relate only to their instrumental value; that is to say, we behave immorally if we do so. The main debate with regard to this notion and this theory has been whether we can know (and what it means to assert) that intrinsic value exists in 'nature', 'trees', 'animals', 'the environment', and so forth.

In general I would accept the theory of intrinsic value, but with a modification. Accordingly, intrinsic value will apply to individuals in the environment but not to the environment.[23] I will demonstrate this by discussing Rolston's theory in the light of the argument so far.[24]

---

[23] In fact, the question of whether any theory of intrinsic value is sound is irrelevant. I do not argue in favour of a theory of intrinsic value, but rather suggest that, *if* one accepts such a theory, then it should be applied to individuals rather than to ecosystems. I should also mention that there is another possibility, namely ascribing intrinsic value to activities; but this is beyond the scope of this chapter.

[24] Another implication could be that environmental philosophers are primarily educators

Rolston suggests a theory of what we can call 'pluralistic intrinsic value'. He finds different categories of values in nature: life-support value, economic value, recreational and creation value, scientific value, aesthetic value, diversity, unity, historical, stability, spontaneity, wildness, historical, religious, and other values. I could not agree more with regard to the intrinsic value of individuals, such as particular deer, or species. But, although he does not directly say that there is value in the relationships themselves, Rolston does mention the value of systems, or 'systemic value'. He discusses the value of non-biotic *things*—humans, sentient fauna, e.g. squirrels, endangered species (1988; 223–4)—but at the same time claims that 'nature [as a whole—AdS] is an objective value carrier' (1988: 4). He then goes on to identify 'the projective system', which is 'the most valuable phenomenon':

The shallow reading . . . [of this is] . . . that humans, when they arrive, are able to value the system out of which they have emerged. A deeper reading means that the system is able to project values, among which are humans. (Rolston 1988: 225)

And:

What humans value in nature is an ecology, pregnant Earth, a projective and pro-life system in which individuals can prosper but are also sacrificed indifferently to their pains and pleasures, individual well-being a lofty but passing role in a storied natural history. From the perspective of individuals there is violence, struggle, death; but from a systems perspective, there is also harmony, interdependence and ever-continuing life. (Rolston 1988: 225)

Thus, Rolston sees 'systemic value' on the level of ecosystems, especially where it seems we cannot speak in terms of intrinsic value in individuals or species because the good of an object is partly its good for others, or its role in sustaining the system, its ability to maintain the 'fitness in a pervasive whole' (Rolston 1988: 223).

If I read Rolston correctly, he may mean that relationships have intrinsic value, and it may even be argued, as Judith Scoville (1995) does, that his theory may be recast in terms of Richard Niebuhr's relational value theory, in which value is a basic of relationships. I think that, while it is clear that the rest of what he says is welcome—i.e. that there is intrinsic, objective, and non-anthropocentric value in individual objects, species, etc. (even if the intrinsic value is embedded in systemic relationships, just as long as the value relates to an individual or a species)—this particular idea (i.e. the systemic value) should be avoided, because otherwise we immediately fall into the trap of conceptual

rather than philosophers. This is admitted by Callicott in discussing the works of Leopold, and by Rolston (1988: ch. 1 and 192) in his assertion that 'no education is complete until one has a concept of nature', and when he discusses 'following nature in the axiological and tutorial senses'; when writing about the environment, environmentalists seek to educate rather than simply convince in the usual philosophical way. This may also support my argument that environmental theorists use the term 'environment' instrumentally in order to produce a certain political behaviour. On the other hand, one may claim that in this case an educator uses all her concepts instrumentally.

instrumentalism. Unlike objects such as trees, donkeys, human beings, and so forth, an ecosystem is a description of relationships. As such, it is mediated through language,[25] which is changeable and social, and hence cannot be a source of value and, even less, be emancipated. In other words, the 'environment' is a description of relationships, which when described may already be oriented towards a certain telos; hence the 'environment' cannot be a source of value, especially not intrinsic value. (This is not to say that relationships cannot have *instrumental* value!)

By way of illustration, consider the family. Obviously, Rachel, John her spouse, and their children have intrinsic value; but the family is a description of legal relationships and certain obligations that John, Rachel, and their children have to each other. In other words, the family is a description of relationships which guarantee the individuals' intrinsic value. If the family ceases to exist—that is, if John and Rachel get divorced—they all still have an intrinsic value, although the relationships between them are different. Indeed, if they get divorced there are now other means (i.e. a new mode of relationships) of respecting the individuals' intrinsic value. For instance, there is a divorce agreement, which is supposed to ensure that the new relationships will guarantee respect for the intrinsic value of John, Rachel, and their children. It may still be true that the family is the best guarantee for these people's intrinsic values (as well as for their love to each other), but then the family has an instrumental, rather than intrinsic, value.

Some may defend the position that intrinsic value can be ascribed to relationships by arguing that relationships might exist prior to individuals. But such a claim would be unreasonable. Relationships cannot be prior to the objects whose affiliations they describe, because in order for there to be relationships between objects there must first be the objects which relate to each other. At this point one may still insist that attaching ontological primacy to objects seems to separate the inseparable: objects emerge or are born into a world of relationships. Moreover, these objects are at least partly constituted by these relationships. Notice, however, that I do not claim that relationships lack *any* value: only that they lack intrinsic value. Indeed, I am constituted partly by my relationships, but these relationships have value in so far as they constitute me, the person, the object in the system.

To see this, try to imagine two situations. The first is where there are only relationships, but not objects (a community without people, an ecosystem without objects). It seems to me that this is meaningless, or not conceivable at all. The other situation is when there are only objects, e.g. persons, without relationships. It seems reasonable to argue that these persons still have intrinsic value. My conclusion is this is *not* a case of the chicken and the egg. Objects

---

[25] Of course, life exists 'out there' independently of humans, but is the lion chasing the antelope or is the antelope running away because of the lion? The answer is provided by human language.

come first; they then may form relationships, which then have value, for the newborn or newly emerging objects. But relationships must have objects in order to exist and to be of any value. So relationships *per se* cannot be of intrinsic value, although they have other values.

Again, I do not wish this argument to be interpreted as a call to eliminate the idea of intrinsic value from environmental ethics. Rather, I would suggest a modification of this theory in the light of my argument, and would ascribe intrinsic value to objects within the environment, but not to the 'environment' itself.

Neither do I wish to dismiss using the concept of the environment in environmental philosophy or its use as a metaphor. In fact, it has been suggested that the terms 'environment' and 'ecology' contain metaphorical elements, e.g. when we speak of 'the economy of nature' or of 'biotic communities' (Callicott 1986: 307; Dryzek 1997: 17). I think this is indeed correct: we do use metaphors when speaking of the environment. Thus, for instance, my saying that I care for, and about, the environment is short for saying that I care for, and about, objects in the environment, or that the relationships I would like to see between human beings and other objects in the environment are better than those that, say, a capitalist polluter would see, in that they guarantee greater respect for objects in the environment. This respect includes respect for the relationships between these objects (i.e. the particular mode of ecosystem balance).

This is, in fact, the 'happy ending' of my otherwise critical chapter. I do not believe we should dispense with environmental philosophy, but I do suggest that environmental philosophers should acknowledge that:

1. the 'environment' is often tacitly a politically-loaded concept; and
2. one should therefore be cautious about using this concept; and
3. one should be careful about deducing the 'ought' from the 'is': there is no neutral 'is' in this case; and
4. any theory of intrinsic value should be modified to apply to objects rather than to relationships (i.e. to the environment); and, finally,
5. there are philosophers who are too keen on combining environmental philosophy with political theory. Although the two may be related, it seems that these philosophers substitute political theory with environmental (meta-) ethics too hastily, or even claim that we need new psychological theories rather than environmental policies.

It seems to me that philosophers have not been cautious enough: it may be better for the environment if we concentrate separately on the moral grounds for environmentalism, i.e. on environmental ethics (often meta-ethics), and on the political theory concerning the institutions that best guarantee a cleaner environment, animal welfare, etc., let alone social justice. Again, this is not to say that environmental philosophy has no political implications. The contrary is true, but we should not use environmental philosophy (and the concept of the environment) to save our souls and abolish bourgeois democracy, or at least we should not do so and at the same time pretend to be protecting the environment. While philosophy should include both environmental ethics and political theory, these two 'branches' of philosophy relate to two different questions. Environmental ethics should answer the question, What moral grounds are there for a more environment friendly attitude? Political theory should answer the question, What sort of human institutions are conducive to, and able to sustain, environment-friendly policies? I believe that, if environmental ethics is approached modestly, as opposed to pretentiously, if it does not claim to solve meta-ethical questions, if it is more accurate (e.g. acknowledging that intrinsic value can apply to individuals only), and if it does not seek to replace political theory, then it will be regarded as reasonable. The practical results will be much more far-reaching than at present: greater numbers of people will be convinced and will develop environment-friendly attitudes. It might even be argued that if this stage is reached there would be no need for the paradigmatic changes in morality demanded by some environmental philosophers,[26] and that the time will then be ripe for political theory to turn its focus on our (human) institutions.

As for environmental ethics, I feel I have said my word (de-Shalit 1994*b*; 1995*a*), and that others have done so even better. I would now like to further the discussion by addressing political theory, asking how liberal, communitarian, democratic, and socialist theories and institutions may, or may not, be harnessed for the benefit of protecting the environment.

---

[26] Compare with Dryzek's claim that ecological modernization 'posits a structural transformation' of capitalism without collapsing into green radicalism. And yet, the irony is that 'if this transformation succeeds it will deprive green radicalism of its bite by showing that transition to a totally different political economy is unnecessary' (Dryzek 1997: 188–9).

PART II

Protecting the Environment: From Meta-ethics to Political Theory

In Part I it was argued that those philosophers and theorists who have been impatient with political theory are mistaken in their thinking. The argument they have suggested has been that, because environmental ethics is based on a revolutionary conception of ethics—non-anthropocentrism—it implies the abolition of the contemporary 'order', or 'system', for the sake of a 'new collective psyche', or 'Green, a-political vision'. It is my contention that these scholars have confused environmental ethics with political theory, failing to notice the different questions to which these theories relate. Environmental ethics answers the question, What are the moral grounds for an environment-friendly attitude or outlook? whereas political theory answers the question, What are the most equitable institutions for promoting environment-friendly policies?.[1] Of course, the two are strongly related, and environmentalists should find interest in both environmental ethics and political theory. However, finding one redundant because of the existence of the other seems not only mistaken philosophically speaking, but also damaging politically speaking.

Thus, in the first part of the book I explain how environmental ethics and political theory have been wrongly integrated, and what should be done to revive theory relating to and justifying environmental policies. I argue that we are in need of a political theory. In the second part I discuss this political theory itself. I apply the mechanism of public reflective equilibrium by referring to works of philosophers, political theorists, environmental consultants, and activists.

Earlier, I raised, though without developing, the argument that any answer relating to the nature of the type of institutions needed should derive from a theory of relations between human beings, which takes the environment into account. This claim will be developed in Chapter 4, where I dismiss the idea of an interspecies community, and present an analysis and subsequent endorsement of the conception of a human, environment-friendly community. I will maintain that a *genuine* community is likely to be environment-friendly. A 'genuine' community is characterized partly by the qualities of democracy, participation, and egalitarianism; this will be further elaborated in Chapters 5 on democracy and 6 on socialism. However, we must examine the alternative position, namely, that it would be more advantageous to the environment if everything were left to the market, and, moreover, that a system based on private property would provide the best means of protecting environmental 'goods'. I will therefore begin my examination of political theory with liberalism rather than with communitarian, democratic socialism.

---

[1] There is another relevant question, namely, What are the most *efficient* institutions for promoting environment-friendly policies? And yet this is a question which political *science*, rather than political philosophy, should answer. This is to say that the answer should be based on empirical evidence. The answer to the question I put (with regard to the equitable institutions for promoting environment-friendly policies) would be normative, although part of the justification for these or other institutions might be their efficiency.

(Although, of course, not all liberal theories are market-based. I elaborate on this below.)

This may seem odd to some who might ask, What hope does liberalism offer environmentalists? Liberalism, it might be argued, rests on the capitalist, Lockeian assumption that human labour adds value to previously valueless objects in nature. The response to this would be: What kind of environmental position can emerge from this kind of disposition towards the non-human?

However, I examine liberalism from a broader perspective than that of an economic theory relating to property and the market, and therefore I believe I offer a less critical perspective on liberalism. My argument here is that the relationship between liberalism and the environment is indeed complex, and that in the final analysis, although liberalism does not provide full answers from the point of view of those concerned about the environment, it does have merit in its own right, and moreover has contributed to the emergence of what I call 'environmental literacy' and 'environmental awareness'. In the following chapter we shall see how this works, and shall consider what remains lacking in liberalism.

3

Is Liberalism Environment-Friendly?

Introduction

There are those who believe that we can expect scientists, or engineers, to solve or at least suggest solutions to all environmental problems. This attitude is often called 'technologism' (O'Riordan 1981; also Shrader-Frechette 1993) or 'technological fix'. However, while, theoretically speaking, science can provide solutions to many environmental problems (a fact that many environmental philosophers have rejected too hastily), in practice, such solutions are thrust aside by economic criteria and considerations. Now, economic criteria reflect nothing but social and political ideologies; and so, in fact, environmental policies involve decisions on public priorities, the allocation of financial and time resources, and the distribution of money and political power. Consequently, the solution to environmental problems becomes political (Goodin 1992a; Yearley 1991). This is then the core of the problem of liberalism vis-à-vis the environment: namely, that liberalism offers an inadequate political theory for dealing with these questions. I will explore the reasons for this later.

In addition, it may be argued that at first sight a connection between liberalism (in its currently most popular form, i.e. contractarianism) and environmental philosophy cannot exist, since the most fundamental feature of liberalism, the contract, disenfranchises those incapable of entering into it, i.e. trees, rocks, rivers, animals, etc. The most prominent of contemporary liberal theorists, John Rawls, for instance, would rather leave the issue of the environment to metaphysics (Rawls 1973: 512). Others have tried to follow Rawls's path, either by modifying liberal theory so that it generates an animal rights ethics (Singer 1988), or by demonstrating that implicitly, the theory does require extensive environmental policies (R. Taylor 1993; Miller 1999; Wissenburg 1999).

Another claim against liberalism in this context is this: the most that contractarian liberalism can achieve is to generate obligations among humans *with regard to* the environment. However, these can always be overridden by other obligations that humans have towards one another. Nevertheless, there are reasons why environmentalists should have a strong respect for liberalism, and I will therefore begin by being positive about liberalism.

But before elaborating further, let me first identify the three concepts I mean to use. The first is *environmental literacy*, which is a function of the information available to citizens on the environment; one is 'environmentally literate' when one knows about the greenhouse effect, the ozone layer, biodiversity, radioactive waste, and so on. Literacy in this sense does not necessarily mean that the information carries any particular moral implication, and yet it is a rather important concept: environmental literacy is the precondition for there to be a meaningful environmental discourse. As an example, it is said that Ronald Reagan once announced that 'ninety percent of pollution is caused by trees'. Whether this story is a myth or not (I hope it is, but I suspect it is not), it reveals a certain ignorance among politicians and the general public about data and processes. This ignorance prevents the opportunity for a meaningful discourse on the environment from taking place, whatever the participants' normative positions about the environment.

The second concept, *environmental awareness*, describes a state of mind which acknowledges that environmental matters affect our life to such a degree that they pose certain moral dilemmas, such as human environmental justice and even responsibility for non-human animals. The third concept, *environmental consciousness*, represents a deeper level of concern, where one understands that environmental matters constitute a political issue which should be treated not merely as a technological case, but rather as a political one, if it is to be resolved.

My argument here will involve three stages. First, I claim that liberalism, for a number of reasons to be examined, provides a sound framework for the evolution of 'Green' ideas and environmental philosophy. The first stage relates to informing citizens about the problems; this leads to increased 'environmental literacy'. However, 'environmental literacy' is not enough, even if we assume the citizens to be responsible people. The problem is that so much information is available in the world today that people are motivated to study something, or search for a specific piece of information, only if they believe it to have direct bearings on their lives.[1] It is therefore crucial, from an environmentalist point of view, that people not only learn about biodiversity, air pollution, the contamination of water by chemicals, the life of the Indo-Chinese tiger, etc., but that they understand how these issues affect them. In other words, there is hope for environmental literacy if it is linked to 'environmental awareness'. Indeed, environmental lawyers dealing with contamination issues, etc., present them as a threat to the public *right* not to be exposed to unnecessary risk, often relating to the works of Ulrich Beck (e.g. 1995).

---

[1] This is not a misanthropic observation, but rather a sympathetic and diagnostic comment. Among all the flashes of information one is exposed to, and between one 'surf' through the network and another, wouldn't we all tend first to pick up information that concerns us?

Consequently, it is within the context of the liberal discourse of rights and their violations that information about the environment is often conveyed.

'This is fine,' sceptics might argue, 'but it only confirms our suspicion that liberalism can only be compatible with one aspect of environmentalism, namely risk and pollution prevention, since these can be easily grasped and "addressed in the language of liberal self-interest", whereas preservation, protecting endangered species or wilderness, etc., cannot. This means therefore that liberalism would reject protecting endangered species on the grounds that it means sacrificing short-term human interests for animal interests in the long run' (di-Zerga 1992, 1995).[2] Not only do I believe this attitude to be wrong, but I also think that liberalism offers the basis for a position that sees animals as having equal moral status with humans. Therefore, in the second stage I shall suggest that liberalism is responsible for the evolution of environmental awareness mainly through its strong attachment to anti-chauvinism.

In the third stage, however, I argue that liberalism runs into difficulties with regard to environmental *policies*. The paradox, then, is that, while on the one hand liberalism allows and encourages discussion on environmental issues, on the other it cannot permit the outcome of the discussion, namely the implementation, maintenance, and justification of environmental policies. Thus, it precludes constructive public action that is meant to protect the environment.

It is important to note that there is extensive empirical evidence to support my claim regarding liberalism. In other words, while in liberal societies there is growing environmental awareness based on a high level of environmental literacy, there is nevertheless a low level of environmental consciousness. According to Sharon Witherspoon's survey in Western Europe (Witherspoon 1997), there are high levels of concern for the environment, expressed in concern not only for humans' health, but for the 'environment' *per se*. And yet, there is only moderate support for environmental policies. As Whitherspoon herself claims, since in these surveys people were first questioned about their concern for the environment, and only when they indicated caring a great deal were they asked about their support for environmental policies, one could expect an even higher level of support for environmental policies, at least in order to show consistency. However, even when people expressed a readiness to make personal sacrifices to protect the environment, their support for environmental policies and their readiness to engage in politics to achieve such policies was not high. Data published by Robert Worcester, chairman of MORI and vice president of the Royal Society for Nature Conservation, also indicates that environmental awareness does not guarantee readiness to act politically, or what I call 'environmental consciousness'.[3]

---

[2] di-Zerga himself does not accept this claim, but he rejects it on grounds different from mine here.

[3] For example, to the question, 'To what extent do you agree or disagree: pollution and environmental damage are things that affect me in my day-to-day life?' 69% answered that

This ambivalence towards liberalism and the environment may appear confusing, since there does not seem to be any sharp and unequivocal assertion for or against liberalism in the context of the environment. On the contrary, the intrinsic complexity of liberalism, and the gap between the theoretical discussion and praxis, only serve to expose the complexity of liberalism's relationship with environmentalism. Nevertheless, the present chapter may provide indication that a more 'social' type of liberalism could well deliver the goods. On the more 'social' type of liberalism, namely the communitarian theory, I elaborate in the next chapter.

Liberalism and Environmental Philosophy

In this section my aim is not so much to show that liberalism and environmental philosophy may be regarded as identical twins, or as ideal ideological bedfellows, but to argue that liberal societies have become a fertile ground for promoting ecological attitudes and environmental philosophy. There are four main reasons for this. The first two lie in the sphere of philosophy or theory and involve both the content of the liberal idea and the tradition of liberal thought.

Let us begin by examining the content. As mentioned before, one of the main components of liberalism is anti-chauvinism: the moral agent does not automatically exalt its own virtues and discredit those of others. (The moral agent could be a single individual or a collective body joined voluntarily, e.g. a party or a company, or else a collective into which they are born, e.g. a nation, race, gender, class.) Chauvinists do not consider 'others' on equal terms—an attitude rejected by liberals in favour of the idea that all people are equal since they are all human beings cast in the same mould. Hence liberals contend that all humans deserve equal rights, and that we should follow a policy of 'respect for others' and 'respecting others as equals'.[4] In short, liberalism as a social philosophy rejects all expressions of chauvinism ranging from national to male chauvinism.

they agreed or strongly agreed, only 15% answered that they disagreed, and only 2% 'strongly disagreed'. However, when asked whether there was much people could do to help protect the environment, 27% thought there was not much they could do; see Worcester (1997: 160–1).

[4] The latter is Ronald Dworkin's formula (1991a: 223–40; 1986). But see also John Locke ('This equality of men by Nature . . . [is] so evident in itself, and beyond all question . . .' in his *Second Treatise of Government*, ch. 2: 5), the French first declaration of the rights of man and of citizens ('Men are born, and always continue, free, and equal in respect to their rights'), the American Declaration of Independence, Thomas Paine's *Rights of Man*, and Alexis de Tocqueville's *Democracy in America* (since everyone is equal, no one is entitled to be a despotic ruler: pt 2, ch. 10).

At the same time, human depletion of resources and damage to the environment has been described on several occasions, and quite rightly, as 'man (or human) chauvinism' (Collard and Contrucci 1988; Routley 1979) with respect to the ill treatment of non-human animals (sometimes even plants or ecosystems) and their exclusion from the ethical community.

It is only natural, then, that many liberals, both theorists and politicians, have adopted Green ideas and ecological attitudes, the essence of liberalism being, as indicated above, the philosophy of 'respect for others'. An environmental attitude (here I use the term in a broad sense) is also based on the respect for other; however, it implies extending the notion of 'others' to include non-human animals, or 'all sentient creatures'.

Most liberals would find it difficult to adhere to 'holism' or to Aldo Leopold's 'Land Ethic', which rests on the premiss that the individual is a member of a community of interdependent parts; but, since there is more to environmental theory than this holism, it may be arguable that the elements of anti-chauvinism and 'respect for others', which have characterized liberal thought, have influenced and contributed to the emergence of 'environmental' ideas, at least in their defence of individual entities in the environment.[5] Roderick Nash has drawn an interesting analogy in this connection between the liberal political campaign against slavery in America and the environmentalists' attempt to persuade the public that the circle of the ethical community should be widened to include animals, and even plants or ecosystems. Just as the 'Abolitionists' were considered radical when they claimed that Blacks were being ill treated and denied any moral status, so environmentalists today are regarded as radical. Consequently, Nash (1989: 200) may be right in claiming that environmental ethics is a 'logical extrapolation of the powerful liberal tradition' (see also Paehlke 1989: 7–9). Nineteenth-century liberals passed from male chauvinism and racism to moral universalism; environmentalists today are moving from a human chauvinism towards a broader moral universalism, arguing that 'the conscious suffering of a sentient creature is indeed intrinsically bad from that creature's standpoint'. Thus, they claim, we look at other species

[as] we look at ourselves, seeing them as beings which have a good they are striving to realise just as we have a good we are striving to realise. . . . [Hence] their lives can be made better or worse by the way humans treat them, and it is possible for humans to take their standpoint and judge what happens to them in terms of *their* well-being. (P. Taylor 1981: 217; 1986: 56–7)

In fact, there is no need to talk about intrinsic value here. We can look at it this way. Liberals in the first half of the nineteenth century adopted the idea of progress wholeheartedly, and for the sake of progress were ready to turn a

---

[5] Admittedly, many environmentalists are keener on groups of living objects, e.g. species, rather than on individual entities. This will be discussed below, where I suggest that a more social type of liberalism suits environmental issues.

blind eye to its victims, such as the working class. In the second half of the nineteenth century, liberalism, while maintaining its faith in progress, developed a concern for the well-being of groups vulnerable to the side-effects of modernization (Goodin 1985, 1988), initially conceived exclusively in terms of human beings (the working class, the elderly, etc.); and in our century liberals have become much more egalitarian[6] and sensitive to the victims of progress. Contemporary liberalism has extended its recognition of vulnerability to children or gender groups, for instance, and supports affirmative action to protect them or ensure that they receive justice. However, in view of the particular evils resulting from modernity and progress, e.g. heavy pollution, toxic, nuclear and radioactive waste, and misguided urban development, it is easy to see how the league of victims should come to include endangered species and other aspects of the non-human environment.

So much for the content of liberalism. But there is a second aspect of liberal theory built into the tradition of liberal philosophy. Liberals have always subjected their positions, values, ideas, and theories to critical scrutiny and have propounded openness and tolerance not only in political life, but in the academic and philosophical debate as well (Popper 1945; Horton and Mendus 1985). Even philosophers and theorists who attack the liberal tradition for its inability to tackle, understand, or solve ecological problems (Gunn 1983) must admit that this is possible for them because they live and work in a liberal and tolerant society.

Moreover, in order to accept environmental philosophy (I mean accepting it in general as ethics or meta-ethics), one must remain relatively open to new ideas and maintain a tolerance of criticism—not only of one's own theory, but also of one's methodology. This is because environmental philosophy is (mostly) *bio*centric or *eco*centric, rather than anthropocentric; and, unlike traditional morality, it discusses the moral relationship not only between human beings but also between humans and non-human entities. So, while one should be careful when claiming a similarity between liberalism and environmental philosophy simply because the former argues for tolerance, it seems fair to maintain that environmental philosophy has emerged at least partly as a result of liberalism's rejection of methodological monism and the fostering of a philosophical and intellectual milieu in which new and provocative ideas can flourish.[7]

The third reason for liberalism becoming the breeding ground for a flourishing of environmental attitudes lies in the sphere of internal politics. I refer here to a tradition of defending the individual against the church, the state,

---

[6] To the extent that it is now claimed by Ronald Dworkin (e.g. 1986) and others that liberalism's most fundamental value is equality rather than liberty.

[7] Anna Bramwell (1991) traces the origins of environmentalism to romantic philosophy and right-wing political theories. But she fails to distinguish between anti-rational, anti-modern *ruralism* on the one hand, and modern, scientific-based and democratic *environmentalism* on the other (de-Shalit 1996).

large-scale industries, and firms. This began in the eighteenth century with the defence of the individual against the state or church, followed by a warning that democracy might still yield despotism. The twentieth-century ideology of citizens' rights, prompted by a wish to defend minorities, especially intellectuals, from the masses, grew out of the liberal fear of despotic majority rule. More recently liberalism has become the defender of the underdog, a crusader against monopolies, and a supporter of proper government and universal law (Freeden 1978; Dworkin 1986: 187–8).

The same stand is taken today by environmentalists who feel they must challenge the activities of huge industries and conglomerates, mainly because they fail to adjust themselves to the demands of *sustainable* development. Such companies, for purely profit-making motives, often pollute the air or the water, decimate forests, and in general neglect the right of individuals to a clean environment. The state should be in the business of imposing regulations, but very often, for economic or other reasons, it chooses to ignore the dangers to individuals. The role of environmentalists in such cases reminds us of the role liberals have taken upon themselves in cases of human rights abuse: it is to document these cases, publish warnings, and occasionally take the liberty to act.[8]

Indeed, this stand has been taken by many environmentalists. Even Jonathon Porritt, founder of Forum for the Future, ex-director of Friends of the Earth in Britain, and one of the 'founding fathers' of the British Green Party, who attacks liberal politicians for their lack of support for the Green cause (Porritt 1988: 71–6), employs the liberal terminology of rights when presenting his Green philosophy:

The fact that people's *rights* are being denied is in itself a serious enough problem. . . . And the fact that there are so few . . . who are prepared either to inform people of the denial of their *rights* or to help them to fight for those *rights*, turns a problem of indifference into crisis of inaction. (Porritt 1984: 115; emphasis added)

Finally, a fourth reason why ecological attitudes have taken root in liberal societies rests in the sphere of international relations. Here one particular element inherent in liberal thought should be highlighted, namely, internationalism. Admittedly, this notion sometimes stands for 'free trade', which, according to many environmentalists, is not environment-friendly (Irvine and Ponton 1988: ch. 10; Vira 1998). Nevertheless, internationalism embodies a strong belief in, and reliance on, multilateral agreements and international organizations, and reflects the conviction that political problems may be solved by sometimes tiresome negotiations, and that national interests do not necessarily run counter to international cooperation. While many consider

---

[8] Three good examples of Green publications that warn of the dangers to individuals' rights are Price (1983), Ferencz and Keyes (1988), and May (1989). A famous Green act was Greenpeace's attempt to stop French nuclear tests in the Pacific, which ended with the blowing up of the Greenpeace boat by members of French intelligence in 1985.

the international arena a place where 'might is right', and where those whose interests are harmed can only complain *post factum*, liberals have regarded international relations as a sphere in which it is possible to foresee problems and apply treatment before damage occurs.

All these elements are crucial because environmental problems can, and must, of course, be tackled through international cooperation. This is precisely the element that is both lacking and needed in contemporary politics, where the solution of environmental problems that are rarely entirely local is concerned.[9] Indeed, the idea that prevention is better than cure has been the underlying rationale for the 1972 Stockholm Conference on the Human Environment, the Toronto Declaration, the London Dumping Convention, 'Our Common Future', the 1992 UNCED in Rio de Janeiro, and other notable international agreements.

At this point, it may be argued that at least some of the features of liberalism discussed so far characterize other currents of thought and ideologies as well, e.g. socialism. This may be true, although the second feature, i.e. the rejection of methodological monism and advancing academic pluralism, is I believe characteristic mainly of liberalism. But even if this is not the case, my argument is neither that liberalism is a necessary condition for the emergence of environmental philosophy, nor that it is a sufficient condition, but rather that liberalism—as a philosophy and a political attitude—influences, stimulates and encourages environmental deliberation and the emergence of environmental thought (hence environmental literacy and awareness).

Liberalism as a Philosophy of Government

Although much thought has been given to ecology in recent years, it appears to be inadequate all the same. The damage to the environment has now reached such horrifying proportions that many believe there is a call for radical and urgent solutions, an approach not necessarily compatible with traditional liberal democracy's reluctance to undertake dramatic change. And yet, now at the end of the 1990s, we are witness to a process of world-wide democratization and the flourishing of liberal–democratic ideas, and no one should be required to abandon this trend.

The highly complex political mission for the twenty-first century is thus twofold: on the one hand, to stop trying to relieve ecological 'suffering' and

---

[9] Consider, for instance, the damage being caused by all nations to the ozone layer, the problem of acid rain, or the contamination of the Mediterranean Sea. For further discussion of the international aspects, see Porter and Brown (1991), Benedick (1992), Brundtland *et al.* (1987) and Grubb *et al.* (1993); for a survey of the treatment of environmental issues in international relations see Vogler and Imber (1995).

instead to introduce reforms radical enough to save the environment and reverse what is still reversible; and, on the other hand, to ensure that this does not occur at the price of imposing regulations that limit or reduce liberties. Thus, there are two dimensions to this mission: to sustain the growing enthusiasm for democracy and liberty, and at the same time to save the environment.

As already indicated above, these two dimensions are closely correlated. Too many environmentalists, both political theorists and philosophers, have expressed pessimism and anxiety regarding the future of liberal democracy in the light of environmental problems including scarcity of resources and pollution (see also Chapter 5 below). Lack of resources on the one hand, and selfish, or self-interested, behaviour on the other has given rise to the belief that the only solution might be to impose regulations and policies against people's wills. William Ophuls, for example, wrote that 'the return of scarcity portends the revival of age-old political evils, for our descendants if not ourselves' (Ophuls 1977: 145). As Paehlke (1988: 293) points out, all these writers fear that the only possible outcome will be 'severe economic restraints, self-discipline beyond that which is likely to develop voluntarily'.

But Ophuls's prophecy need not necessarily come true. For instance, while his suggestion of replacing the market by political action is, I believe, welcome (see below), it is still questionable whether liberty should give way to authority, and whether egalitarian democracy should be abandoned for the sake of 'political competence and status' (Ophuls 1977: 227). Ophuls's appeal for a strong leadership (p. 159),[10] reminiscent of George Bernard Shaw's *Man and Superman*, is not the only alternative.

So it seems that democratic societies should be looking for a middle path, which might, at least prima facie, include non-coercive, planned, and consistent policies. These policies must be in line with sustaining and promoting democracy and individual liberty, and yet they may also imply a shift from discussing environmental issues politically to a *politics of the environment*. But liberalism hinders constructive public action to secure environmental protection. To see why, let me first discuss the liberal belief in the market.

Environmentalism and Liberalism: Individuals' Economic Behaviour

The most radical liberal argument is that the state should limit its own intervention because individuals' economic behaviour is the best basis for tackling environmental issues. This needs to be refuted before we come to discuss the

---

[10] To be fair, Ophuls denied that he wanted rule by an elite (Ophuls 1986: 287–8).

more moderate liberal arguments. Here, although I offer a critical scrutiny of the 'market approach' to the environment, I deliberately refrain from claiming to actually refute it. This approach is a much debated issue, whose ramifications would require a separate book.[11] However, I do wish to examine the literature on the *premisses* of the market approach in our context, with special attention to the 'correct' (not in the sense of politically correct) role of politics. My arguments concerning the premisses of a market economy and how they relate to the environment will be mainly non-technical and philosophical.

First of all, let us note that there are many empirically based arguments against the market approach (or, as it is often called, the 'individuals' economic behaviour' approach) to the environment. To mention but one, the assumption that if a certain agricultural product is not healthy people will refrain from purchasing or consuming it, which will in turn force producers to make sure they keep to certain standards, is wrong. Indeed, recently the British government set up an independent Food Standards Agency, and granted it a research budget, to guarantee investment in food safety (Porritt 1998). Therefore, according to some activists, we may no longer trust the magic and invisible hand of the market to do the work for us, but instead must assume responsibility for planning and initiative. Individuals' economic behaviour has proved both inefficient and inequitable in coping with ecological missions, let alone ecological disasters.

The question then arises, Why, if this is the case, do so many people still believe in the 'market' as the mechanism for solving all our environmental problems? Environmental activists who criticize the market tend to answer

---

[11] See e.g. Eckersley (1995*b*). For a libertarian attitude, see Anderson and Leal (1991: 147): 'A truly free market approach to pollution control would require polluters and recipients of the discharge to bargain over the level of pollution. Bargaining may take place in the form of an exchange of property rights, where the discharger pays the recipient for disposal before the fact or in the form of payments for damages paid after the fact. Either way, both parties have an incentive to consider the trade-offs associated with more or less pollution.' In this chapter I do not relate to 'truly free market' approaches as such, for two reasons. First, they are rare among activists and politicians; second, they are incredibly implausible. (Does one see people engaged in this process of bargaining? Can it take place without politics intervening, at least when it comes to deciding upon the level of pollution permitted?) The more sophisticated approaches that regard the economy as 'free' and 'market-oriented'—even when there are some regulations and state intervention—are therefore not only more realistic, but also more interesting. However, I should distinguish this declaration from the one made by Marcel Wissenburg in his very interesting and optimistic book (1998, 213): 'There is no such thing as a society without a free market. Not only in planned economies, but even in the direst of times and under the most oppressive systems of government, something called "the black market" operates—and it operates on the same principles as the free market: demand and supply.' I think this is wrong. A black market cannot be said to be a 'free market'. In order for an economy to be a 'free market', there should be either lack of direct, centralist intervention in the process of pricing or free flow and exchange of goods and human labour. The former does not exist in the black market because prices, while being a function of demand and supply, are still restricted by the alternative options in the state economy, which are decided upon by the centralistic state. The latter does not exist because trade is not free and not all goods are available, even in theory.

this question with sociological and psychological explanations. For instance, Jeremy Seabrook, an ex-member of the British Labour Party and a Green activist, contends that the market is the best and most efficient mechanism to *ruin* the entire universe. In spite of this, however, people all over the world have been attracted to the idea of the market and its promise of a better material future on the grounds that 'the economy became the arena in which the guilt for what had happened [in the Second World War] was to be assuaged.' The market, argues Seabrook, has become 'the object of a superstitious reverence: if only this could be made to work, to grow, to provide, we would surely gain exemption from any recurrence of the barbarities of the recent past.' The market, he contends, has successfully done just this. Nevertheless, it cannot provide what people really need and long for, namely a pleasant and harmonious life. In the East, he claims, the imported idea of the market has ruined the traditional rural way of life and its social manifestations through the process of urbanization, whereas in the West the market has ruined our conception of nature (Seabrook 1990: 13–14, ch. 7). My response to Seabrook's fascinating theory is that, while this psychological explanation is illuminating, it overlooks serious philosophical and economic arguments put forward in support of a reliance on the market to do the job, i.e. protect the environment.

In general, it seems that these arguments fall into two main categories: welfarist and non-welfarist. The former relates to the increase in individuals' welfare thanks to the market and its role in protecting the environment; the latter relates to other values such as liberty or property rights, which, it is claimed, are better protected under the market system. Let us start with the welfarist claims.

Some market advocates believe that markets and market prices will indeed succeed in co-ordinating production in a way that maximizes the benefit (including environmental benefits) of everybody.[12] While many of these market advocates acknowledge that in practice markets in environmental goods do not always exist, they nevertheless claim that markets should be created and market mechanisms (e.g. incentives, pollution rights) introduced to achieve public ends such as protecting the environment. This attitude is called by John Dryzek 'If you can't privatize it, market it anyway', or 'economic rationalism' (Dryzek 1997: ch. 6).

Why do these people think that market-based mechanisms are better than regulations or legislation? David Pearce claims that they 'serve to keep down compliance costs' (with the real prospects of rising environmental standards and hence costs of control this is important, he argues), and they serve to 'force' technology on a continuous basis: that is to say 'the polluter has a repeated incentive to look for cleaner and cleaner technology' (Pearce 1992: 10). It seems, however, that another important reason why market-based

---

[12] Sagoff (1994) analyses this claim, which, he thinks, is a dogma.

mechanisms are thought by market advocats to be better than legislation and regulation is that they save governments the need to radically reform their policies, a very difficult mission in political terms. Thus, these mechanisms have been used in several countries. Tradable pollution permits and Green taxes on air and water pollution, waste and noise, and fees on fertilizers or batteries exist in at least fourteen countries (L. Brown *et al.* 1995). Whether they do indeed manage to protect the environment is controversial: many people doubt that these market-based instruments have been the cause of improvement even when things did improve. For instance, in the UK, the market share of unleaded petrol rose from 4 to 30 per cent within a year (March 1989–March 1990). Some have linked this to the higher tax on leaded petrol introduced at the time; but it has been argued that these taxes and tariffs were set too low to motivate any serious change in behaviour (L. Brown *et al.* 1995)—in fact, they were not intended to cause behavioural change, but rather to raise a modest amount of revenue for specific environmental purposes. The change in behaviour should therefore be explained differently; for instance, it remains to be examined whether the shift in petrol consumerism was not due to intensive propaganda and growing public awareness of the dangers of CO pollution.

Another welfarist argument in favour of the market is that the latter is based on a system in which property is private. Environmental problems do not occur because of the endless quest for private profit, but, on the contrary, because of failures by governments to specify (private) property rights. (For a discussion of this claim, see Dryzek 1997: 104–5.) Markets maximize welfare, and by extension, *environmental* welfare. They can do this because individuals tend to care for anything if, and as long as, they hold it privately. If they hold it commonly they care for it less; for example, people tend to be more careful about not littering their private gardens and less careful about littering parks. This is a complex issue, and I would like to leave the discussion of this claim to Chapter 6.

As for non-welfarist reasons for continuing to believe in the market as the mechanism for solving our environmental problems, these entail arguments about liberty and the way it is protected in the market. The claim is simple: the value of liberty supersedes any other value, and therefore, even if the market does not promote the best results with regard to protecting the environment, we must adhere to this system, because in any other system, the price—limiting liberty—is too high to pay. It is interesting to note that non-welfarist arguments in favour of the market may appeal to many environmentalists as well, because these arguments seem congruent with ideas such as 'small is beautiful', 'human-scale institutions', 'decentralization', and 'the retreat from politics' (Eckersley 1992a: 141). I would like to leave the discussion of this to the next chapter, where I criticize the idea, quite popular among many romantic environmentalists, of local, a-political communities. Here I wish to analyse the welfarist and non-welfarist arguments in greater depth, because this reasoning is also used by environmental activists who criticize the market.

Now, the critique of the economic behaviour approach in relation to the environment is also based on economic arguments and the use of 'market' terminology to demonstrate that individuals' behaviour cannot tackle the environmental issue. According to these arguments, the consequence will always be greater pollution, since the costs are borne by nature and by those who share the environment, and not by the polluter. The polluter does not have to be motivated by ill-will: this problem is ingrained in the idea of the market and its very 'imperative', as Eckersley calls it: 'grow or die' (Eckersley 1992*b*: 319). Such private attitudes cannot respect environmental notions of limits to growth and carrying capacity. An environmentally friendly product is likely to be more expensive than its rival product, and hence no 'rational' (i.e. profit-seeking) entrepreneur is likely to consider such a product.

Add to this the following, and you have a structural problem. Often firms pollute as a byproduct of a process that generates substantial sums of money. The question then is, Should manufacturers reduce production (or, at least, introduce filters) in order to pollute less? The question arises since reducing production (or building filters) will increase production costs and hence generate less profit. Since market economy goes hand in hand with private property, we may assume that these firms are privately owned and managed. Thus, most, or at least a great part, of the profit is distributed among a limited and small number of people: the management or owners. For these parties, the question is slightly different: Should *we* earn less for the sake of *other people* not being exposed to the pollution? These owners and managers usually do not reside near the polluting outlets (factories, dumping sites, etc.) and therefore will tend to think in economic rather than environmental terms. It might be different if the firm were owned by the public or the firm's employees: then, the cost of reducing production or introducing filters would be spread over a greater number of people, making the marginal cost to each relatively meaningless. In addition, the public and the employees probably live closer to the polluting sources and therefore are more likely to suffer directly from the pollution, which would make them more inclined to view the matter in environmental rather than merely economic terms.

At this point, market advocates would suggest a system for penalizing the polluter. Let us intervene slightly in the market, they would say, and charge the polluter for any damage sustained.[13] Thus, anyone who pollutes, depletes,

---

[13] It is interesting to note that John Stuart Mill (1990: 7) already thought this could be a solution to air pollution. As for contemporary discussion, Dryzek notes (1997: 105–6) that such an act need not be regarded as an intervention in the market: instead, the fact that one owns a house or a piece of land can imply that she has a right to breathe clean air there, and hence polluting it is a violation of this person's right. I am not sure that I agree. It seems to me that the only way this is plausible is if the person who owns a house also owns the air around it. But surely this does not make sense.

or utilizes a certain natural resource beyond a certain degree will have to pay for it one way or another. But how do we assess the damage? Can we assess damage that is not local, or within national borders, but rather is international, e.g. acid rain in Canada resulting from air pollution in the USA? How do we assess the damage when only a small and very specific section of a society is hurt (e.g. factory workers, or those who used to play with their children on a playground now up for development)? Moreover, it is very likely that the consumers themselves will have to pay for the pollution the manufacture causes, especially in the cases of monopolies or special products produced by very few firms or perhaps only a single firm. In particular, this is true with regard to energy (where often charges for causing pollution have been transferred to the consumers). So, if all polluting manufactures are charged for the pollution they cause, they will transfer the cost to the consumers. All consumers will then pay the real and full price of energy (including cleaning costs). This in turn will increase inequality, since the proportion of income spent on energy declines as income increases although the use of energy increases. Thus, paying the full price of energy seems unfair to the worst-off.

But there is a further problem with regard to assessing environmental damage. While it may be possible to determine the cost of a particular illness (e.g. it is equal to the cost of hospital treatment plus a certain amount for compensation), how do we determine the 'cost' of a life? Indeed, the very term is strange. We are thinking of the value of life, but can it be translated into the 'cost' of life? To estimate a person's probable future earnings or any other criterion of the value of life is obnoxious, because in that case, theoretically, someone who possesses this amount of money would be able to purchase another person's life. But, if, as some advocates of the individuals' economic behaviour approach have maintained, this question is too artificial or even irrelevant (e.g. because most environmental problems do not cause death among human beings), there is still the question of assessing the value of the lives of non-humans. Thus, how much is the life of a sea otter worth? David Moberg comments that

surveying people about how much the animals are worth to them or measuring lost income if sea otters disappeared may keep a few economists employed, but it does not answer the question. (Moberg 1991: 512)

This is indeed a cynical, albeit serious reply.

If only one respondent said it was of infinite value, that would throw off the survey. If you limit the response to how much a person would be willing to spend, the result would obviously be affected by how much money people have, a standard flaw of market preference analysis. (Moberg 1991: 512)

Yet Moberg's response is only part of the answer. The truth of the matter is that any calculation or assessment of the cost/value of animals' lives is, at the end of the day, hypocritical and weird. What we should do instead is ask the animal to put a price on the value of its own life. Just as, in the case of human lives, we do not ask a murderer what the value of his victims' lives are, but rather (so-to-speak) ask the victims themselves, so we should do in the case of animals' lives. This is true not only in cases resulting in the death of animals, but in any case of environmental damage. Evaluating the cost in terms of how much people *would pay* is mistaken methodologically. What makes a certain good valuable is not the state of mind of the consumer who wants that good, but rather something inherent in that good (Goodin 1992*b*: 25).

Now, some 'individuals' economic behaviour' advocates may remain sceptical with regard to biocentrism, and therefore reject taking into account the animals' perspective. None the less, it is undeniable that these calculations fail to evaluate the cost for other human beings in future generations. Thus, the not yet born are either ignored or 'discounted'. I use 'discounted' in the sense that these economists tend to discount the future; i.e., the future value of a current value x is less than x now, because we have to calculate what x would yield in this future if it were invested now and allowed to accrue interest over time. This, at least on the face of it, implies that it is not rational to preserve x as it is for the future, an argument that is totally incompatible with any notion of intergenerational equity (Eckersley 1992*b*: 319; de-Shalit 1995*a*: 88–99).

In addition to the above difficulties in evaluating the cost of environmental damage, there is a serious problem with a notion that serves the market advocates in their approach to this issue. They assume that we cannot and should not value objects in nature 'for their existence', but rather should value them for their usefulness to humans. This in itself is one thing; but they then jump to the conclusion that something becomes of value if someone expresses a preference for it. These market advocates then conclude that all we need to do when deciding on environmental policies is to ask people how much they would pay to have their preferences fulfilled, e.g. to conserve a forest, save the life of three whales, preserve a particular building. Economists call this mechanism the WTP (willingness to pay) test.

Now, there are two critiques of the WTP test, one technical, the other more theoretical. The former states that, even if we accept the general approach according to which an item has a value to the extent that people express preferences for it, there are still technical difficulties with a measurement mechanism such as this. The second critique challenges the premises of this approach as well. I will be discussing the more general critique below when exploring the distinction between consumers' behaviour and being a citizen. For the moment, however, I will begin with the technical critique.

Following a psychology study conducted by Amos Twersky and Danny Kahaneman in the USA and Maya Bar-Hillel in Israel,[14] I decided to undertake a simple experiment to uncover the fallacy behind the WTP concept. I asked a

---

[14] Mainly about the effect of numbers and information revealed to people on their assessments of other figures and dates.

group of forty students to imagine that an ecological disaster had occurred, and that consequently there was an urgent need to clean our country's coastline. Twenty students were asked whether they would contribute 1 per cent of their salaries that month to clean the coast. All of them replied positively. Then they were asked if they thought it would be possible to predict the average amount that their fellow students would be willing to pay: 90 per cent replied that it would be possible; the average WTP predicted was 1.85 per cent of one's salary. The second group of twenty students was given the same story and were asked whether they would be willing to pay 4 per cent of their salaries. They all claimed they would contribute this amount and thought that the average WTP would be 6.16 per cent of one's salary. The results are clear: the concept of WTP—a mechanism that has gained legitimacy among economists because it respects individuals' autonomy—reflects nothing about 'individuals' autonomous wills'. Rather, we see that both the format of the question and the starting point affect the WTP.

To be on the safe side, I conducted a further similar experiment. This time I told forty students that the department had decided to allow them to use our common room for their coffee breaks; each student would contribute as much as they wished in order to run this 'coffee shop'. First, a group of twenty students were asked whether they would pay $6 a month. They all answered 'yes'; when asked about the WTP of their fellow students, their answers varied from $2 to $16 with the average of $7.42. Second, another group of twenty students, were given the same story, but each of these was asked to contribute $30 a month: 20 per cent agreed, whereas 80 per cent disagreed, but the average evaluations of their fellow students' WTP was $15! Another group of twenty students were told that many of their fellow students had already agreed to pay $30 a month. This time a much higher percentage of students was ready to pay this sum, though they did complain about it being very high. My conclusion is that, although WTP is interesting, theoretically speaking, it is not a reliable mechanism for revealing preferences of autonomous individuals.

Another technical difficulty with the WTP test is as follows. When people are asked whether they are willing to pay X to obtain Z, it is clear that: the value of X rise the less people want Z. But the experiments I have conducted reveal a paradox: when asked how much they would pay to achieve a certain public good or a public goal, people's answers relate to what they think others would pay (as demonstrated above). The answer people usually give is this: they would be prepared to contribute X if they thought that no one else, or very few people, would, and they are ready to contribute Y ($Y>X$) if they think others will also contribute. The paradox is, of course, that if others contribute as well, the individual will not need to pay so much: if everybody contributes, each one will have to contribute T ($T<X$).

Advocates of the WTP measurement can still claim that, if one has market efficiency in mind, the WTP mechanism should be used. According to this view, the market is efficient when goods are allocated to the people or organizations who want them or need them the most. The best way to learn who wants these goods the most is the WTP test. Such arguments are often expressed by economists and market advocates, and I must confess that I find this very surprising. It seems clear to me that the WTP test is biased and cannot help us discover who really needs or desperately wants this good. (Notice that I do not challenge the more philosophical idea that the economy should work this way, i.e. should allocate goods to those who want them most.) To see why, consider the following case. Suppose we are all asked about our WTP for Z. Suppose, also, that Mr Poor says he will pay X whereas Mr Rich says he will pay $3X$. The result will be that Mr Rich will get Z. But the fact that the rich Mr Rich is ready to pay three times as much as the poor Mr Poor does not necessarily indicate that Z is three times more important to him, or that he is more desperate to have it. What if $3X$ is not much for Mr Rich, whereas X is all that Mr Poor has?

It goes without saying that these technical questions do not exhaust the discussion of the relationship of liberalism to environmental concern, but they do point to the difficulties regarding the political and practical implications of liberalism in this context (and I discuss these below). However, beyond all these difficulties with the 'individuals' economic behaviour' approach, there is—according to the critique of the market theory—another, perhaps greater, difficulty. This is the belief that individuals' economic behaviour yields the 'best results'. Do such results include the difficulties in breathing experienced every summer by the people of Athens owing to traffic pollution? Indeed, one could legitimately ask: 'best' results in what sense? This is not a simple question. Michael Jacobs, an economist and a professional consultant on sustainable development policy, who is in general not happy with the market approach, concedes that economists do not pretend to claim that these results are 'best' in the sense that they reflect the actual optimal (or 'right') level of environmental protection: rather, he argues, they merely claim that cost–benefit analysis can reveal social objectives without attaching any *ethical* status to these objectives (Jacobs 1995*a*: 51). I must, however, disagree: the economists' approach does reflect a conception of the good. According to them, the 'good' is what individuals want, as reflected in their actual decisions and the choices they make. However, even if we do accept Jacobs's claim regarding the market economists, and use 'best' to denote people actually getting what they want, there is very little empirical support for this claim. As many activists argue, it is not at all clear that the market yields better results in terms of satisfying people's preferences when it comes to preferences concerning the environment. Poor results of using 'economic instruments' with regard to the anticipated environmental impact have been reported by Australians Peter Christoff (1995: 176) and Peter Kinrade (1995: 91). Notice that these activists do not doubt that, for example, incentives often work (e.g., if I am required to pay for each cubic metre of water I consume, I shall have an extra inducement not to waste water): rather, they doubt whether incentives and mechanisms such as this are sufficient, or if they alone can indeed yield the 'best' results.

Moreover, the problem with the market is that it seems that the list of goods whose supply cannot be guaranteed by individuals' economic behaviour is quite long and includes some significant examples, in particular cases in which the good is desired by only part of the population. Think, for example, of a remote forest. Individuals' economic behaviour will not save this forest, because its economic value to timber merchants is far greater than the amount environmentalists could pay to save it for aesthetic reasons.[15]

At this point non-welfarist arguments arise once again. Some market advocates respond that the question is not one of metaphysical belief, but rather of an ethical belief in the idea of freedom. Recognizing the fact of environmental damage to our world, they have suggested that firms should be allowed to react to changing market needs, including the need to be more environment-friendly, in their own ways and using their own approaches. This, as Eckersley notes (1992b: 318), 'is not simply a defence of economic efficiency; it is also linked to a defence of political freedom'. Thus, for example, if there must be less pollution, then a system of selling pollution rights could be introduced.[16] Pollution rights would be distributed to firms, so that if x is the degree of pollution tolerable and n is the number of firms, each firm will receive x/n pollution rights. Those in a position to continue manufacturing under the constraints of limiting the resultant pollution will do so, and will cover the costs by selling pollution rights to other firms.[17]

All this is fine. But if the issue is one of ethical belief, as market advocates claim, we should consider not only liberty, but also egalitarianism. While some firms would adjust to the new circumstances by limiting pollution, and others by purchasing pollution rights, the problem that remains is the distribution of exposure to hazardous waste and pollution. Third World countries have long been disproportionally exposed to dangerous waste. For instance, in the 1970s it was quite common for African countries to 'export' land to Western firms for burying toxic and radioactive waste. And in the Western world, the poor find themselves unable to buy houses in safer, less polluted, areas, or to find safer jobs. Even if taxes are introduced, those who find it most difficult to cope will again be the least advantaged (Centre for Science and Environment 1992; Martinez-Alier 1993, 1997a). Many questions regarding

[15] This relates to the question of whether only *use* value should count, or whether *option* value (i.e., whether I can use and enjoy this environmental good in the future) counts as well; see Randall (1986).

[16] Here we have the 'market fix': problems caused by the market will be solved by letting the market play an even greater role.

[17] Steidlmeier (1993), for example, argues that pollution permits have a legitimacy as 'a second-best solution'.

distribution of cost and of power seem to arise; for example, Why should we wait until there is a mess before mopping it up? Why not prevent pollution before workers—who often live near the factories that employ them—are forced to breathe in smog, or before people are hurt and the environment damaged? Why should we allow the private sector to decide where to pollute? Are such decisions private at all? Should they be in the hands of those who run the industries and pollute our rivers, meadows and seas? (I must ask readers to wait for the last chapter, where I again raise these questions and discuss them. I have raised them here only as a quick response to the market advocates claim about ethical beliefs.)

At this point many market advocates accept these problems. Nevertheless, they fear what they call the diametrical: opposite to a market economy. Thus, many of these people doubt not only whether full state or public ownership is congruent with liberty, but also whether such a system would be better for the environment. As Goodin (1992b: 7, fn. 30) notes, 'the environmental consequences of public ownership in Eastern Europe do not serve as a happy precedent'.[18] Thus, they seek to modify, refine, or correct the market in order to make it more environment-friendly. While not rejecting all that liberalism stands for, they nevertheless think that, if liberalism implies an 'individuals' economic behaviour' type of economics, then it is inadequate in the sense that it neglects aspects of ecology, wilderness preservation, etc. The right question, these environmentalists argue, is not how to get rid of the market, but what sort of environmental goods can it deliver, and what it cannot.

It seems to me, though, that changing the question does not solve the main problem: namely that the market economy is based on premises that do not take the new environmental problems into account. For a start, the market economy has a wrong conception of compensation: it does not compensate or reward individuals and firms that *do* act to conserve the environment. A person who lives in an historic house and preserves it is not usually compensated for doing so; however, if the house is sold to a developer, the owner may make a lot of money. Similarly, the capitalist who invests huge sums of money in order to recycle his industry's waste is not rewarded by the neighbour capitalist who pollutes a nearby river.

Moreover, since market advocates are interested primarily not in the environmental problem but rather in satisfying people's preferences, they do seek to solve not environmental problems, but rather the human problems caused by these environmental problems, namely that people cannot satisfy their preferences. And so, if the quality of the water is bad, we do not solve the problem of water quality, but instead switch to mineral water; if there are no green areas left in town, then a farmer opens land up to the public and we take our car, drive out into the country, and pay the farmer to enjoy nature; if there is

---

[18] However, in Ch. 6 I argue that the poor state of the environment in Eastern Europe was due to the lack of democracy rather than to public ownership.

too much noise, there are glass factories to offer us double-glazed windows. But on top of the obvious and very serious questions—Are we satisfied with these solutions? Is this what we wanted? Can we *all* afford them?—the even more crucial question in this context is this, Can the market, even if it does solve one or two problems related to satisfying preferences, provide the solution to the ecological crisis in general? (B. Barry 1991*a*; Eckersley 1993). In other words, suppose the market does solve the question of how to satisfy people's preferences: isn't this achieved at the price of ignoring the environmental problems themselves? It seems that it is, because the market does not see *the environment* as the problem in the first place. The market approach translates any such issue into questions of satisfying individuals' preferences.

So, even if we accept the market as a system relevant to the 'environmental era', there is still a strong need for 'politics'. In other words, we eventually come to realize that the economy cannot be a genuinely market economy, and that the pro-market economists have failed more in their political than in their economic theory. They either chose to solve environmental problems by ignoring the social implications, or else decided to solve the economic problem of satisfying wants, but gave up on the environmental problems. They failed to notice that, besides the question of which instruments should be chosen to protect the environment, the question of the social costs and benefits associated with these measures should also be addressed.[19] Therefore, in addition to dealing with the issue of a 'market or non-market' economy, the question of the most appropriate kind of politics should also be considered.

I would therefore like to turn to this question and argue that liberals have to come to terms with the political fact highlighted by the need to promote environmental policies: namely, that the state of the environment is closely related to our view of 'the political' and the political process, including the debate on the good life, and furthermore that the issue of the environment involves the very goals of our political life, not merely the means of achieving certain goals. Notice that my claim is more than a simple claim in favour of additional state initiatives (taxes, incentives, subsidises, and so forth). Rather, it is an argument in favour of a different form of politics, in which it is assumed that, not only can individuals identify and express their self-interest preferences, but they also have moral ideals. Individuals can, and will, relate to other individuals and their ideals in a process of moral deliberation. But can liberalism sustain such politics in the context of environmental policies?

[19] A debate has been taking place among economists—between 'environmental economists' such as David Pearce and 'ecological economists' such as Herman Daly. Daly and his colleagues suggest that environmental economists are wrong in their premisses about the goal of economics, which they regard as an optimal allocation of resources. Ecological economists, however, assume that humans act within 'finite and non-growing ecosystems', and therefore ecological economists seek an optimal scale of resource use in addition to the optimal allocation of resources. This optimal scale means that it should be sustainable. By doing so, ecological economists add the protection of ecosystems as a legitimate economic goal (see Daly 1991, and Eckersley 1995*a*: 7–46).

Environmentalism and Liberalism: Conceptions of Politics

There are two conceptions of politics which represent two interpretations of liberalism. One, which is generally speaking more common to contemporary mainstream American liberalism, is based on the value of neutrality (hence what falls under the category of the 'political' is rather limited), and amounts to minimal state intervention, opposition to regulation, and a concept of politics as an aggregate of autonomous decisions—all of which are antithetical to environmental policies. The other interpretation, sometimes referred to as 'social liberalism', is not hostile to advancing certain ideas of the good (e.g., conservation), and is more open to state intervention (de-Shalit 1993).

When discussing the inadequacy of liberalism's image of politics in the context of ecological policies, I must refer first to the impossibility of neutrality in the context of conservation or any other environmental policy. The idea of neutrality, as advanced by many prominent liberal theorists, is that the state should keep out of the debate on the nature of the good. Official policies should not promote or reflect any conception of what constitutes the good life; on the contrary, the state should be indifferent to any discrepancies between those ideas. For example, while discussing distributive justice, Gauthier writes:

An essentially just society . . . does not need to shape individuals in order to afford them justice . . . .. In saying that an essentially just society is neutral with respect to the aims of its members, we deny that justice is linked to any substantive conception of what is good, either for the individual or for society. (Gauthier 1986: 341; see also Rawls 1993; Kymlicka 1989; but see Raz 1980)

But can one remain neutral in matters of conservation? A neutral argument in favour of conservation must make a fair political procedure the only criterion for choosing a policy. Suppose a liberal holds a belief about the importance of preservation. She may hope that a way of life related to the environment (e.g. a beautiful forest), will be available for posterity. But she would fear that, owing to the destruction of the environment, this way of life would be endangered. The destruction of natural objects in fact destroys the very possibility of certain competing ideas of the good life. The liberal (e.g. Dworkin 1986: 202) fears that in the time of future generations one may not be in a position to make a neutral choice from among the ideas of the good life *now* available. Notice that, instead of a concern for the environmental quality enjoyed by future generations, this is a concern for the choice employed by them.

Moreover, this way of reasoning is misleading. If you and I are choosing between x objects and I say that we should choose between $(x+1)$ objects, you will probably ask me why I insist upon object ($x+1$). I cannot answer 'because it exists', because then you may wonder why I do not advocate object ($x+2$). I therefore have no other choice than to explain why ($x+1$) is especially desirable, significant, important, or whatever. We wish posterity to enjoy a certain object precisely because it has been 'desired and found satisfying in the past'. Moreover, we do not preserve—indeed, we sometimes try to destroy—what we think is wrong or bad, e.g. nuclear weapons. Ironically, according to the above liberal argument, we should conserve nuclear weapons and perhaps even the idea of war itself as a way of life, so that future generations may have an awareness of it and have an opportunity to choose between a larger variety of ideas of the good. This, of course, is unwise, if not outrageous. In short, an argument in favour of the conservation of a certain object must be based on the claim that this object is in itself good, especially when conserving it contradicts the interests of certain people at the present time (e.g. higher salaries, more jobs).

It is possible at this point to defend the 'neutral liberal' stand by distinguishing between things that are good in themselves and things that are instrumentally valuable, arguing that nuclear weapons fall into the latter category. Leaving aside the empirical question of whether or not there are people who regard nuclear weapons, or wars, as a good, this is exactly the point: 'neutral' liberals usually find individual well-being the most proper, if not the only, moral basic consideration for social policies. They tend to define individual well-being in terms of satisfying personal, *subjective* individual wants (Brecher 1998). But they could also have defined well-being according to *objective* wants (preferences a person would hold if fully informed, not confused and rational—Hare 1982). Otherwise it is enough to assume that there may be someone who thinks that wars are good to imply that the idea of war should be preserved. We must therefore assert that wars are not good, and we should do this according to objective wants. In other words, the challenge of the environment is such that objective wants should also be considered and that well-being should be an account of final goods (O'Neill 1993).

In the above liberal argument, however, the concept of neutrality is, in fact, derived from the more fundamental values of choice and autonomy, which are, it has been suggested, basic to American contemporary liberalism (Scanlon 1988; Galston 1991; Beiner 1992). The latter is therefore considered to be highly democratic inasmuch as, according to its doctrines, political decisions should respect individuals' choices and reflect nothing other than the aggregate of people's preferences. For example, environmental policies are congruent with liberalism if and only if a majority (or winning coalition) is in favour. Thus, private preferences and economic measures backed by the legitimacy of 'rational behaviour' have supplanted the debate on political ideals and the image of the good life. This philosophy holds that society is an instrument for the benefit of individuals; all the more, therefore, should nature be subjugated by humans, who fulfil their individualistic desires through its progressive transformation (C. Taylor 1975: 540–3). According to this conception of politics, everything is reduced to private interests which are held in balance by a market or exchange (Elster 1986; I discuss this view in Chapter 5).

But if any methodological innovation existed in the environmental perspectives regarding the relations between society and nature, it would be the removal of the distinction between what is considered nature or the environment on the one hand, and what is considered culture on the other. Thus, the concept of the environment becomes part of our culture, and deliberation on the environment a part of our politics. Therefore, it is repeatedly argued and widely accepted that what environmental politics needs now is something more sophisticated. We are talking here about an environmental politics that is more than simply the political discussion of environmental matters. This does not simply imply policies that are responsive whatever the individual preferences or whatever the outcome, but policies that, while being responsive, also take into account the good of the community as a whole and offer solutions to problems that are rarely considered, and still less resolved, by individualistic, self-involved, short-term interests.[20] Moreover, there is a good chance that, in the environmental context, individual and private preferences will in fact contradict the general good. Thus, Jonathon Porritt writes:

There may well have been a time, at the start of the Industrial Revolution, when Adam Smith's assertion that the sum of individual decisions in pursuit of self-interest added up to a pretty fair approximation of public welfare, with the 'invisible hand' of the market ensuring that individualism and the general interest of society were one and the same thing. But in today's crowded, interdependent world, these same individualistic tendencies are beginning to destroy our *general* interest and thereby harm us all. (Porritt 1984: 116; emphasis added).

Indeed, economic and self-interested individualistic preferences could easily lead to the continuing depletion of scarce resources, be they oil, clean air, or scenic landscape. As Ted Schrecker (1991) writes, the resistance of business to environmental regulations has been 'bitter', and firms have fought 'long and expensive court battles to avoid conviction', sometimes issuing threats to shut down firms.

Garret Hardin's well-known 'Tragedy of the Commons' (1968) demonstrates this claim. According to Hardin, the state of the environment resembles a pasture open to all. Each herdsman seeks to keep as many cattle on the common as possible, but the carrying capacity of the land is insufficient. Each herdsman is interested in improving his own position. If he asks himself what is the utility of adding one more animal to his herd, he answers that the advantage is +1 (the herdsman receives all the proceeds from the sale of the additional animal), whereas the disadvantage is only a fraction of –1 (the effects of overgrazing when the land is shared by all the herdsmen). The tragedy, of course,

---

[20] See David Miller's account (1992) of energy policies to two models of politics.

is that all herdsmen arrive at the same conclusion and fail to see the issue in the right terms: i.e. that the pasture is a public good. Similarly, the question of how to reduce, say, pollution on the roads illustrates the fact that environmental issues involve concepts of 'public good', 'collective action', and 'free rider', and that the state should provide the necessary solutions through environmental policies.

It is at this point that we come to the second critique of the WTP mechanism. Earlier I mentioned the technical critique, which I have discussed, and the more theoretical one. According to the latter, one must concede that 'environmental imperatives are basically matters of principle that cannot be bargained away in an economic fashion', and that 'not all of us think of ourselves primarily as consumers; many of us regard ourselves as citizens as well' (Ophuls 1977: 186; Sagoff 1988: 27). As citizens, we are concerned with the public interest or the good of the community rather than with our own personal interests. As citizens, we have obligations that are not always compatible with our private preferences as individuals:

[The] cost–benefit analysis . . . prevents us from achieving a certain kind of self-determination. . . . It prevents us from deciding who we are, not just what we are. . . . There is a right and a wrong way to manage those national parks. . . . The wrong thing to do is to make a big drive-in for Winnebagos. This has nothing to do with what turns a social profit or maximises wealth. . . . (Sagoff 1984: 172–3)

I would like to discuss this issue of citizenship *v.* consumer behaviour. The argument has been stated rather eloquently by Mark Sagoff, and since then has been discussed and 'recycled' by many others.[21] Still, I would like to discuss it again, in order to raise an additional related argument. Sagoff's argument is that using cost–benefit analysis in the domain of politics is wrong because it is based on a misconception of politics. Those who do so think of politics as a process in which we should consider consumer preferences; instead, politics should be seen as a process in which we consider citizens and their 'convictions' (Sagoff 1984: 170). Therefore, to think of environmental problems as questions of preference satisfaction without relating to ethical, aesthetic and political questions is wrong. It is especially wrong to legislate on the environment on the basis of cost–benefit analysis. Some laws should be passed for ethical reasons rather than economic ones. Hence they should have nothing to do with cost–benefit analysis. 'Self-respecting and dignified societies', writes Sagoff, 'on ethical and aesthetical grounds do not trade a magnificent natural heritage for a bowl of consumer porridge' (1984: 170). He goes

---

[21] For such a claim by an activist, see Kinrade (1995) This is a very interesting discussion of a similar argument using different terminology. Kinrade argues that in fact markets should have no role in determining environmental objectives: rather, they should be limited to forming part of an integrated set of policies aimed at achieving sustainable development. But the goals should be decided outside the market, and by the participatory democratic process that I associate with this claim in Ch. 5.

on to distinguish between citizens (and what they want) and consumers (and what they want); public and private interests; and virtues and methods.

Now the point I wish to make is that Sagoff's claim that using cost–benefit analysis with regard to the environment is 'wrong' can be understood—indeed, I think that Sagoff means it so—as both immoral and implausible, or meaningless. It seems to me, however, that most of the discussion of Sagoff's thesis concentrates on the immorality of the cost–benefit analysis, whereas its being meaningless has been neglected. I want now to review the discussion of the immorality of this attitude and then to analyse its implausibility.

Sagoff claims that a society that regards itself as decent should not base environmental policies on a cost–benefit analysis and on individualists' economic behaviour. He calls the clash between ethical and economic approaches to the environment a 'fundamental ideological conflict' and asserts that 'turning the management of national parks over to hucksters . . . is a moral failure' (Sagoff 1984: 151, 173), because as citizens we are concerned with public interests of the community rather than private interests (Sagoff 1988: 8).

John O'Neill argues that these distinctions are inadequate. He would like Sagoff to go a step further towards a profound critique of the system itself. In fact, O'Neill introduces two important arguments. First, he thinks that using the cost–benefit analysis to measure just anything is a moral failure because it fails to comprehend the deep moral significance of commitments:

To treat price as a neutral measuring device and acts of buying and selling like an exercise in the use of a tape measure is to fail to appreciate that acts of exchange are social acts with social meanings. Consider the most famous example of assignments of 'willingness to pay'—that of Judas accepting a price of thirty pieces of silver for taking soldiers to Christ (Matthew. 26: 14–16). The act of so putting a price on Christ is not merely an act of measuring badly done—what is wrong with the act is not that thirty pieces of silver was a poor evaluation, that he should have gone for more. What is wrong with it is that it is an act of *betrayal*—that a person's commitment to another is treated as something that can be bought or sold. . . . A person who would be willing to put a price on a friend simply has not understood what it is to be a friend. The commitment of friendship is constituted in part by a refusal to treat the friendship thus. (O'Neill 1993: 119–20)

In other words, O'Neill sustains Sagoff's claim that cost–benefit analysis fails to distinguish between 'convictions' and preferences, and that, since acts of exchange are also social, they have a social meaning and therefore ought not to be priced. This is, I think, a very important claim. So monetary comparisons between, say, something I could buy with my money and a certain commitment to a friend, or any person, fail to account for this commitment; thus, such comparisons are morally wrong. (At this point I think O'Neill goes a bit too far. He also says so with regard to commitments to *policies*: 'Commitments to others—to friends, family and to items one values, *to the preservation of particular landscapes, species,* and so on—are constituted by a refusal to treat them as commodities that can be bought or sold' (O'Neill 1993: 120; emphasis added). As much as I agree with him with regard to commitments to friends or any person, it occurs to me that O'Neill is wrong to bracket commitments to people with commitments to policies. I would argue that, on the contrary, often commitments to policies contradict commitments to persons, especially if the policy turns out to be rather harmful to many people. Even in environmental cases, a commitment to preservation that disregards the fact that many people may starve or die sounds far-fetched.[22] But this is a minor point.)

O'Neill goes on to criticize Sagoff for limiting himself to drawing the distinction between citizenship and market, public and private interests, values and preferences, without questioning the institutions themselves (especially the market). In other words, while Sagoff claims that 'social regulations ought to reflect the community-regarding values we express through the political process, and not simply or primarily the self-regarding preferences we seek to justify in markets', O'Neill contends that it is also important to ask why markets encourage one to think and behave in an egotistic and anti-environmental fashion, and asks how we might reconcile the attitude we should have (as citizens) and the one we often have in the current system, so that we stop thinking primarily as consumers. In other words, O'Neill is seeking to extend the moral critique of the cost–benefit analysis.

However, it seems to me that Sagoff's methodological critique is also very important, and that it should be revised and reinforced. According to Sagoff (1988: 92), applying cost–benefit analysis to environmental matters is a 'category mistake'. This is the kind of mistake that arises when one 'predicates on one concept another that makes no sense in relation to it', for example asking what the average American is called, or claiming that 2 plus 2 is blue. But Sagoff goes on to say that the category mistake here is that 'public and private preferences also belong to different logical categories'. I think it is better if we don't think of the objects as *private* and *public* preferences, because the very distinction we wish to make is that between *preferences* and *values*. The claim here is that values are not preferences, rather than that they are public preferences. So I would describe the category mistake here as a confusion between values and preferences. This, then, is the methodological critique of the cost–benefit analysis: it does not make sense.

At this point an advocate of the cost–benefit analysis would argue: 'Yes, perhaps it is true that an agent does not price and cannot price his or her values. So when people refuse to put a price on, say, the aesthetic value of an unpolluted river, they may legitimately be expressing their sense that "this is incommensurable with the value to them of various purchasing commodities".'[23]

---

[22] Although many philosophers have tried to claim that these do not clash, or that indeed sometimes it is important to save animals or forests rather than human beings (see Rolston 1996, and the response by Brennan 1998).

[23] See Keat (1994: 338) and Keat (1997), where he analyses critically the role of the utilitarian calculation in cost–benefit analysis.

'But', the cost–benefit analysis advocate would claim, 'an inspector, an outsider, could analyse this person's *revealed* preferences.' This could be done, for example, by looking at the trouble this person takes to defend the river (e.g. demonstrating, writing letters, sending petitions).

However, this is incorrect. Let us consider the following example. Suppose John's mother is ill. She is so ill that it is very likely that she will die soon, and yet the more people care of her, the greater the likelihood of postponing her death. John takes care of her, but he also has young children who need him. He sees himself responsible for both his mother and his children. But time is limited. He must make tragic choices. So, since he is responsible for his children, he leaves his mother every evening to help his children with their homework and cook dinner for them. 'Right', says the cost–benefit analyst, 'this reveals that his mother's life, or being with his ill mother, has a price, which John is not ready to pay.' But this is exactly what I suspect is completely wrong. No preferences are revealed here. John is responsible for his children, and he is in the almost impossible situation of making a tragic choice. Not every time we do X rather than Y are we acting according to some list of preferences. We sometimes ought to behave in a certain way, or believe that we should behave so, without it having any relation on what, ideally, we would like to do. Perhaps John would rather stay with his ill mother, but he has other responsibilities and obligations.

To sum up the difference between Sagoff's methodological claim and mine, Sagoff argues that what is wrong with using the cost–benefit analysis in relation to politics and environmental policies is that it fails to see that 'when an individual states his or her personal preference, he or she may say "I want (desire, prefer . . .) x." [Whereas] when the individual states a view of what is right or best for the community—what the government should do—he or she may say "We want (prefer, desire) x".' I think that, although Sagoff had the right intuition, his readers might miss the main point: namely that values are not preferences, not even public ones.

Thus, the problem with cost–benefit analysis is that we should distinguish between *what is good* and *what I am prepared to do*. The two are not the same, although they may be related. I may, for instance, think that it is good that elephants are conserved, and I may be ready to contribute £100 to fight the ivory trade. But the two questions need not be the same. The question of what is good is not a function of what I can do to achieve or fulfil it, and should not be related to the general opinion about the good. For example, I may think it would be good if people used their cars only four days a week. However, at the moment I understand that there is little I can do to make this come true, at least outside my country, so I am therefore not ready to do a lot to achieve this goal. (But I still think it is good.) By contrast, the question of what I am ready to do (and the amount I am willing to pay) is a function not only of what I believe to be good, but of what I see others doing or being willing to do.

To return to Sagoff's and O'Neill's claims, environmental attitudes reflect ideas of the good rather than what one is ready to do. Therefore environmental policies should be made by reference to people's values, as expressed in political debates about the good, rather than by reference to their preferences, as expressed in market behaviour. Or, as Russell Keat (1994) puts it, both attitudes should be in the domain of politics: one is related to the shared values of consumption, the other to the shared values of nature and its protection.[24] Moreover, it is not enough, as O'Neill argues, to claim that market preferences differ from citizens' preferences. It is also important to realize that environmental questions are a matter of values and are discussed in terms of the good. Thus, if we are to discuss the way we (as citizens) would like our environment to be, we should discuss the institutions that 'act as a bridge between the individual as a "self-maximising agent" and an individual as a "citizen", whose behaviour is founded in the public discourse about value' (O'Neill 1993: 176). This should be accompanied by the question of how to organize citizens collectively to achieve the good. I shall refer to the former in Chapter 5 on democracy, and to the latter in Chapter 6 on socialism.

So when environmentalists make their claims, they are actually discussing their ideas of the good. They claim that one way of life is better than another. One must be aware of the fact that there *is* a debate here on the idea of the good. In the final analysis, this should be obvious. Indeed, the language of the debate reveals this. Any Green, or counter-Green, argument must make some assumption regarding the idea of the good, since the argument rests either on a theory of value (e.g. Rolston's theory of intrinsic, non-instrumental value), or on the idea of preservationism (*vis-à-vis* development, and vice versa) being the good, and so forth.

Thus, the state of the environment calls for politics of the common and a debate on the good. At this point, an objection has been raised that, all the same, the concern expressed by environmentalists is no more than an expression of an individual's private preferences. Moreover, the argument goes, a contractor's wish to develop a particular valley (which is, for that matter, another private preference) is in no way inferior to the environmentalist's demand that all work should stop and the beautiful valley be preserved. So why should we discuss these preferences publicly as ideas of the good that have to be considered? And, the argument might continue, why should we engage in a debate on a certain caprice of an environmental 'freak'? At the end of the day, the environmentalists' claim that the world will be destroyed if

---

[24] I elaborate on what people regard as their ideas of the good, and how it should affect environmental policies, in Ch. 5 in my discussion of deliberative participatory democracy. Unlike several theorists who think that these expressed ideas of the good construct a debate which leads to collective decisions about policy-making (see Jacobs 1997b), I analyse the process as one of trial and error: policies are decided according to a limited debate, which flourishes and becomes richer and more comprehensive only afterwards, when citizens reflect on policies, and regard them as new inputs to the deliberation.

their suggestions are not implemented is similar to the warnings issued by an almost unknown candidate for the 1992 American presidential campaign, John Huglin, that, if he were not elected and his proposals not taken seriously, there would be a world-wide holocaust. More serious an example would be the religious fanatic's prophecy and demand for us to all attend churches, synagogues, mosques, etc.

But this criticism of environmentalism is deceptive. With regard to the first point, the issue here is not which view is inferior or superior—both developers and environmentalists express ideas of the good life and conjure images of how this world should be and how humans should live. They sometimes even use the same arguments. For instance, developers put forward the psychological argument that if we have more roads and more jobs, then people will experience less stress. Environmentalists argue that, since stress is caused by noise, traffic, and the fast rhythm of our lives, then if our goal is to reduce tension, we should limit growth, build fewer roads, etc. But these are not preferences that can be bargained over until compromise is reached. The two sides represent opposite conceptions of a good world—of what is and what is not desirable.

Now with regard to fanatics, the challenge is easily answered: environmentalism is based on *rational* evaluations and on scientific, empirical data, whereas religious fanatics do not appreciate such evaluations. Their system is irrational in essence, while the environmentalists base their call for change on scientific grounds and on empirical, though admittedly controversial, data. So environmentalists do not simply express private preferences, but put forward ideas of the 'good' phrased in moral terms and based on scientific knowledge. We should now ask if there isn't a price to be paid for the liberal insistence on viewing politics as a matter of autonomous decisions made by individuals. The answer is: there must be if limits are placed on consideration of the good of the community, of welfare policies, etc. For the environmentalist, politics *must* provide the framework in which common and general interests are discussed and protected, if not promoted.

Now, since the state seems to be the 'only institution with the necessary resources to provide environmental policies' (Walker 1989), we are probably speaking of state intervention. Some people think that this isn't a strong challenge to liberalism. Many liberals would argue that one can remain neutral with regard to the idea of the good but none the less advocate interventionism—that you don't have to debate the nature of the good in order to justify state intervention. The Rawlsian theory of justice is neutral but nevertheless favours state intervention. I subscribe to the view that Rawls cannot in fact offer the idea of interventionism without a commitment to some idea of the good (Nagel 1975; de-Shalit 1992*a*). This debate, however, is beyond the scope of this chapter. For our purpose, it is sufficient to claim that, even if Rawls, or any other liberal, starts from the idea of neutrality yet justifies a certain kind of interventionism, this would not be an interventionism appropriate to the case of the environment. As we have seen, where the environment is concerned, interventionism is based on and justified by the debate on the good. Any less weighty reason for interventionism would not justify what many consider to be the drastic policies necessary to deal with the present ecological risks and disasters we face and the political difficulties accompanying them. Indeed, if such radical policies were implemented without their being based on a genuine debate concerning the good, they would turn out to be nothing more than what Ophuls fears they would be: i.e., regulations imposed on a large section of the population without it understanding why they are needed.[25]

To conclude this chapter, although liberalism has provided fertile ground for environmental philosophy, environmental literacy, and environmental awareness, it seems to have a fundamental problem with regard to public environmental policy and its justification. Most liberals adhere to neutrality, and regard liberal–democratic politics primarily as a matter of individual wills and preferences, whereas environmental issues call for a politics of the common and the good, and consequently for interventionism.

Does this imply that liberal governments cannot tackle the environmental challenge? My argument is that, if liberalism limits itself to a policy of neutrality and an aggregate of autonomous decisions, then it is most likely to fail. Environmentalism implies state intervention justified by a consideration of the common good, and hence the relinquishment of neutrality as a justification for the liberal state and its policies. A sense of community is needed since social and environmental responsibilities in the environmental era ought to take precedence over self-interested profit-making motivation. If we want to see policies protecting the environment, but at the same time do not wish to retreat into totalitarian regimes, we must take the opportunity that liberalism as a philosophy offers us (as I argued in the first part of this chapter), and look for a theory that is more socially oriented. The politics of the aggregate of autonomous decisions and an economics of individual preferences are of little benefit. A politics of the common, however, which at the same time does not arbitrarily restrict liberties, may perhaps be found in the more neglected tradition of liberalism when it is coupled with a strong welfare state. (For an analysis of this liberalism see Holmes 1999.) Such a political theory might allow for a justification of environmental policies in non-totalitarian terms and so might be far more appropriate to the environmental era. I therefore want to move on and discuss the idea of community and its role in justifying and sustaining environment-friendly policies.

---

[25] It is sometimes suggested by environmentalists (e.g. Spretnak and Capra 1985: 157–81) that *international* environmental concern is also crucial for the much needed international cooperation in any valid environmental policy. But this raises another issue (see Caldwell 1984).

4

The Community of Nature and the Nature of Community

Introduction

Two points discussed in the previous chapters give rise to a debate on community. First is the question that seems to have arisen from the introduction and the first two chapters, namely, what, if any, is the relationship between reasoning about nature, and reasoning about human beings and their politics? Some may say there is no connection at all, others would claim we need a unified mode of thinking to embrace the two. Any answer to this question raises further questions related to other issues. For example, with regard to democracy, if animals should enjoy equal status with humans, and if reasoning about them should use the same terms (rights, representation, etc.), the question arises: is the claim still valid that democracy is 'the rule of the people by the people for the people'? This chapter, however, does not discuss the implications for democratic theory. Rather, it discusses the idea of community according to two modes of reasoning: environmental philosophy and political theory.

The second point, already mentioned in Chapter 3, is that one reason for clinging to communitarianism might be that individualism and liberalism are held responsible for many ecological tragedies in nature; to put it less harshly, these approaches are considered incapable of delivering, justifying, and sustaining environmental policies. The claim in Chapter 3 is that, even if liberalism has been the background for the emergence of environmental awareness, liberalism—at least in its individualistic version—is insufficient for the emergence of environmental consciousness. For this reason, several activists and philosophers have suggested that 'community' is an idea capable of inspiring citizens and sustaining environmental policies.

One such argument has been put forward by Michael Jacobs (1997c). Liberalism, he argues, fails to explain to people the relationship between social goods and their own well-being. It is difficult to establish the link between certain policies and their effects on different aspects of quality of life when people perceive these aspects and their well-being as a function of their access to goods that affect their personal life. For example, if the issue is the government's contribution to my well-being, and if I think of my well-being as a function of the number and quality of services that I personally enjoy, I will not regard a very good elementary education system as something that contributes to my well-being if I don't have children. If I personally experience crime, then I will appreciate any new initiative by the state to prevent crime; if, however, I do not experience this fear of crime, I shall be less concerned about these new policies, and I will not regard them as contributing to my well-being.

Jacobs argues that 'community' and a community-oriented outlook will make the difference. The reason, he argues, is that the issue of community brings in the question of identity, of who I am, rather than simply how well I live. And so, if I now care about my identity, the elementary education system becomes important to me even though I don't have children. I know that part of, say, being 'British' involves having a good education system, or that being 'Canadian' includes allowing citizens free dental care—even if I don't personally need this service.

We can agree with Jacobs with regard to his claim about community and identity. However, we could also claim that this argument can be related to the idea of well-being. The way to do this is to adopt a revised notion of well-being. Accordingly, part of a person's sense of well-being is feeling at ease with his or her identity. Feeling ill at ease with your identity causes a reduction in sense of well-being. In other words, when I know that being 'British' includes living in a society that takes education seriously and is ready to supply its children high-quality education, I feel more happy and content about being British, and therefore gain a lot in terms of my well-being.

The same can be said about environmental policies. It may well be the case that I live in a place far away from my country's shores, but my well-being gains from knowing that my society keeps its shores clean and doesn't pollute its rivers. However, in order for my well-being to gain from this, I have to think of my life in *communitarian* ways: I have to feel that my identity is related to my community and to the way it behaves.

Indeed, the concept of community has been the focus of numerous environmental philosophers who hold that communitarianism is a proper theory for reasoning about the environment and our relationships with it. Sometimes, however, communitarianism is upheld on the basis of metaphysical beliefs concerning the natural order. In fact, the writing on the environment and environmental policies in communitarian terms contains three basic conceptions of 'community'. The broad conception is the *multi-species community*, where humans and nature together form a single large community. (I shall also show that there are two versions of this multi-species community: metaphysical and egalitarian.) A less broad conception is the '*from nature to politics*' model, which posits a community of nature and a separate political community of humans, with the former serving as a model for the latter. The third, even narrower, conception confines communitarianism to the *human domain*, whereby, although the community may be quite strong, it is nevertheless a *human* object and project.

I plan to dismiss the first two conceptions of community on both methodological and pragmatic grounds and will offer a theory in favour of the latter. But there are several models of human community as well. Thus, I will discuss the kind of political and human community needed to implement environment-friendly policies, arguing that this is the community of 'collective rational reflection.' However, among environmental activists, the most popular idea of community is the local, small, community. And so, applying the methodology suggested earlier, namely 'public reflective equilibrium', I take these activists' theory seriously, even though I am critical of it. My conclusion is that the preferred conception of community, from the standpoint of environmentalists, should be that of a political—and not necessarily a local—community, and that, in order to fully grasp its character, there is a need to discuss democratic policies. This I will leave to the next chapter.

The Multi-Species Community

According to this mode of reasoning about nature and humans, we all belong to a single multi-species community, and our obligations to other human beings therefore extend to other members of that multi-species community. This conception of community, then, is very broad, in terms of both the variety and the number of community members. However, there are two versions of this theory. One is metaphysical and ontological, and argues not so much that humans are part of nature, but that nature is part of humans in the sense that nature and human beings' relations toward nature are part of being human.[1] This theory informs the politics of spiritualistic environmentalism, or Western environmentalism, inspired by indigenous peoples in the 'Third World'.

To a large extent, the metaphysical version derives from Leopold's theory (1949) of the 'land community'. Despite the claim made by certain writers that Leopold's talk of land as community is simply a rhetorical device intended to stimulate us by 'loosening language' (Weston 1996: 150), it appears that for Leopold, and many of his followers, land is indeed a community. Morality, then, is nothing other than sustaining the balance within this community by

---

[1] A very powerful expression of this attitude can be found in a poem written by the Jewish Ukrainian poet, Saul Tchernichovsky, who immigrated to Palestine in the early 20th century, and experienced great longing for his homeland. In an apologetic poem, he writes: 'Man is nothing but the pattern of his homeland's landscape.'

transforming *Homo sapiens* from conqueror, or at least owner, of this community to member of the community. From this, multi-species theorists deduce that the biotic and human communities overlap and in fact collapse into a single community. Baird Callicott's monistic theory is an example of such holistic communitarianism. According to Callicott, 'all our duties—to people, to animals, to nature—are expressible in a common vocabulary of community' (Callicott 1994: 53). Callicott believes that the tasks of environmental ethicists is to come up with a principle or theory capable of orchestrating all aspects of our moral behaviour that involve humans and non-humans simultaneously. Notice that by this Callicott commits the methodological error referred to in Chapters 1 and 2: he combines environmental philosophy and metaphysics with political theory in a single theory, using a single mode of reasoning.

Besides being both methodologically and practically unfortunate, it seems to me that Callicott's reasoning reveals the possible poverty of this conception of community. Such a multi-species community is, admittedly, broad in one sense—in so far as it embraces a variety of species together with human beings. However, this is at the cost of the community being very narrow, or thin, in another sense: the content of this community—the values, the debates, the moral reasoning of its members—must be very limited if it is to be shared by all members of this community or, as it is often put in the communitarian discourse, if it is to 'constitute' the community's members. This is because, while some human characteristics are shared by non-human animals, there is very little more that can be said about their having things in common. Now, one may ask, What's wrong with a community being thin, or narrow? The answer is that, if this multi-species community is in fact so narrow, why should moral principles derive from it rather than from a thicker community? Why should humans conduct environment-friendly policies, if so little is common to humans and non-humans?[2]

Another challenge to this metaphysical multi-species community is the following. According to this theory, community encompasses human beings, mammals, other animals, non-animal objects, and so on. 'Nature' is part of us humans, and therefore we care about it and have obligations towards it. But this knowledge is intuitive; it is private knowledge in the sense that one 'feels' it. Consider, for example, the following characterization of these relationships:

---

[2] It should be noted that several theorists have suggested that humans belong to layers of community, and that one of these layers is the biophysical community (e.g. Benton 1989, 1993). While this approach makes the metaphysical multi-species less vulnerable to the critique that it is too wide and open to include species that have nothing in common with humans, it can still be argued that there isn't enough common to, and shared by, those species in this community to make the community constitutive to humans and the moral ground for policies. In other words, if by 'community' we refer to something more serious than a group of entities who feel nice together, but rather as an object that constitutes the members' identity, then it seems we cannot talk of a community of just all species. There are very important differences between the identities of various species. For example, lions eat gazelles, but gazelles are vegetarians (and are eaten by lions).

Morality from this perspective does not rely on tablets of commandments, or rules of conduct, but trusts our own responsiveness to those we know and about whom we accordingly care. . . . for it is in small, face-to-face communities that people can achieve genuine interconnectedness through sustained experiences. . . . face to face relationships with a variety of particular non-human beings on a day-to-day basis . . . through communication. (Mathews 1995: 74, 76, 79)

I would question whether we can indeed base moral relationships on intimate intuitions. Moreover, is it not reasonable to claim that in fact where such close relationships exist no moral principles are needed; rather, there is a need for 'morality' (as in binding rules of conduct) when we deal with relationships with those we do *not* know? And if the community is based on face-to-face communication, how can it embrace so many species? Suppose I do 'feel' that the ponies of Exmoor are part of me because I have known them intimately: what makes me feel the same about the various monkeys of northern India, whom I have never seen, or about the Tenrec Ecandatus, who (so I hear) lives in Madagascar? It seems to me therefore that the metaphysical multi-species community is not a conception that might be used as a rationale for environmental policies.

Several theorists claim that it is still possible to sustain the concept of multi-species community. However, while the first version of the multi-species community is founded on an assumption that nature is part of being human, these theorists base their conception of the multi-species community on the idea that humans are part of nature. This could carry important implications if the theory implies a community of equals. Indeed, the second vision of the multi-species community theory is an egalitarian one: since humans affect nature and are affected by it, they are nothing more than one species within a large ecosystem, no different from any other. There is therefore no moral ground for any different, privileged treatment or respect for humans. This is the theory that informs, for example, the politics of animal welfarists. (Justice should include animals, and reasoning about justice should include the animals' perspective: Thero 1995.) In fact, these egalitarians place the burden of proof on those who claim the existence of more than a single community. As noted in Chapter 1, the latter are often depicted as chauvinists since, it is argued, they supply no sufficient or relevant reason for the distinction between their moral attitude to humans and to non-humans.[3]

A more sophisticated egalitarian argument has been suggested by Tim Hayward (1994; 1998). Hayward examines the implications of the Enlightenment for the relationships between human beings and nature. He claims that one reading of the Enlightenment—although not necessarily the correct

[3] See Ch. 1, p. 15, on the discussion of Regan's position on animal rights. Also, Mike Mills (1996) argues that the question of expanding the moral community and the implications of this expansion are of moral and logical superiority to any other issue. Indeed, he claims that 'eco-authoritarianism' and 'eco-radicalism' fail to do just that, and that any notion of democracy or authority should apply to our relationships with the non-human.

one—is that, in their search of emancipation, humans have dominated nature. This would mean that humans are outside nature. But Hayward thinks a much better understanding of 'domination of nature' is the quest to *understand* nature—not to be alienated from it because of ignorance and consequential superstitious beliefs. In other words, Hayward suggests that we should know more about nature: this knowledge, he hopes, will allow us to develop an attitude to nature that I have called 'egalitarianism'. This will be an attitude of 'being with, belonging to a community, not only of humans but of animals and plants and even inanimate nature too' (T. Hayward 1994: 31).

It seems that the position favouring a single, multi-species community also emerges in the debate between animal welfarists, who must assume such a community, and conservationists, who appear to assume two separate communities. This debate, to which I have also referred in Chapter 1, is eloquently discussed by Kate Rawles (1997), when she relates to deer culling. She distinguishes between the standpoints of these two groups. Readers may recall that, while conservationists are concerned with species and ecosystems, animal welfarists are concerned with individual animals, and that, while the conservationists' aim is to preserve biodiversity and balance in nature, welfarists aim at minimizing misery and pain. It seems to me, however, that there is more to these distinctions. Animal welfarists must assume a single community in which principles of human conduct apply to relationships between humans and non-humans, whereas conservationists think in terms of two communities, one consisting of humans, and the other comprising the rest of the species.

Kate Rawles herself argues in favour of sentimental approaches to questions of relationships with animals and suggests empathy as the key sentiment. Empathy, however, is the power to enter into the feelings of others. Pushing aside the question of whether this is possible (we may wonder whether it is possible to enter into the feelings of animals and whether, owing to lack of communication, we will ever know what their feelings are; in other words, we question whether 'thinking like a mountain'—or, in that case, animals—can be any more than a metaphor), the point is that such a standpoint must assume some kind of similarity in reasoning about feelings. In other words, it must assume a community. Any call for empathy, even among human beings, assumes not only the absence of relevant dissimilarities which may become obstacles to our capability to show empathy, but also 'community', because only within a community is it possible to know the feelings of the other in such an intimate way.

I must admit that the idea of a multi-species community is thought-provoking. However, the multi-species community challenges some very basic intuitions regarding everyday life. Consider for example a situation in which I witness one dog chasing another. I consider it my responsibility to prevent the one dog from harming the other one, and if it turns out that the dog gets injured then I should take it either to the vet or to its owner. However, if I am walking in the mountains and see a bird attacked by a bird of prey I should not intervene, because this is 'nature's way'. Perhaps the death of the quarry helps maintain equilibrium in the ecosystem; moreover, if I prevent the bird of prey from attacking, it may die of weakness or hunger. So if indeed my obligations to domestic animals are stronger than, or at least different from, my obligations to wild animals, it seems reasonable to claim that there are different levels of human obligations to animals implying that different communities are at stake. If so, why then is it unreasonable to claim that a superordinate level of human obligation exists, namely to other humans? To this, one could reply that different degrees of obligations prove nothing; at the end of the day, obligations may differ also between humans. My answer is that among humans some obligations do indeed derive from a sense of, or membership in, a single community. These obligations may be stronger than other obligations that can exist between any two human beings. (For at least two levels of such obligations, see B. Barry 1991*b*.) Thus, if I am right, not all obligations we have are communitarian, and therefore it may be argued that humans and animals do not necessarily form a single, multi-species, community, even if at the same time humans have many obligations to animals.

Another challenge to the egalitarian multi-species community theory is that it may contradict the basis of ecological thought, i.e. that in ecosystems there are some species whose 'function' is to maintain and sustain the lives of other species. At the end of the day, how can we call for environmental policies—policies intended to preserve ecosystems where some species have been, are being, and will be exploited by other species—on the basis of such an egalitarian assumption?

From Nature to Politics

Some people acknowledge that the idea of a multi-species community is controversial, but nevertheless contend that a link of some kind exists between the two separate communities of humans and other species. For example, it is sometimes argued that we can learn from ecology and such ideas as holism not only (or necessarily) that nature is part of humans (metaphysical multi-species community), or that humans are part of nature (egalitarian multi-species community), but also that humans are indeed a community, and moreover, that there is a model of community—that existing in nature—which by virtue of being *natural* constitutes the ideal features of a human community. According to these theorists, the human mind is natural, and human societies are natural: humans form the *sort of* community that is formed in and by nature. Put in other words, since all species form a community, so does the human species. Although Leopold's theory has already been mentioned as a starting point for the 'single community' model, it seems that in it we can find the inspiration for the 'from nature to politics' model too. There is cooperation in nature, claims Leopold; we call it symbiosis. Politics therefore should attune itself to nature: instead of competing, we should be adopting cooperative mechanisms (Leopold 1949: 202). Thus, political institutions should be subjugated to the message of ecology. (Notice that this claim reaches beyond ontology: it is a normative one.)

This theory has also been suggested by theorists of bioregionalism. For example, they argue that the boundaries of a region are, and should be, determined by natural rather than political dictates. In other words, a region is an ecosystem, not a political system, and can be political only to the extent, and inasmuch as, it is already an ecosystem distinguished from other systems by its distinctive flora, soils, etc. These theorists claim that we should live 'bioregionally'; i.e., we should rely on the resources within our territory (rather than, for example, on international trade), live in communities of intimate size, aim at sustainability through self-sufficiency, and let the 'natural world determine the political, economic and social life of communities' (Sale 1984: 284; quoted in Dobson 1990: 119). This, however, only hints at the possibility of forming a political community based on the community of nature.

Perhaps the best known example of the 'from nature to politics' theory appears in Andrew Dobson's analysis of Deep Ecology referred to in Chapter 2. Dobson writes that for 'ecologism' there is a 'strong sense in which the natural world is taken as a model for the human world':

The principal features of the natural world and the political and social conclusions or prescriptions that can be drawn from them are: diversity—toleration, stability and democracy; interdependence—equality; longevity—tradition; nature as 'female'—a particular conception of feminism. (Dobson 1990: 24)

So, for example, the objective of tolerance should derive from ecology: the more diverse the flora and fauna, the more stable the ecosystem. The same goes for humans: the more diverse our community is, the more it tolerates others, and the more stable it will be. Now, it is difficult to say whether the approach is inductive or deductive, namely whether we start by looking at nature, and see first that it has diversity and second that it is a sustainable community, and then conclude that we humans should follow this successful line; or that we start by thinking that we should be tolerant and live in a pluralist community, and only then find 'proof' of this in nature. Whichever of these represents the environmentalist's view, I would now argue that the view is wrong for two reasons: first, it is methodologically false, and second, it is pragmatically dangerous.

The very idea of deriving rules of conduct for one sphere (relationships among humans) from another (relationships between and among species) is thorny. Although we often have an intuition that 'things are just the same', we should be cautious about importing paradigms from one sphere to another. In the case discussed here, there are two difficulties. First, in order to show that X can be extrapolated from sphere A to sphere B, one must show that sphere A is similar in relevant matters to sphere B, so that X in B is like X in A. Thus, extrapolating from nature to human matters involves arguing that nature is similar to, or even identical with, human society. This prima facie is problematic, if one accepts the definition of nature as 'things out there', i.e. the a-human. If, after defining nature as the a-human, one moves on to extrapolate from nature to humans, there seems to be an inconsistency. So the only way that one can take this step is if one defines humans as part of nature and nature as part of humans.

Second, in this case we are asked to transpose nature not only on to human beings, but also on to politics. Herein lies a problem. Nature is, of course, natural, whereas politics is artificial and man-made. Whatever may be said about the similarities between the way humans and other species organize themselves, the latter do not have politics; they do not discuss matters, they do not vote, form institutions, or demonstrate. Learning from nature seems impossible in this sense.[4]

In fact, there is no reason to infer harmony as opposed to any other characteristic from nature. It seems either arbitrary or, even worse, intentional to derive harmony rather than, for example, conflict and competition. And there is no reason why one should find balance and stability in nature rather than cruelty, constant change, and misery. Nature encompasses so many phenomena that it is possible to 'find' almost everything in it. Consider, for example, the behaviour studies of wolves, discussed by Jeff Turner, who, together with his partner Sue, made wildlife films about wolves. He argues that wolves behave more or less like families rather than in hierarchical societies:

Results from wolf studies in the wild indicate that, by three years of age, almost every wolf pup has left home. That means that, in any one wolf pack, the chances are that you would find only two animals over the age of four—the breeding pair. This is not the image of the wolf which we are accustomed to. We have been brought up with the idea of a pack—a word that implies a loose association, which needs to be ruled by a strong leader, who, like a human tyrant, secures sole breeding-rights and dishes out punishment whenever his subjects step out of line. (Turner 1998)

Why did this happen? Why have scientists been describing a different wolf for several years? The dominance order of the wolf pack was suggested in 1947 by Rudolf Schenkel, of Basel University, who studied wolves in captivity.

---

[4] I am aware of the post-modern claim that nature and the objects in it are also 'cultural', but I see no reason to refute this here, since the whole project of environmental philosophy is to protect nature as natural, and my point is that *this* cannot live in harmony with the idea of deriving politics from nature.

Turner suggests that, 'when Schenkel described the dominance order of wolf society, the world had just been through a devastating global conflict, in which an autocratic and insane man almost brought the world to its knees'. So what Schenkel saw in wolves and their behaviour was none other than what he saw in human society. And therefore, writes Turner, 'if we are to even understand the true nature of wolves, then we must always be aware of the context in which they are studied'. What we can learn from Turner's article is that whatever we 'find' in nature may represent an arbitrary choice on our part. In fact, it may be the projection of human values, rather than authentic 'natural' values, since nature neither has, nor is operated on, the basis of values. (Notice that I do not claim that human beings cannot ascribe values, e.g. aesthetic ones, to natural phenomena.)

It seems, then, that an attempt to find harmony in nature may be nothing but a romanticization of nature and, by extension, of politics. This may lead to ridiculous suggestions, such as the attempt by several Greens to form a 'politics which is innocent of politics'. Politics, which is usually the art of living together in spite of disharmonies and tensions, has, under the magic of these theorists, become the art of avoiding conflict by ignoring or denying its existence.

Still, an anarchist could claim that this only proves her point: if there is no politics in nature, then neither should humans have politics. (Remember that the idea is to learn and infer from nature to human society.) 'Let's organize in natural communities', the anarchist would argue, 'Let's return to nature.' However, there is a further complication here: some of the elements and processes within nature are positive in the context of nature, but negative—indeed, harmful—in the context of human society. In other words, if there is a community in nature, the processes that sustain it would cause damage or be considered immoral within a human community. Consider for example the act of killing, which is part of everyday life in nature, but is either immoral (murder) or irregular (war) in social life. Or think of premature death, which is sometimes required by nature to renew life and sustain the ecosystem, but which in human society is regarded as a tragedy that has the potential to destroy a system such as the family. (This provides further supports for my earlier claim that the multi-species community is not a conceivable concept. In a community, rules must apply equally to all members. If a multi-species community were to exist, then all species should be liable to the same rules. But this is not the case.)

So far, I have criticized the methodological premises underlying the claim that reasoning with regard to the environment and the human community can be the same or similar. I will now move on to the pragmatic critique. It seems counterproductive to advance this mode of reasoning if one wishes to influence politics and contribute to the effort to make our policies more environment-friendly. At first appearance, deriving ideas about politics from nature seems attractive because it can be easily understood by the general public. But it is also dangerous. If one suggests that the public seeks guidance for its politics in nature, one might see many people adopting Social Darwinian and other anti-liberal and a-democratic positions. The reason is that, since what each of us sees in nature is the projection of values we already have, those who are already anti-liberal and who accept authority and hierarchy more readily will tend to see authority and hierarchy in nature, and will ascribe to these the moral status of philosophical 'proof', without acknowledging that these attributes already reflect their political anti-liberal and a-democratic positions. (Just as those with already liberal and egalitarian beliefs tend to find harmony and equality in nature.) As long as the philosopher suggests we should learn and make our inferences from nature, he cannot object to dangerous sets of ideas and values derived from nature. If he does wish to object, there are no grounds other than claiming that his interpretation is true and the other false. Such a claim would be difficult to support in a political debate based on 'learning from nature' (because anything can be seen in nature, as argued above).

In other words, even if nature is referred to as community for *rhetorical purposes*, it should be avoided, since it opens the door to interpretations capable of supporting a regime harmful to the environment and the public.[5] Environmental activists and philosophers should distance themselves from such repugnant results. I will therefore conclude this section with the claim that politics should not depend on whether or not nature is community, and I advise the rejection of modes of reasoning about the relationships between humans and the environment which argue that we should extrapolate from the community of nature to the community of humans. This should be added to my previous conclusion that the multi-species community, despite being attractive, is in fact a problematic conception of community.

Three Models of Human Community

So far I have rejected arguments favouring an environmental concern based on a concept of nature as a community, being able to provide a model for the human community or of nature being part of our own community.[6] However, regardless of whether nature is community or not, and whether humans are part of this community, we have politics at our disposal to enable us to care

[5] A question arises as to why Social Darwinism and other a-democratic theories should be rejected. This calls for an argument from democracy (e.g., Social Darwinism is disastrous for humans and contradicts autonomy), which, I believe, can be taken for granted here. As for why democracy is good for the environment, I elaborate on this in the next chapter.

[6] Notice that I have not rejected the idea that humans are part of nature, or that this could serve as a basis for environmental concern, but only that this 'fact' implies that we all form a single *community*.

for nature. The question now remains, What kind of politics and political theory do we need to implement environmental policies? In the previous chapter we saw that individualistic liberalism is not the answer. So let us then turn to an examination of communitarian politics. Since this also involves a variety of conceptions of community, we will now embark on a rather long voyage during which I hope to explore a model of a human community that is consistent and coherent, as well as appealing, in the sense that it is not authoritarian and that it can help solve environmental problems.

The liberal community

Several models of human community have already been suggested by numerous philosophers and theorists. The first model—the liberal community (e.g. Gauthier 1986:, ch. xi)—is an instrumental community since it involves a set of individuals who, having already defined their interests in a private, detached process of reflection, enter a community in order to use it instrumentally to further and actualize their interests. The test of this community is its ability to satisfy its members with minimal intervention, and to limit itself to fulfilling the original preferences of its members. Moreover, it is assumed that the preferences are a given and that they are to be respected rather than debated. If there is any debate, then it involves a process of bargaining over the fulfilment of these interests. Here, the role of the community is not to transform the individual, or to make one understand the other's conception of the good, etc., but to allow people to pursue their own ideas of the good without interference. If John and Rachel have a preference for conserving wildlife, whereas Nick and Margaret have a preference for rapid development, their sharing a community implies that they will respect each other's preferences, but will adopt the policy resulting from a certain mechanism or decision-making process (perhaps cost–benefit analysis or a majoritarian vote), rather than a profound deliberation of the morality of the various preferences. In other words, John, Rachel, Nick, and Margaret wish to live as a community, but to regard its function as a general and rather vague framework for individuals.

So in this instance 'community' takes second place to the values of liberty and autonomy and its form is therefore rather weak. That is not to say that this type of community would not be stable: it may 'work', 'function', etc., but only because it limits itself. Ironically, this model of the community might be self-destructive: the more the community gains in power, the more it loses in legitimacy. For example, if the community embarks on a moral debate about preservation with the aim of changing individuals and making them believe that ecosystems should be preserved, or that the community has 'duties towards the environment', (liberal) members will not be able to tolerate the community. Their view would be that the community should not engage in such debates. But, as argued in Chapter 3, being environment-friendly is an idea of the good that must be debated publicly. So, if one is looking for a concept of 'community' that suits environmental politics, this model would not be appropriate. At least it can be claimed that this model would not make a difference, compared with liberal individualism.[7]

The historical model

The second model is the historical model. Here, the community is basically a question of 'gut feeling'. It is beyond reason, and therefore represents a state of consciousness based on basic and immediate intuitions. However, it is also related to certain social institutions, such as 'shared understanding', 'norms', 'myths', etc. This is a more 'historical' approach (often attributed to Ferdinand Tonnies and his notion of *Gemeinschaft*) to membership of a community: if one is born into a community, one probably remains there. In the final analysis, what binds one to the community is something one 'feels' and acknowledges, regardless of rational consideration.

But what can we say about members' relationships with one another? Since these relationships are beyond critical reflection, it appears that they resemble the relationships within a family, albeit a rather extended one. One has certain feelings towards one's fellow members which are distinguishable from feelings towards non-members. These are feelings, emotions, and sentiments—e.g. feelings of care and love—rather than rational attitudes, or interests. But does this make sense?

Again we come to the question of the size of the community. Nowadays a community may be so large that it is impossible to actually love or even to know everybody within it. Theorists who support the historical model of community are aware of this. Thus, their answer is that there is a *chain of care*, or love. Because one cares for (and loves) one's own relatives or dearest ones, one in turn cares about (and perhaps 'loves' in a weaker sense) their relatives and dearest, and *their* dearest, and so on.

But this theory can be demonstrated not to work. In the first place, when it comes to policies, the theory collapses because it mistakenly bases political

---

[7] It is sometimes claimed that this model nevertheless does allow for the transformation of individuals. The process of transformation, though, is regarded as a byproduct of everyday interaction. Although basic to our routine experiences, everyday interaction does manage to transform the individual, for instance by originating altruism. So, for example, by working together, shopping in the same grocery, and so forth, a sense of community—care, empathy, etc.—emerges. But I wonder about the relevance of such a model to our times. Interaction was once perhaps an indicator of community, in times when human beings lived in small groups; but this is not the case anymore. 'Community' should not necessarily imply localism: nor should it imply any physical restriction or boundaries. A community, as I explain below, can be based on spiritualistic or moral interaction and thereby can have no relation to physical criteria. For example, there is a strong community of 'Greens', which is international. I elaborate on this in the final section of this chapter.

obligations on affection. If this were adequate, love would lose its meaning as an exclusive emotion. Community and political obligations, however, are *inclusive*. But more importantly, the chain of care or love suggested by these theorists requires that I should love that which is loved by the object of my love. In other words, if I care about my wife, and she cares about her mother, I must care about her mother; or if Jack cares about Janet, but she, unfortunately cares about John, then Jack should care about John, which contradicts every intuition. The reason is that caring and other similar emotions are not contagious, and therefore do not provide sufficient justification for political obligations towards our fellow community members.

So other theorists have developed an alternative rationale for this community, namely the idea of 'shared understanding'. Here, the community has a special status ('constitutive') because it is based on a *shared understanding*. But it seems to me that we aren't actually given a clear definition of this 'shared understanding'. On the other hand, it may be a promising idea. So what is shared understanding? Who shares what? And what does it mean to share ideas?

According to the historical community model, shared understanding involves a set of given norms to which the members of the community try to measure up (Bellah *et al.* 1985). So important are these norms to the constitution of the 'self' that, when the member does indeed measure up, he or she is said to gain self-respect (Walzer 1983: 278). But how can an individual's self-respect depend on pre-set norms? Does this imply subordination of the search for self-respect to the already given community and communal framework? Does it imply, for instance, that non-conformists can never gain self-respect because they wouldn't measure up to any given norm? But most importantly, how does one discover these norms?

Certainly, if we wish the community to be constitutive, i.e., to transform or shape the individual members, then we would like the process by which transformation takes place, i.e. the search for shared understanding, rather than the values alone, to form its essence. However, while the liberal model does not take the transformation of the self seriously, since it sees these norms as an instrumental compromise and hence as external to the individual, the historical model too fails to take the transformation of the self seriously while maintaining that the community is constitutive, i.e. that it transforms the self. This is because there is no genuine inner struggle in the process of reaching this shared understanding. The self is not given the opportunity to debate, reflect upon, weigh norms against other norms, analyse them, and so on.

In fact the concept of shared understanding is itself paradoxical. If there are norms that are said to constitute all members (hence they are shared), it is not necessary that they be understood in the same way. On the contrary: these norms are a product of the debate about them. If so, we can't have shared 'understanding': we have instead shared 'debating'. This implies that communitarianism should emphasize the process of collective reflection rather than the values themselves. In other words, communitarians put forward two important ideas: the transformation of the self, and the significance of belonging. But if they seek the latter, they must have the former, and they must allow for an open process there.

In fact, it is not surprising that the historical model does not include a genuine transformation of the self, although it claims that the community is constitutive. According to this model of community, the virtue of community lies mainly in belonging to it. This does not leave enough room for transformation of the self; rather, it makes belonging a rather passive quality in that it does not relate to the person's personality and character as for example in the case of belonging by birth—in other words, by chance. Thus, belonging reveals or indicates nothing, morally speaking, about the person who belongs. This must be wrong from a communitarian point of view. To see why, consider the following.

The Nazis claimed that being a German by birth was morally superior to being a Jew by birth—by virtue of being German. This is not only complete nonsense but also meaningless, since where no choice exists there can be no moral significance. The Germans by birth never chose to be Germans, and the Jews by birth never chose to be Jews; hence they cannot be praised or blamed for their identity. On the other hand, suppose I make a choice which involves joining Friends of the Earth (FoE) or the racist group KKK. If my membership is based on identification with the norms of these communities, wouldn't it be reasonable to claim that I am a better person if, after reflection, I choose to become a member of FoE? And wouldn't such an assertion be based on the fact that I weighed the values of these two communities and decided that one set of values was moral and the other immoral? So actually, it is the process of weighing norms and transformation, rather than the belonging, that are indications of one's morality.

My main critique of the 'historical' model of community, therefore, would be that it places value in belonging rather than in search for community. It is my contention, then, that the source of the community's value should be the ongoing process of search which starts from within but then continues by reflecting and applying critical scrutiny whose goal is the evaluation of one's community-by-chance versus a potential community-by-choice. This is not to say that whenever such a process is applied it results in leaving one's community—on the contrary, usually it ends in accepting the community-by-chance and perhaps making efforts to modify it from within—but the point is that this process is indeed applied, and that without it there can be no real value in community if this community is to be constitutive in a meaningful sense.

Before we turn to a discussion of the third model of human community, I would like to raise another objection to the historical model, namely that this type of community cannot suit the environmentalist goal either, precisely because it regards primordial obligations so highly. Ideas for environmental policies must be based both on reason and on a profound examination through rational deliberation of all alternative policies. Where policies are concerned, the fear is that the policies' impact on the environment will be not only harmful, but irreversible. In this respect, it is important that, if we cannot be immunized against wrong decisions with respect to the environment (say, because ecosystems are so complex that it is impossible to consider *all* effects of our policies on the environment), then at least we must allow ourselves a process of self-correction. (I elaborate on this in Chapter 5 below.) We need to submit our positions to re-evaluation. The historical model of community however is far from supporting this process. If, as is in case of the historical community, relationships are not vulnerable to criticism, and if belonging and loyalty are prior to one's choice, then the community is less likely to engage in any reflection on its values, and therefore is less likely to subject itself to a review and critique of its policies and its environmental attitudes. Environmentalists should therefore look for a community of *thinking together* rather than of *being together*. This will allow a continuous flow of criticism and a re-evaluation of policies and their environmental impact.[8]

Community as collective rational reflection

The third model I wish to suggest here, the 'community of thinking together', consists of three elements: reflection, rationality, and collectivity. I now wish to explore these, starting with reflection. All theories of communitarianism conceive of the individual as bound by social relationships and cultural connections in a way that the individual is defined by obligations. Thus, 'to divest oneself of such commitments would be, in one important sense, to change one's identity' (Miller 1988: 650). But according to the third communitarian model, these social relationships are not beyond reflection. Since these relationships constitute one's personality and identity, they must be compatible with (i.e. not contradicting) free and rational agency.

To see this, let us re-examine the communitarian claim that the community's ideas of the good 'constitute the self'. We must explore (1) what is meant by 'ideas'; and (2) what 'constituted' means. So, first, an 'idea' encompasses two elements: one declarative, the other argumentative, contentious, or even polemic. The latter provides the rationale, explanation, and defence of the

---

[8] An advocate of the historical model could claim that in the past such communities have evolved norms to regulate interaction with the environment which ensured that the environment would not be damaged, in order for these communities to survive: they were sustainable. But in today's complex ecological crisis these traditions would not meet the challenges. As argued below, these necessarily local answers do not answer today's environmental problems.

former. For example, when I claim that 'post-modernism is false', I declare a position that immediately calls for an explanation and defence. It is therefore impossible to separate the declarative element from the argumentative, because if we do the declarative element loses its status as an 'idea', collapsing into a groundless, hence superstitious, belief. Of course, no rational person wishes to be constituted by a superstitious belief. Therefore a person should acknowledge the importance of the argumentative element in the process of constitution of the self. Thus, the concept of 'constituting' beliefs implies a place for reasoning and for a debate of different arguments.

Let me elaborate further. 'Historical' communitarians believe that the community constitutes the self inasmuch as the declarative elements of its 'beliefs' are *intuitive*. For example, as long as my intuitions are that socialist assertions (e.g. that classes should be abolished, that equality is a highly important value, and that the 'market' should be limited or controlled) are right, I see myself as part of the community of socialists, and my identity as a person is constituted by these socialist assertions. Historical communitarians also assume that if I am born to such a community I am very unlikely to leave it.

Contrary to this approach, I claim that the community constitutes the self inasmuch as the arguments supporting the declarations seem *reasonable*. John cannot seriously claim that he is *constituted* by the community, and so in that sense is a socialist, unless he examines socialist values and finds them convincing and appealing. Presumably he weighs the pros and cons of socialism. He has, so to speak, decided that he favours, for instance, egalitarian to libertarian policies. This then involves a process of weighing the arguments concerning and justifying socialist values, ideas, etc. Before claiming to be a socialist, and demanding egalitarian policies John must be convinced—he cannot just feel or believe—that this is what he believes. This is particularly so if the ideas at stake are controversial and he will need to justify his position to others. He has to know *why* he believes in whatever he does.

So, in order for John to be convinced, he must know that the argument is reasonable. Thus, he must relate to the different (either contradictory or similar) arguments put forward by, say, Amy. Hence the rationale, and therefore the idea of the good, is related to the deliberation in which John and Amy are involved. Therefore the deliberation about the idea, including reflection on, and change of, one's conviction, is a crucial element in the constitution of the 'self' by the community. [9]

[9] Another important comment is that reflection does not constitute a necessary part of what every community is, analytically or anthropologically. Rather, it is a normative demand presented here as the basis of any *rational* idea of community. There are cases of communities—or so they are called—in which there is no process of reflection; examples are a football club or a spiritualistic sect. But it seems to me that no rational person would like to define herself in terms of potentially false opinions and values. We have an interest in holding valued beliefs (see Raz 1986: 310).

So now let us look at what in fact is constituted. In an exchange between Simon Caney (1992*a*, *b*) and Mulhall and Swift (1992), the authors discuss whether the assertion that 'society shapes one's character' is philosophical or sociological. But the term 'character' is misleading. Indeed, the claim that one's character is shaped by one's social interactions is sociological, but also trivial. The issue is how is one's *identity* constituted, and how one perceives oneself. It is about the question, 'Who am I?' rather than 'What kind of person am I?'

At this point historical communitarians suggest that our attachments constitute our identity, and that since these attachments are 'deep' they cannot be changed (Sandel 1982: 55, 62). But, as Caney argues, there is no reason why changing one's commitments and ideas of the good should be incompatible with experiencing constitutive attachments. On the contrary, I would add that, since these experiences are not limited by the time and place in which they occur, there should be no reason why such new experiences cannot cause one to change one's ideas, especially when something is discovered to be wrong with previously held ideas (e.g. if the arguments supporting them are not consistent, or contradict other intuitions we have). Again, these new ideas often derive from dialogue related to one's ideas in the broad sense (debate, reading, theatre, studying and teaching, etc.), which, as argued above, already encompass deliberation. Therefore, this model of community identifies community with a process of collective reflection on ideas and identity. In this sense, the model sees community as a matter of *consciousness* and level of relationships, rather than as particular *institutions*. (de-Shalit 1995*a*: 22–61). However, I also maintain that the community is 'rational'. With respect to this point, it is important to add that I am not suggesting that only rational ideas should be discussed. In fact, I do not wish to consider the question of which ideas are rational and which are not. To clarify, let us say that all ideas should be discussed, so long as they do not call for, or imply, the restriction of other ideas. The main point is that the discussion itself should be critical, open, sincere, and in that sense rational: no reasonable idea would be rejected outright, emotional manipulation would not be used in the debate, and the debate would not be censored or controlled by those initiating or conducting it. (This in itself might not be enough to secure rational decisions; I elaborate on this in Chapter 5 below.)

Community, Equal Respect, Openness, Liberty

It may be argued that, since community contradicts other desired values of democratic societies such as equal respect, openness, and liberty, it should be rejected by environmentalists sensitive to the democratic aspects of public life.

I now wish to argue that this model of community is compatible with, rather than contradictory to, these values. First, let us look at equal respect. Among other things, this principle implies impartial consideration. It has therefore been suggested that communitarianism, which stresses special obligations to fellow members of the community, does not meet this principle. And yet, the model proposed here is open to outsiders and is therefore impartial as well. In order to see this, it would be helpful to distinguish between harsh and flexible partiality.

Harsh partiality means something like racism. Since you belong to a different race, I exploit you or discriminate against you. *Flexible partiality*, on the other hand, means that our attitude towards George may change as his beliefs and behaviour do. So, yes, I may discriminate in favour of Stephen, who shares my ideas and behaviour, but if George comes to share them too, he will be treated exactly the same way as Stephen. I think that even liberals are flexibly partial, inasmuch as their theory of toleration limits what is to be tolerated (e.g. fascism, racism). However, their toleration is flexible also in the sense that, if the person changes her beliefs and ceases to be a fascist, liberal society will willingly embrace her. At this point a liberal could agree, but could still contend that the borderlines drawn by liberalism are ideological, or normative, and hence relevant, whereas communitarians' borderlines are ethnic, and hence arbitrary and irrelevant. I have already given my answer: this model's borderlines are drawn according to belief systems and the debates about them, rather than according to ethnic or other morally arbitrary criteria.[10] So this model does contain flexible partiality, but this should not imply any immoral exclusion.

Indeed, according to this line of argument, this model of community does not prevent minorities from having their say and therefore does not deteriorate into a simple crude form of majoritarianism and imposition of values. Therefore it can be said that this is not a model of community vulnerable to the liberal critique of communitarianism, i.e. that it treats the 'other' or some minorities as not equal. Not only are the institutions open to procedures that allow minorities to express themselves, but minorities are encouraged to do so, since the majority needs its beliefs to be questioned in order to maintain their vitality. Thus, this communitarianism not only is tolerant of minorities, but genuinely regards them as equals, not only with regard to distribution (their being minorities does not involve any partiality in distribution of goods), but also in the much stronger sense of their being regarded as equal contributors to the discussion of, and search for, a common good. Thus, their citizenship status is equal.

As for openness, communitarians have been accused of depicting a community that conforms to a certain idea of the good, and is therefore already

---

[10] This is not to say that this community cannot also be an ethnic group; and yet the constitutive element is not ethnic, but rather the collective rational reflection.

closed to new ideas and thoughts and is in that respect conservative or even chauvinist (Keteb 1989). This may be true with respect to the more conservative conception of the historical community. However, the model of community advanced here is of a community that, while being oriented towards a good that will direct its members, does not conform to any particular idea of the good as a final and complete answer to moral and ethical dilemmas. Pluralism, then, is part of the process of the 'constituted self'. The essence of communitarianism according to this model is not that Daniel is constituted by his community (and by its values, rather than by Ralph's community and its values), but rather that Daniel's and Ralph's membership of their communities serves to enrich their 'selves'. So, just as in liberalism the individual is strong when autonomous, in this model of communitarianism the community is strong when it engages in debate rather than when it upholds its values without ever questioning them.

Another liberal principle that is often said to clash with the idea of community is negative liberty, i.e. the absence of external coercion related mainly to choosing behaviour, attitudes, etc. This freedom is thought to be the starting point for many liberal theorists, and is regarded as an individual's right. It has therefore been claimed that the community represents such a form of coercion, or at least that, in its attempt to promote a general good, it limits negative liberties and clashes with individuals' rights. This may be true in so far as the community is indeed an institution determined along non-flexible lines such as ethnicity. However, as already discussed, the model proposed here is a flexible one, so that, if someone wishes to evaluate the common good and challenge it, he is most welcome to do so.

Indeed, I see no reason why this model of community should obviate negative liberty. Here, the community, understood as a collective deliberation which sustains personal reflection on ideas, is nothing but a genuine catalyst for the fulfilment of negative liberties: it sustains negative liberties (without dismissing positive ones—unlike liberals, who do dismiss them), and provides a framework for flourishing and actualization. Again, this is because the community is regarded as a level of consciousness dependent upon an open process (in which each member's effort to rethink values is supported by fellow members, who do so because they also need the collective process of reflection in order to know that they are not constituted by false beliefs), rather than an institution with existing ultimate goals or ideas of the good. Unlike the liberal community, in which the greater the debate and challenge, the more the community collapses into sheer atomism, in this model, the greater the debate, the greater the community's authenticity and spirit. (See below, where I elaborate on the differences between this model and other conceptions of community.)

Community as Collective Rational Reflection and its Appeal to Environmentalists

What makes this model more attractive from the environmentalist perspective than other models? There are three main reasons beside those already raised in my exposure of the other models' disadvantages. First, we are discussing the *constitutive* community, which, as noted earlier, cannot be founded exclusively on the basis of sentiment. Given that the obligations community members have to one other are rather strong, sentiment may be too weak to engender and support these obligations. People may experience sentiments such as sympathy for the struggle led by conservationists against widening the A34 at Newbury, but they do nothing—indeed, they have no obligation to do anything at all. This is not to deny the importance of sentiment in every community's life, or the place of emotions in the creation of communities and the myths that sustain them. Sentiments may even serve as a catalyst for social and political mobilization. Nevertheless, sentiments and emotions are inadequate to explain the constitutive community, and in fact may even be suspect when they provoke negative reactions such as the rejection of the stranger or the nonconformist.

Second, in so far as it is pluralistic, this model is more attuned to modern times. In large communities nowadays, although people do not actually know each other, if they do meet they immediately feel they have 'something' in common, and that they are members of the same 'community'. But then, this 'something', which I have described as the process of collective reflection on the common good, cannot be satisfied with only a single common good. In the modern (and sometimes multi-ethnic and multi-cultural) community, there is a call for several ideas which together inspire this reflection and form the common good. However, to accomplish this, and for these ideas to be defined, there has to be a collective process of reflection, in which ideas are challenged and where we can go beyond intuitive instinct and primordial relations. So, while the historical model perceives existing social values, customs, and traditions as exerting constraint on moral reforms, the present model sees these as the starting point in the evaluative process and is therefore more conducive to the emergence of much needed and sufficiently radical environmental policy reform.

Third, one of the most important critiques of liberalism by communitarians is that, by emphasizing individual rights and the priority of the right over the good, a gap has crept in between politics and morality and hence between politics and ethical considerations. The fact that politics has become manipulative, cynical, and power-seeking is a crucial critique made by many communitarians and environmental activists. So we have the historical communitarians offering us an intuitive community based on emotions rather than reason, and we are left to wonder whether such a community would be open to ethical considerations. While the historical type of community could lead to the enforcement of a particular code of behaviour, it does not imply, let alone guarantee, any ethical considerations. Rather, in order to have the latter, we must have first ethical judgements, i.e. the weighing of several ideas or values against one another. This means openness to other ideas, including those from outside the community, and careful consideration of these ideas. Environmentalists argue that, in order to protect the environment, politics should be reunited with ethics; or as they often claim, politics should be less about power and more about the morality of our public domain and our obligations to the natural world. They also want to see the economy guided by moral considerations rather than by a single principle of growth (Kemball-Cook *et al.* 1991; Shiva 1989; Ekins 1986; Capra and Charlane 1984). All these imply that there should be moral debates in the political arena. If so, then environmentalists should support the free flow of new ideas and the exchange of opinions about them—in other words, the model of community that I have offered.

According to this model, the communities undergo common political, social, and cultural experiences; they reflect and interpret the significance of these events through discussion, debate, literature, arts, and so forth. They then become engaged in political debate through the political and social institutions, and regard the goal of politics as the transformation of ideas through rational discussion rather than an enumeration of certain preferences resulting in compromise. They wish to convince and be convinced, rather than to find a middle way. They are interested in the moral aspects of their decisions.

The same can be said of environmental activists. They are not only interested in compromise: they want at least to try to convince the public that their position is moral and therefore seek to grasp the moral content of relevant policies. Hence environmentalists will consider policies moral regardless of whether they provide or reflect consensus or compromise. It is not the fact that these policies allow this community to live together that makes them moral: it is that these policies are moral because, after long and profound deliberation, the community realizes that a particular act reflects an idea of the good with regard to the environment. For the community to reach this conclusion, it needs to open itself to reflection and critical scrutiny. This is why, when an environmentalist wishes to construct environment-friendly policies, she will need this model of community.[11]

---

[11] I have just rejected the idea that, if a given environmental policy reflects compromise, it should be respected as moral. Environmentalists have long been arguing that the criteria for the moral status of environmental policies is their proper treatment of the environment rather than their treatment of ourselves. Of course, the environment includes human beings, so there is a place for 'enlightened' anthropocentric considerations (T. Hayward 1994). However, the argument goes, we should reject such instrumental considerations as this policy is good since it enables more cooperation between human beings. An exception to this would be

However, this is an ideal model, meaning that often, when this model is hard to achieve, 'community' as such will not be sufficient to guarantee environment-friendly policies. This is why I shall move in the next chapter to discuss participatory democracy. But this is also why so many environmental activists have been suggesting a shift from national and international politics—spheres in which we are less likely to achieve a sense of community as described in the model here—to 'local' politics, to the diffusion of power from the centre to local authorities, neighbourhood organizations, etc. These activists believe that, if we concentrate on local ties, local relationships, and local organizations, we are more likely to arrive at environment-friendly policies. So to end this chapter I shall now turn to 'localism', its benefits and its drawbacks.

Community: All the Way to Localism?

On first appearance, it seems as if 'localism' naturally derives from the model of community I have been suggesting. The latter identifies community with the process of collective deliberation on ideas and identity. It regards the community as a level of relationships in which one questions one's own beliefs and ideas through sympathetic considerations of others' beliefs and ideas. But since this consideration must be sympathetic—one cannot question and change one's ideas without being genuinely open to those of others—it cannot be a process involving unlimited numbers of people. It must relate to a group of people who already have a sufficiently common background for their

urgently needed cooperation with regard to the environment. For example, if policy X is the only policy we are ever likely to agree upon with regard to radioactive management issue P, then there is a good reason to adopt it; even though the environment has not been treated properly, just because P is such an urgent problem that we must have a solution at hand. Having said that, readers may misinterpret me as saying that we should reach a majoritarian or, even better, a consensus agreement about the morality of a certain policy. But I am not so naive as to believe that such a consensus could easily be reached. This is not only because there are 'bad guys', i.e. those who oppose environmental policies, say, because they are in favour of development and industry, but also because the 'good guys' are likely to differ in their view as to what constitutes a better understanding of our duties to the natural environment. A classic example is the following. In areas where there used to be an ecosystem E1, but, owing to human activities centuries ago there is now ecosystem E2, including a variety of species, should we preserve and protect E2, or should we intervene and restore the original E1? (To make things even more difficult, imagine that several species may become endangered if they are not brought back to this area and protected, whereas if they are brought back, species recently coming to this area be threatened.) Environmental philosophers have argued about this, and it seems that there is no clear-cut answer as to which policy is right. I therefore believe that unanimous agreement on such questions is impossible, at least in many cases. Still, it is crucial that we have the deliberation first and make the decision afterwards. It is important because it allows people to reflect on the ideas and rationale behind any policy, and to decide according to the morality of the policy, rather than its contribution to cooperation within society.

debates. There are therefore many activists who claim that we need to translate the idea of community to 'localism'.

I would now like to analyse this claim. I will start with a summary of the
arguments in favour of localism as put forward in recent years. I shall then suggest several arguments which at first sight appear to support localism much
more strongly. However, I shall then suggest that these arguments are still
problematic, and that the combination of community and environmental
policies does not necessarily imply localism. On the contrary, I shall argue, it
may be better for the environment if we think of community as a level of relationships, rather than as a concept describing geographical boundaries of
groups of people. Notice that I argue both that the 'community' does not necessarily imply localism, and that communities do not have to be local to protect the environment.

What are the arguments used to justify and support localism? First, we
should distinguish between two kinds of argument: that which regards community as a source of support for environmental policies, and that which
regards community as part of what is often called a 'Green lifestyle'. With
regard to the latter, I have very little to say. I believe that, empirically, localism is indeed a crucial part of the Green lifestyle. The rationale often given by
the advocates of this idea is based on claims put forward by, among others,
Schumacher (1973) and Roszak (1978), who claims that 'both person and
planet are threatened by the same enemy: the bigness of things'. However, I
have no intention of discussing this here. Although I have a lot of respect for
the Green way of life, at least for analytical purposes, I accept Goodin's well
known distinction between what we should do politically about the environment and the way individuals should live (e.g. be vegetarians, live in remote
villages) (Goodin 1992*b*).

So why do environmentalists believe that localism could help us construct
environment-friendly policies? First, if we think pragmatically—and this is
also claimed by many activists[12]—the language of 'localism' may be more
appealing to a larger number of citizens and to many authorities. Citizens
who are asked to contribute and to make a sacrifice for the sake of their own,
immediate and surrounding community (e.g. neighbourhood, village) are
more likely to feel that this is a reasonable request, indeed not a sacrifice at
all. For example, local (council) taxes are often advertised or justified as 'the
tax that returns to you', because taxpayers can see and feel the way their
money is used. Authorities also tend to be enthusiastic about localism.
Stephen Young reports that there was a positive response among local
authorities to the Local Agenda 21, following the Rio summit. Local author-

---

[12] They emphasize that local-oriented arguments relate to small-scale problems, and therefore more people can comprehend them; see, e.g. Die Grunen (1980; 1983, as well as its plat-
form for Europe from 1989). For a comprehensive discussion of Die Grunen's ideology and its
attitudes to community and localism, see Talshir (1998).

ities and environmental journals alike were 'full of policy initiatives to promote sustainable development', he writes. Many authorities began by analysing their own impact on the environment. Authorities have initiated different means of getting people to discuss matters concerning their towns or neighbourhoods (S. Young 1997).

Secondly, many activists claim that small communities that relate to their locality can live in harmony with their surroundings more easily (Bookchin 1988: 88–9). The reason, these people argue, is that globalization and the international capitalist system are the cause of both environmental degradation and cultural impoverishment. Communities lose both their ability to control changes in their surroundings and their cohesiveness, and therefore their unique cultures. Moreover, the circumstances of having to cope with immediate, small-scale environmental problems help people understand problems more easily, and can change their attitudes from apathy to care. International or global environmental problems seem to many activists to be too heavy and complicated to be grasped readily, not to mention to be controlled. Thus, protection of the environment on the one hand, and of locally developed values and cultures on the other, may be reciprocally sustaining. As Bryan Norton and Bruce Hannon write:

Taking local values seriously may also call into question the contemporary wisdom favouring free trade, international capital markets, and the pervasive search for competitive advantage. The world economy, as currently organised . . . may be incompatible with protecting locally developed values and the cultural practices local people have evolved for living as a human community within a distinctive, local ecological community. (Norton and Hannon 1997: 241)

Third, many activists see localism as an opportunity to enhance democracy (Hall 1976). Reflecting on the attitudes of both activists and authorities to the Local Agenda 21 programme, Stephen Young concludes that 'there is a tremendous opportunity here for the innovative, people-centred approaches to participation of the mid-1990s to become established as best practice'. And he adds: 'Reaching the watershed on participation that is now coming into view ahead would have a much broader significance for the regeneration of local democracy' (S. Young 1997: 146).

However, all these factors fail to supply good enough reasons for believing that localism is the only way we should think of community and environmental policies. For example, the argument that small communities can easily cope with small-scale local problems is challenged by the fact that most environmental problems are regional, national, and international, rather than local, and that attitudes of localism might lead to transference of problems to other places rather than to a solving of them. I elaborate on these and other difficulties below. But before moving to this critique, I would like to touch on what I regard as some of the stronger arguments in favour of localism, namely the theory put forward by Bryan Norton and Bruce Hannon (1997).

Norton and Hannon's starting point is that people think locally. This is not only a psychological fact which cannot be ignored while contemplating environmental policies, but also a fact that could be used to sustain these policies. The 'intensity of one's opposition to unpopular industries, and the strength of approbation for desirable land uses, vary inversely with the distance of that activity from one's own geographic "place" '. By nature, people wish to be near the things they like, and far away from things they dislike or fear. But, more interestingly, they *like* what they are near and they like less things that are distant from them. Norton and Hannon further claim (1997: fn. 6) that the place one comes from affects one's attitudes to objects, problems, issues on the political agenda, and so on: 'There may be an innate tendency to perceive and value from a specific local space.' Thus, they argue that environmental values are nothing but cultural values that are constructed from a given perspective in space and time. 'The intensity of environmental valuation is highest in the here and now.' If so, they argue, all we have to do is cause people to develop a full sense of place. It will inevitably involve a recognition of the 'various scales on which one interacts with nature from that place'.

But it seems to me that Norton and Hannon are not aware of the relativist implications of their theory. If environmental values are nothing but cultural values, and if one's location affects the way one evaluates environmental values, then this perhaps may help in forming local groups for the protection of the environment (on the assumption that all members of this community do share the same perspective—not an easy assumption), but it will also undermine any attempt to construct a national or a global environmental protection policy. In particular, this will be problematic when the issue is seen differently from different places owing to the encouragement of such particularistic outlooks.

Take the following example. During the 1980s countless trees were cut down in East Nepal to warm the water used by thousands of tourists trekking in the mountains. According to some reports, up to 90 per cent of the trees were cut down. As a result, during the monsoon season soil was swept away from the Nepalese mountains to the rivers all the way down to Bangladesh, causing floods in Bangladesh. Environmental reasoning regarding this case would conclude that there was something wrong. But the 'local attitude' theory would tolerate what the villagers in Nepal did. They perceived of their 'place' as a source of income. Their culture and local values meant that, although they did not have a right to harm others, it was legitimate—indeed, obvious—that they need not consider the consequences of their acts thousands of miles away. If we accept Norton and Hannon's theory, we may run out of arguments to oppose Nepal's policies of cutting down forests.

At this point (I will return to the Norton–Hannon theory below), another strong argument is put forward to support localism. This is the argument that self-reliance and local organizations will limit unnecessary trade while not ruling out trade relations (J. Barry 1999; but see Pepper 1996: 306–19 for a review of such attitudes). In fact, this principle is the motto of already existing local organizations, called LETS (Local Employment and Trade System). These organizations, most of which are in North America and the UK, are voluntary organizations of people who are already living together or who decide to live together. They aim at limiting their own use of money and reliance on real market trade, instead forming local markets, organized voluntarily and without profits. Each member declares what he or she can do in exchange for other services and how much of the internal, local, 'money' (an accounting fiction) they wish to accept for their services. For example, George is a plumber and will work for 3 'Green pounds'. He fixes Jane's sink. Jane can teach French. She will teach Julia's son for 5 'Green pounds'. Julia is a mechanic who will fix George's car for 2 'Green pounds', and Michael's car for 3 'Green pounds'; and so on. People will not pay interest on their debts, and all exchanges will remain within the local 'system'. (For more about LETS see J. Barry 1999: ch. 6.)

The LETS organization has several benefits in environmental terms. First, because trade is confined within a local network, and because products and services are created only when asked for, there is less temptation to accumulate, and part of the production is directed towards non-accumulative economic activities. Moreover, if needs are met by local supply, and if, as LETS advocates predict, preferences gradually change so that one wants what is already available locally rather than objects that must be imported from afar, there will be less production and less use of all forms of transportation, and therefore less pollution. The price that people have to pay is what many call 'voluntary simplicity'. For example, one would drink herbal tea rather than coffee, buy locally produced chairs, rather than the more beautiful ones produced in another town, be satisfied with locally produced vegetables, perhaps give up using olive oil (in northern countries), and so on. If people are ready to accept this, there will no doubt be less pollution. The rationale is simple: it is widely acknowledged that environmental degradation is a function of the scale of the economy, so the more local the economy is the narrower is its scale, and hence the less harm it does to the environment.

John Barry specifies another advantage of the LETS organization, deriving from narrowing international trade. He claims that, since the system most of us live in and by is too dependent on international trade, communities become too vulnerable to sudden changes in global demand. If, for example, the price of copper falls, not only do the miners in a certain community lose their jobs, but also, consequently, the whole community collapses. To avoid this risk, people should be less dependent on international trade, hence the advantage of LETS.

Another social benefit has been suggested by David Pepper—who nevertheless is critical of LETS: 'People do not seem to behave in LETS as they do in capitalism, for example running up bad debts (by leaving the system in deficit, whereupon all remaining members would share the loss). Members usually justify the trust invested in them' (Pepper 1996: 315). John Barry predicts an environmental benefit deriving from this social one: since people behave responsibly, and since there is local control of the technology used within the neighbourhood, there will probably be fewer chances of exporting and importing toxic and other types of waste.

Notice that the premiss of LETS advocates is that, if people feel attached to policies, they become more responsible. The main reason, it seems, is that, when people comprehend both the problem and the policy, they accept responsibility. Humans tend to be irresponsible and selfish with respect to the environment because they do not understand the implications of their acts. However, the solution offered by LETS is only partial. LETS advocates claim that, since people are ignorant about the world, we must change the 'world' to scales that can be understood. But why shouldn't we, instead, improve people's abilities to understand the complex world? This could be achieved if, for example, the state offered people better education on the subject.

In addition to this criticism, I see two main problems with the LETS organization, in terms of both its social and economic implications and its impact on the environment. To begin with, neighbourhoods are not always mixed in social–economic terms. As a matter of fact, they are more likely to be more or less homogeneous. Now suppose a wealthy neighbourhood organizes itself on the basis of LETS. This means that members of this neighbourhood will earn less in terms of 'real' currency. The reason is that a person who is, say, a plumber will work part of his time within the community, accepting services rather than money in exchange for his work. This 'income' cannot be taxed by the state. Under this system, therefore, the plumber will pay less in taxes than if he had worked under the current system because his economic activities within the state (taxable) economy are reduced. As a result, people from this rich neighbourhood will pay less in taxes, and therefore less money will be transferred from the rich to members of another community, who happen to be poorer.

At first sight this seems to be only a matter of injustice. But it is more than that. Consider serious environmental problems, such as cleaning coasts, reducing pollution in the rivers, producing safe energy. In order to solve such problems, large sums of money are needed, and therefore only states are likely to be able to solve these problems. However, under LETS, states will have less tax income, whereas needs for environmental services, as well as other services, will remain the same. The state will have to lay roads and pavements, it will have to provide education, to supply and organize the health services, to invest in scientific research, and to spend money on the protection of rare species. At the same time, it will lack adequate financial resources.[13] We see,

---

[13] To be precise, the state could declare that, since its income is reduced, it imposes new, or higher, taxes on income that is taxable. This, however, may be unfair to those who do not

then, that LETS raises a question of social justice and of environmental efficiency.

LETS advocates might claim that ideally we could indeed limit the role of the state in our life. This would be consistent with a romantic–anarchist tendency among several environmental activists. But unfortunately, this is misguided. LETS in fact must assume the existence of the state. Its claim that 'no real money exists' is not an accurate description of the system. To see why, let us examine a LETS advertisement (from the LETS information pack, quoted in Pepper 1996: 313). 'I did not know what to do about my broken window' announces a LETS member. 'How was I going to get the cash to have it fixed? Then someone told me about the Green pound. So I rang up. Pretty soon Liz was round to fix it. I phoned in to debit my account and credit hers [by] the amount we'd agreed. I've not got many skills to offer but I did babysit for Karen, and I fixed John's bike. And then I was able to buy bread with Green money too. Everyone is now better off and *no real money* has been spent' (my emphasis).

Notice that this person uses the phone. This means that he needs a telephone, which was made in a factory using knowledge developed in laboratories or universities. The latter were subsidized by the state, and many of its scholars had studied with the help of state grants. This person also needed the telephone company services. Liz fixes his window using glass, which was, again, made in a factory, or even imported from abroad. Perhaps the factory belonged to another, poorer, community. This means that she did pay for the glass, and presumably she needed money—real money—to pay for it. John's bikes are fixed. Perhaps John 'bought' this bike from another member of the community in exchange for a certain service or good. But somebody purchased the bike from its producers some time ago (unless there is a bike factory in this community). So LETS does assume that other economic activities will continue and that other people will continue living in accordance with the current system. More important, exchanges in LETS are limited to *prevalent skills*. Once it comes to scarce skills, the LETS principles may come unstuck. In both cases, either services are not provided, or they are provided for a flexible price (which is, presumably, determined according to demand[14]).

In other words, LETS can either assume the existence of a state, in which case the system is a limited model and its impact on the environment therefore marginal, or it involves a very complicated system of exchange between communities. In the latter scenario, all communities would be organized as LETS communities. A mechanism of regulating and conducting exchanges

---

belong to a LETS, either because they choose not to or because there is no such system in their communities.

[14] See the case of flexible prices discussed by Pepper (1996: 351–6).

would then be introduced.[15] In addition, if controversies arose, people would need to decide who, or which community, was right. Then other people would have to ensure that nobody cheated on the system. Thus, legislators, administrators, judges, and police emerge. In short, we have a state that organizes these communities. This *may* be much better both for the environment and for society than the current system. However, it would bear more resemblance to a *market–socialist state*, where cooperatives are constructed on the basis of place, that is communities, than to a system of spontaneous local organizations. In Chapter 6 I elaborate on such a system, analysing its advantages, though claiming that it rests on principles that are remote from those of localism.

In these last few pages I have discussed the drawbacks and problems of localism only when it is organized as LETS communities. However, localism as a political idea can be realized in other social arrangements. I would therefore like to return to my analysis of the problems of localism in general. To do so, let me again refer to environmental problems in terms of problems concerning public good and collective action. But notice that most environmental problems are far more than local problems: they are regional or even global. Admittedly, prima facie, some environmental problems are local by nature; for example, the dumping of sewage in streams or the leakage of toxic waste from a silo have local impact on such things as water quality. However, most of the serious, most threatening, problems impact on a larger area. Examples are the ozone layer, the greenhouse effect, air pollution, old and unreliable nuclear power stations, the toxic waste trade, the extinction of species, and the overuse of forests. Thus, for example, in order not to damage the ozone layer, all individuals should reduce their use of CFCs. Nevertheless, several countries have announced that they will continue to use CFCs until they are as technologically developed as the states that have already benefited from the use of CFCs (in both industry and domestic refrigerators). The issue becomes, therefore, a matter of collective action not only of individuals, but of countries as well. If only one country used CFCs, the damage to the ozone layer would be marginal. And yet, each state would like to be the only state to continue using CFCs. The result is that collective action must be organized among countries; but, since in the international arena there is no coercive power such as the state and its police, organizing and conducting such collective action would most likely be very difficult.

One very important way of coping with this difficulty is by raising awareness and environmental consciousness. It is at this point that I regard localism

---

[15] Some activists claim that just like in nature, things will be organized by themselves. This either implies radical libertarian, pro-market attitudes, which contradict these people's claim to offer social justice (Goodin 1992*a*: 154–6; Pepper 1993: 173–4), or a genuine belief that things can be learnt from nature. This, however, is philosophically false, as I have argued above.

as a hindrance, rather than a help, to environmental policies. Localism will fail to sustain environmental policies for two reasons.

First, people with locally oriented attitudes will fail to understand the international and global aspects of environmental problems. Their perspective on life will become narrow and shallow.[16] For example, Stephen Young explains how localism works: 'Visioning techniques are used to get people to discuss how they would like a neighbourhood to be, prior to discussing the action needed to change it. Community profiling and village appraisals involve local people doing surveys to identify local needs' (S. Young 1997: 140). Gradually, the issue that becomes the core of this activity is the way the community lives and its welfare, rather than the environmental problem. The latter is subordinated to the main goal, which is the flourishing of the local community. This might actually lead to the neglect of environmental questions, and to very narrow interests.[17]

The tendency of these people to become provincial in their outlook would be further enhanced by a combination of a political process and a common psychological fact. Localism will allow people to have a lot of control over many, though often minor, issues. Now, when people have control over issues, they tend to ascribe importance to them. Thus, they will tend to regard these minor issues as very important ones. As a result, they will lose interest in other, larger problems. Believing that what matters is that they have control over their lives, they will become obsessed with the minor issues over which they do indeed have control, and indifferent towards the larger problems (which, actually, have a larger impact on their lives).[18]

Moreover, if what we have in mind is constructing communitarian attitudes, this is not the way to achieve it. Why have theorists and activists been misled to believe that localism is communitarian? Because when people adopt an attitude of localism they identify an interest that appears to be beyond their own self-interest as an interest of themselves, with regard to their surroundings. This

---

[16] This is the slippery slope that also leads to chauvinistic attitudes. Community as such should not imply chauvinism. For a good defence of community against the claim that it leads to chauvinism see Herman (1996) Notice also that as Eckersley argues (1992a: 173–4), historically, most progressive changes have tended to emanate from central government rather than provincial or local decision-making bodies. Perhaps this is why Goldsmith *et al.* (1972) insists that small-scale communities must not be 'inward-looking'. But it is not enough to say that they 'must not' become inward-looking, because eventually this is what will happen if society encourages and emphasizes localism.

[17] It is interesting to compare my argument here with Nancy Rosenblaum's recent book (1998). Membership in voluntary groups and organizations has dropped, she tells us. She claims that the way to revive these organizations is by valuing not what they do for society in general, but rather what they do for their individual members. These organizations meet the psychological and social needs of these individuals, and this is their main rationale. Indeed, Rosenblaum is right. But then I am right to claim that these organizations do not help the environment because they sustain inward-looking attitudes and concentrate on local and particularistic issues.

[18] Here I argue that one way of avoiding this process is to think and act beyond the local. I set aside for the next chapter another way, which is even more important.

process may have led activists to believe that people would tend to develop an interest in a cleaner and safer environment. However, this is mistaken; at best it may lead people to include in their own interests a cleaner and safer *immediate* environment. They will therefore do everything they can to *distance themselves* from hazardous waste, nuclear power stations, sources of pollution and so on; or, if they cannot distance themselves from these threats, they will do all they can to *remove the threats*. Such behaviour reveals that, rather than communitarian, localism is extended self-interest.[19]

This is the second way in which localism would fail to sustain environmental policies. People would act to remove threats rather than to abolish or solve them. The goal would be to protect one's own, immediate environment. Groups would therefore develop a collective attitude of NIMBY (Not In My Backyard), or, essentially, an attitude of NIOBY (Not In Our Backyard). They would care not about pollution as such, but about pollution not existing in their locality. For instance, in 1996 a new foundation was announced in Israel, its aim, to support local groups of citizens who wished to take an active part in protecting the environment. Since 1996, as many as two hundred applications have been reviewed, and about forty groups were granted a significant sum of money to help them hire lawyers and conduct campaigns against specific environmental threats. Unfortunately, however, most of the applications were meant to help remove a certain threat from the locality, rather than to help abolish it altogether. As a result, when these groups did receive help and were successful, the financing foundation received in the following year new applications from other groups that wanted to remove the same threats (e.g. construction of a polluting factory, a waste disposal site, and so on) from *their* towns, neighbourhoods or villages. It is also safe to argue that, in places where the local people were more skilled, enjoyed greater access to decision-makers, or had more political power, the campaigns were more successful and more of the programmes they fought were cancelled. But they were not abolished: rather, the waste disposal sites or polluting factories were built in other, less powerful, neighbourhoods. So not only did localism not help solve environmental problems, it also caused injustice: those who were already less powerful, less rich, etc., suffered even more.

At this point let us return to Norton and Hannan, and their defence of localism along the lines described above. A 'preference for the near', they observe, is 'inherent in human behaviour'. That is to say, they treat localism not as an attitude that has to be developed but rather as an inherent psychological tendency. When relating this attitude to NIMBYism, Norton and Hannan claim that NIMBY sentiments already exist, and therefore there is no need to create a new type of consciousness. What politics should do therefore is take NIMBY

[19] Notice that this relates to my critique of the historical model of community: it belongs to the family of 'localism', which is not good as a basis for solving most of current environmental problems.

sentiments into account and channel them towards a policy of environmental protection that is 'developed from many local perspectives' (Norton and Hannon 1997: 243). To see how localism and NIMBY could become legitimate, Norton and Hannan draw two distinctions. The first is between *economic* NIMBY and *place-oriented* NIMBY. The former is NIMBYism that 'degenerates into a game to ensure adequate compensation': people then protect themselves rather than their localities. However, Norton and Hannon claim, if NIMBYs show no interest in compensation, and if their NIMBYism is accompanied by an active search for 'local sense-of-place values', then this NIMBY attitude may help to protect the environment. The second distinction Norton and Hannon draw is between two implications that people draw from their own NIMBY attitudes. Thus, NIMBY A would conclude that, if X is not to be done in her own backyard it should be done in another backyard, whereas NIMBY B would imply that X should not be done in anyone's backyard.

I am afraid the concept of NIMBY is misleading. With regard to the first distinction, it is clear that those who use NIMBY as a tool in order to strike a better compensation deal do not express any genuine local or environmental sentiments. Furthermore, even when people do express place-oriented (uncompromising) NIMBY demands (e.g. claiming that their 'place' is so important to them that they will not tolerate any harm to it), one cannot infer that these are genuine environmental arguments. Rather, NIMBY demands are assertions to do with one's extended self. These NIMBYs really care only about themselves; they just happen to regard their environment as part of their 'self'. So they resist any attempt to harm their own environment; but they do not fight environmental damage (e.g. pollution) *per se*. For example, they might express place-oriented NIMBYism with regard to the burial of hazardous waste in their town, without opposing the export of this waste to a Third World country. Does the NIMBY, then, have any environmental attitude at all?

It is at this point that the second distinction is brought in. While I do accept this distinction, I don't think that the attitude expressed by NIMBY B falls under the category of 'localism', nor does it derive from localism. In other words, if B argues that X shouldn't be done anywhere, why should B express it in NIMBY terms at all? B actually argues that X is *wrong*, not that X shouldn't be done to B and in B's locality. Norton and Hannon argue that 'local communities cannot insist on their own self-determination and consistently deny that right to other communities which feel similarly, but from distinct spatial perspectives.' I agree; but, rather than being related to localism, this is the correct generalization underlying any ethical principle. (In fact, this is a good argument against the concept of 'localism' in its common use.)

Interestingly, it has been reported that, when communities did rely on attitudes of localism, this sort of reasoning (the generalization) was omitted from the process of solving environmental problems through policy enactment. As Stephen Young writes, when local communities such as villages, towns, and neighbourhoods adopted the Local Agenda 21 programme and initiated their own policies, it turned out that a 'strategic' (beyond the local) outlook was needed. However, this strategic outlook was based on macro considerations, according to which often another community would be forced to host the new development, waste disposal site, etc. Thus, the macro approach limits options at the 'local' level (S. Young 1997: 143). If, however, citizens develop local attitudes, they might be resistant to the legitimacy of macro considerations, regarding them as a threat not only to their personal well-being but also to their communities and their autonomy.

This, in fact, is another problem with 'localism'. While environmental policies call for individuals who think as citizens rather than as consumers (see Chapter 3 above on liberalism), localism is, in fact a consumerist way of thinking. Recall the examples given in Chapter 3: as a citizen I should think of the general good, and therefore buy a certain product even if it is a little bit more expensive because it is environment-friendly; as a consumer, my behaviour is motivated by my short-term self-interest. Now consider a case in which a dumping site *has* to be found for some kind of waste. No village or town would like to have it within its territory. As consumers—and as 'locals'—the population will try to prevent dumping in their own locality. As citizens, however, they should consider the general good: perhaps it would be best for the community as a whole (and for the environment as well) if this sub-community, this town for example, has the site within its territory, because from an ecological perspective it is the safest place to put it (for instance, this community does not sit on underground water resources). Localism, then, ties in with consumerist attitudes, rather than with citizenship.

Last, but not least, if one of the tests of a good theory is that it is reasonable, localism fails the test because its anthropological assumption is mistaken. Those advancing the idea of localism mention 'villages', 'neighbourhoods', and sometimes 'towns'. Not surprisingly, they do not mention cities. However, most of us live in cities. Moreover, those of us who live in cities move from place to place quite often. Localism ignores this anthropological fact. Organizations such as neighbourhood committees, small discussion groups, round tables etc., can function where people actually live in small communities, and where they tend to stay for long periods in the same house. In contemporary society, however, people tend to move very often, thereby failing to develop a strong relationship to their 'place' (de-Shalit 1997*b*). Theorists should therefore assume that environmental attitudes have to be developed within a society lacking any strong local ties, rather than the opposite. That most people lack these ties should be the premiss of any theory of environmental policies. This fact may be considered by readers as unfortunate; but assuming the opposite is simply wrong.

For all these reasons, it seems to me that community should not imply localism. I return, therefore, to my theory above, in which the notion of community is devoid of any geographical characteristics, but rather is seen as a level of relationships. This is a rather broad sense of community, and one that needs to be discussed further, particularly since I have suggested a community of 'collective rational reflection'. What makes reflection 'rational'? On what can and should we reflect? How would the community be organized so that it is 'collective'? All these questions call for a certain notion of democracy, which I shall discuss in the next chapter.

Summary

Since I have dismissed two strong conceptions of community—both the multi-species community and the local community—one might claim that my conception of community implies a reduction of community to a liberal–individualistic model of human relationships. However, it should be clear that the model of a human community that I have suggested is not a reduction of community, but rather a defence against its being reduced to the random (the liberal community), or the intuitive (the historical community). I would now like to refute these potential claims.

First, one may claim that the argument that there is—indeed, must be—choice in the communitarian theory is in fact a claim that there is no difference between the liberal and the communitarian theories. I would therefore say that here it is appropriate to examine the significance of choice closely. The liberal depicts individual choice in a community as an act of autonomy, choice being the individual's declaration of distancing from the other—i.e. defining what distinguishes one person from another. It is the assertion that she has chosen *her* way. The communitarian described above also chooses, but here it means choosing whatever will connect him to the other; it is an assertion that, although there are several ways of achieving this connection, this is the way he finds most attractive or moral. Finding one's own way does not necessarily imply rejecting that of others, and defining one's 'authenticity' does not necessarily imply defining it in opposition to the other (cf. C. Taylor 1991). The communitarian in this model adds that finding her way implies doing so with reference to others within the community, and their arguments. The idea of an heroic, isolated person making the choice is wrong because choosing is a social process. Moreover, choosing begins with existing ties; nevertheless, I have argued, not allowing one to scrutinize and replace ties is inconsistent with the claim that the community constitutes the self.

Another difference between liberalism and communitarianism which might appear to have blurred, but which in fact remains constant, is the legitimacy of political institutions. It may now appear as if, for both theories, rational consent by all individuals provides the only legitimacy for political institutions. This would not be accurate. While the historical version of communitarianism does not allow genuine consent (instead, institutions form part of the community and hence are part of what already constitutes the self), radical individualism means that *only* consent counts. The model I have suggested embraces both these aspects: while consent is given, it is only a necessary, rather than a sufficient, condition for the legitimacy of the institutions. These institutions must also sustain the ethos of community or common aspirations, goals, etc. Otherwise, why should the community member bother with them, and consent to these particular institutions as opposed to any others? According to this model, an answer to these questions must involve a discussion of the idea of the good. 'Thus, these specific institutions are to be preferred,' argues the communitarian, 'because they advance an idea of the good which I find to be attractive and right.'

To summarize this chapter, then, I started off by examining the role of community in any political theory about environmental policies. I argued that, if individualistic liberalism cannot construct environmental consciousness, there might be a need for a communitarian theory. However, many environmental philosophers have gone too far in suggesting that such a theory would be based on the idea that all species belong to the same community, or that there is a way to derive such theory from a close examination of nature. I also claimed that activists have gone too far in suggesting that we should have a human community modified to 'localism'. I have analysed the pros and cons of the localist system, arguing that it is both socially unjust and environmentally ineffective. I therefore claim that we should be thinking in communitarian terms, meaning that all humans belong to a community which engages in collective rational reflection on values and policies—reflection of the kind likely to sustain environmental policies.

However, the picture is not complete. 'Community' alone is not sufficient to construct environmental policies. It is revealed that environmental planning, conducted by experts, should be respectful of and sensitive to people and their wills—or at least so we want it to be, to the extent that we are democrats. As Huey Johnson, founder of the Resource Renewal Institute in San Francisco, writes, this planning should be 'developed by government with the input of key players in the region it covers—not mandated from the top down—and [it should be] designed to deal with problems appropriately at each level of scale'. Would this imply letting local communities decide for themselves? Or should the experts decide alone? Johnson, unlike many environmental activists, agrees that environmental planning demands attitudes that go beyond the local:

Both the Netherlands and New Zealand delegate the responsibility for managing local environmental problems . . . to local authorities. But both nations also set standards at the regional and national levels, because they realise that many environmental issues cross the boundaries of city and region. The same will be true in the United States. While cities and states will implement their own green plans, federal standards and agreements will be necessary to deal with issues that cross boundaries. Ultimately, some environmental issue will require international agreements and standards. (Johnson 1995: 3)

How should we find the balance between local needs and global perspectives? between global needs and local perspectives? How do we construct environmental consciousness without manipulating people? What kind of institutions do we need for this? To discuss these issues, I turn to the chapter on democracy.

5

Democracy and the Environment: A Radical Theory of Participation

Introduction: The Challenge of 'Survivalism' and 'Eco-authoritarianism'

Community, as described in the last chapter, is a state of mind, just like altruism. Often it is natural and spontaneous, but this is not always the case. In many social and economic circumstances, people tend to lose their communitarian attitudes and practices. There is much sociological evidence to indicate that when this happens people tend to be careless, indifferent towards their chances of effecting change, and alienated not only from the 'system', but from nature and the environment as well. Interestingly, this happens when communities are affected by environmental disasters caused directly by human beings (as opposed to ecological disasters such as tornadoes, earthquakes, etc.). In such cases many communities have been shocked at the extent of their own collapse (Picon *et al.* 1997; P. Brown and Mikkelsen 1990; Edelstein 1988). We find that this effect is doubled in circumstances of poverty and misery (Harvey 1996; Blowers and Leroy 1994).

One may wonder how it is that 'community' disappears so quickly in times of crisis. It would appear that overcoming the state of mind of carelessness is similar to sustaining altruism, a quality latent in human nature requiring encouragement to manifest itself. Care and community are latent in people's dreams and aspirations, but these qualities are unfortunately repressed by economic and social circumstances. This is where politics comes in to expose and encourage a state of mind of care and community. Compare for example post-communist Russia with post-communist Czechoslovakia. In Russia totalitarianism has been replaced by a cynical, chaotic, and corrupt regime resulting in despair, emigration, and even greater indifference. In Czechoslovakia totalitarianism has been replaced by Vaclav Havel's politics of hope, which has given rise to greater participation, a heightened sense of responsibility, increased community feeling, and greater sense of care for the environment.

However, we are not simply searching for ways of overcoming crises: we have also to prevent their occurrence. But the approach to both is the same.

Since community is a state of mind, there are basically two very simple ways to prevent alienation and indifference and to overcome them when they occur. One is by offering people greater equality in their opportunities to welfare; the other is to make them feel more like members of the community and less like bystanders. The first, then, involves egalitarian (in economic terms) politics, while the second signifies participatory democracy. I would like to begin by discussing the latter, which is less controversial in our time, and to follow this in the next chapter with discussion of a theory of democratic socialism.

There is a prevailing school of thought among environmentalists, i.e. *survivalism*, which maintains that democracy is in fact an obstacle towards more environment-friendly policies.[1] At the end of the day, claim the survivalism theorists, people will invariably tend to protect their own interests, especially in situations of 'public goods', the 'prisoners' dilemma', and so on; and the more difficult the times are, the more this is likely to happen. A democratic regime is not suited to the environmental era since it is open to cynical exploitation by those with narrow, short-run, self-regarding interests, e.g. 'more jobs', 'greater consumption', and so on. Serious long-term human interests and the interests of non-human entities cannot be protected or even considered under democratic regimes. Notice that the premiss of these theorists is that politics is not about encouraging the arts, educating our children, holding (international) sporting events, etc.: rather, politics in general, and democracy in particular, is about survival set against a background of cleavages, contradictory interests, enmity, and hostility. Thus, democracy is a luxury that people can afford in times of affluence, when competition is minimal. The main environmental challenge is extreme scarcity entailing a return to premodern era politics, to a Hobbesian world—in other words, to abandoning democracy for the sake of more authoritarian and less tranquil politics. The choice humans have is between 'Leviathan or oblivion' (Ophuls 1992).

The survivalists, however, are mistaken on two grounds. First, while it is true that under certain difficult circumstances people tend to lose faith in community and to care less for one another, it is also important to note that this occurs mostly when the hardship is the consequence of *man-caused* technological disasters. In cases of natural disaster and many crises caused by outside agencies (e.g. foreign governments), people tend to find comfort in

---

[1] A very good discussion of survivalism is in Dryzek (1996: 23–45). As for Survivalism theorists, see Hardin, (1968) and Ophuls (1977). Recently Ophuls revised his attack on contemporary politics (1997). Although I do not agree with Ophuls's thesis, I think that his first book was important and well written, and therefore I shall allow myself not to discuss his new book profoundly. It is not clear what his new book's target is. He mentions 'liberal polity', 'modernity', 'the modern political paradigm', 'civilization'; but then—after claiming that any talk about values is conceptually wrong—he discusses 'liberal-democratic values'. Eventually he challenges the 'Enlightenment'. But this seems strange, because he does accept and internalize important Enlightenment values such as scepticism (see p. x), and he is influenced by Darwinism and socio-biology, which do belong to the Enlightenment.

community and to become increasingly aware of the 'other'. Belief in democratic procedures and way of life also tends to intensify rather than weaken (Goodin and Dryzek 1977; Erikson 1994). Erikson (1994: 22) studied people's reactions to, and behaviour in the wake of, such environmental disasters as the Three Mile Island (radioactive link in 1979), or the case of the Ojibwa tribe in north-western Ontario, where in the late 1970s the tribe learned that the local waterways they had been using were contaminated with metholmercury. According to Erikson, these events, despite not being as sudden or explosive as a natural disaster, are highly traumatic, to the extent that they 'blur the line we have been in the habit of drawing between the acute and the chronic'. Following this study, Maurie Cohen (1996) has compared different environmental disasters. He claims that the taxonomy of disasters must take into account four intervening variables: social class, geographical location, cultural adaptation, and perceptual considerations.

What these works indicate, I believe, is that environmental 'events' are often not perceived as 'disasters', and that under such circumstances the motivation to share and care more is high. This fascinating evidence may imply that the psychological premisses of survivalism are far-fetched. A more careful examination is therefore required to ascertain why communities collapse in the face of man-caused disasters and gain in strength when coping with natural or external crisis. In conclusion, it seems that community and democracy can be a positive factor in helping people face environmental disasters, especially those caused by 'nature'. However, it should be mentioned that, since humans interfere in nature and in ecosystems so often, it is sometimes difficult to distinguish between man-caused and 'natural' disasters.

The second reason why the survivalism theorists are mistaken is that the survivalists relate to a very narrow conception of democracy, namely as an instrumental mechanism for advancing the interests of individuals. If one regards democracy as such a system, then one is likely to accept Hardin's and Ophul's pessimism. However, other models of democracy may better describe the uniqueness of this regime. I therefore wish to analyse models of democracy and to show how faith in democracy can be restored, even in the face of the need for radical environmental policies.

Survivalism, however, represented only the early wave of scepticism towards democracy inspired by environmental thought. The second wave, which typified the 1980s and 1990s, is often referred to as *eco-authoritarianism*. For example, in a series of articles and a book, Laura Westra (1993; 1994; 1995) has suggested that democracy should be replaced by 'some sort of Platonic philosopher–queen'. At times it seems as if Westra is actually criticizing *neutral* liberalism, rather than democracy—for example when she argues that 'rights may be better viewed as means towards justice', or that 'laws and regulations should be chosen according to an ideal goal or "good", rather than represent the haphazard implementation of voters' preferences'. But then she goes on to refer to democracy as a 'sacred cow', arguing that democratic institutions cannot cope with the environmental challenge, and therefore lead to immoral consequences. She justifies abandoning democracy in the name of a 'serious commitment to the public interest'. At the same time, however, she calls for 'governments, professionals, and institutions' to educate the public and to do what is necessary regardless of what the public thinks. This, she claims would be in the public interest (Westra 1994: 196). Readers may think it odd that some environmentalist would wish to ignore what people think, and I will soon challenge this idea of ignoring the public. However, as Pepperman-Taylor argues, this attitude can logically be derived from radical biocentrism. How? Because if one is biocentric, a policy cannot be justified on the ground that it is what people—human beings—actually want, as this would undermine the biocentric argument that human beings and their desires are no more important than other species and their interests, or the ecocentric argument that maintaining balance in nature is a moral imperative of the highest importance. Thus, Pepperman Taylor argues (1996), biocentrics can justify a policy on the grounds that the policy is right, regardless of what people think.

Notice, however, two very important differences between this kind of argument and the more common argument put forward by radicals, communitarians, and socialists: namely that sometimes the aggregation of individuals' wills should not be the guide for policy-making. (In fact, I argue this both in this chapter and in Chapter 3.) First, the popular argument claims that sometimes there is an idea of the good which overrules individuals' interests, i.e. overrides what individuals *want*. Westra, however, wants the philosopher-queen to ignore what people *think*. Communitarians, radicals, socialists do not argue that what people think is irrelevant. On the contrary: the idea of the good that should guide our policies is conceived and developed into a theory by people. Westra's approach, however, is that only highly educated people—philosophers, for instance—should decide on policies, regardless not of the individual's interests, but of what people (or laypersons) think about morality and the good life.

The second important difference is that even these radicals, communitarians, and socialists would eventually subordinate policy to a new process of public scrutiny, and will legitimate revisions in the policy if it turns out that the policy-makers were wrong. (I develop this argument below.) Westra cannot conceive that the philosopher–queen might in fact be wrong. She therefore justifies abandoning democracy to protect the public interest as defined by the philosopher–queen.

There is another argument against Westra's position. Suppose for a moment that the philosopher–queen *should* define the public interest. Surely, the public interest includes autonomy, sovereignty, civil rights, and political freedoms. So, while the environmental critique on current democratic institutions (that they are often incapable of taking sufficient account of 'ecological integrity' or environmental needs) is legitimate, it should not lead us simply to dismiss all other values associated with democracy, e.g. political freedom, when they seem to collapse with the value of ecological integrity;[2] nor should it lead us to abandon democracy for the sake of a regime which in ignoring these values would be even more likely to be immoral.

Moreover, if there are indeed problems with people's behaviour and attitudes toward the environment, the cause could be too *little* democracy rather than too much. The eco-authoritarian's conclusion that democracy is the cause of environmental problems seems arbitrary, over-hasty, and lacking sufficient grounds. Thus, Robert Paehlke recently argued that the relationship between environment, economic growth, and democracy is far more complex than previously thought, and therefore that 'the scarcity-distribution traumas [that eco-authoritarians] feared would now seem more likely in the absence of democratic regimes committed to environmental protection rather than within them' (Paehlke 1996: 19).

Notice, also, that the eco-authoritarian conclusions remove us from the practice of public reflective equilibrium; rather than being engaged in a serious consideration of public attitudes, eco-authoritarianism recommends Platonic politics, regardless of ideas and theories that, for example, environmental activists have put forward. This seems to me not only a threat to activists' ability to have an influence on policies, but also a threat for the environment; I therefore find it hard to understand why many environmentalists and activists find eco-authoritarianism so appealing.[3]

Above and beyond all these reasons for democracy, it should be noted that the question of whether or not we should practise democracy involves more than mere implications regarding the state of the environment. In the final analysis, humanity is faced with a variety of problems, besides those that concern the environment. However crucial solving environmental problems may be, it seems that solutions must be found within the framework of democracy because democracy is needed—in extra large doses—for a great many reasons, ranging from constituting social justice to protecting freedoms, from relieving poverty to reaching peace agreements in areas such as the Middle East, the former Yugoslavia, etc. I am conscious of the debate on this issue: Rudolf Bahro, for instance, is a prominent Green leader, very frustrated with democracy (Bahro 1986: 210–13); but I, for one, am not certain that this debate is one the people of this world can afford. Perhaps those who already benefit from democracy, in whose countries democracy is taken for granted, can afford the luxury of playing with semantics and concepts. I come from a place where

---

[2] Focusing on ecological integrity only is a strange reduction of morality to a very narrow, single-principle theory (see Pepperman-Taylor 1996: 94).

[3] I have in mind organizations such as Earth First! and Dave Foreman's new groups. The only reason I can find is that eco-authoritarianism summarizes attitudes of anti-establishment (see de-Shalit 1996).

democracy is a fragile idea; where the alternative—a fundamentalist, perhaps authoritarian regime—is more than an abstract nightmare. Those of us who experience the real danger of losing democracy cannot play with such ideas, and therefore I will try to convince readers of the need for democracy, and will not simply suffice with an assertion that democracy is needed. After reviewing the various theories of democracy, therefore, and exploring why democracy is beneficial to the environment, I mean to offer a systemic theory of 'deliberative participatory democracy' and explain why I believe democracy is good in general. Only then will I apply this model of democracy to environmental policies.

'Democracy is Good for the Environment': A Short Review of the Literature

Several arguments have been put forward to support the claim that democracy is good for the environment. One reason for this diversity of arguments is that there is more than a single conception of democracy. In general, every democracy involves periodic multi-party elections, separation of powers, and a system of laws and rights (including the universal right to vote) that protects citizens from the arbitrary use of power. Beyond these principles, there are many theories in philosophical and political works on the subject of democracy. Thus, we read about 'representative', 'direct', 'federal', 'participatory', 'deliberative', and other types and models of democracy. Consequently, when activists and philosophers argue in favour of democracy and why it is good for the environment, they put forward different theories. In broad terms, the theories and arguments fall into four groups.[4]

1. Representative democracy is good for the environment because it is more likely than any other regime to represent the interests of future generations and non-human species

Such arguments are put forward by John Barry (1999) and Andrew Dobson (1997), among others. They argue that future generations—people who are not yet born—and animals and other entities in the environment that cannot express their interests do have interests. Since in principle 'anyone whose interests are affected by the government of a country should have the right to vote for (or against) it', and since 'as defined in the Brundtland report of the World Commission on Environment and Development . . . development is sustainable when it meets the needs of the present without compromising the

---

[4] Notice that I do not claim to review all theories about the environment and democracy.

ability of future generations to meet their own needs', and since 'it is indisputable that actions taken now affect future generations [and non-human species]', it can be argued that we should therefore establish representative mechanisms to represent and protect these interests of future generations and animals. (Interestingly, both authors also support participatory mechanisms.) For example, we could theoretically nominate representatives to parliament or any other political institution; these representatives could then represent future generations, so that the future would have a vote.

An immediate problem which Dobson himself raises relates to the assumption latent in this claim, that 'elected representatives will represent the interests of their constituents more effectively than appointees because of the need to submit themselves to re-election'. The problem is that future generations cannot now elect or re-elect their representatives, and non-human species can never elect theirs. What do we mean, then, when we talk of 'representatives'? Dobson's suggestion is a very interesting one. He suggests appointing proxy (substitute) future generations from the present generation. They would function in 'exactly the same way as any democratic electorate. They would debate and fight election campaigns, outlining their objectives as far as furthering the interests of future generations (and non-human species) are concerned. "The proxy electorate would consider the various candidates' merits and then choose its preferred candidates through a democratic election. The [winners] would then sit in the democratic assembly alongside present generation representatives."

This kind of (virtual?) representation raises all kinds of questions which I would rather not discuss here (such as, if this is indeed done, should we also nominate representatives and constituents for people in a state of coma? Should we do this for foetuses (they differ from future generations in that their future existence is certain, whereas the existence of future generations is contingent on our policies, so why nominate representatives to them)? Should we nominate representatives for our dead ancestors?) However, the most salient difficulty is raised by Dobson himself: how do we know, or what kind of guarantee do we have, that the interests of future generations and non-human species would in fact be represented by such a random sample? What if we pick up dozens of George Bushes to serve as members of this constituency? They would not be interested in these interests.

Dobson's solution is to identify a lobby in the present generation that 'has its eyes firmly fixed on the future, as it were. One such lobby is that which argues in favour of environmental sustainability.' Dobson's proposal implies that we should select this group of people from Green voters, or from environmental NGOs. In other words, we should allow the latter to have two votes. But this act may be seen by many, and quite rightly, as undemocratic, biased, and inegalitarian, since it sustains and fosters a certain position and faction (i.e. environmentalists, conservationists, etc.) within parliament. It is inegalitarian because the idea of democratic representation is not only that many ideas are represented, but also that this representation is proportional to the society in which the assembly functions; this is guaranteed by the principle of 'a single vote for each person'. Moreover, this is a biased system, which makes it very controversial, and subject to criticism of illegitimacy. According to this suggestion, we have to decide in advance what is the best way to care for the future, and only then have a debate about how to care for the future. Developers could argue that it is their ideas that really embrace a care for the future, rather than those of the conservationists. Suppose, for example, that in the newly establish parliament in Northern Ireland we were to allow more seats to peace supporters because they care for the future. Unionists or radical supporters of the IRA could claim that these people do *not* care for the future, or that they take a too great risk in the present for the sake of a fantasy of the future. Well, in this case I personally would not mind strengthening the peace supporters, but I hope this clarifies my point: that this move is not necessarily democratic, in the sense that it sustains a certain position and strengthens a certain group or party before the debate begins. Moreover, this move not only sustains a certain position and a certain group, but it also suggests that we can or should relocate certain democratic processes from the general public *to* groups: it thereby makes democracy narrower rather than stronger.

In addition, this suggestion is counterproductive. If we do allow environmental NGOs to form an extra constituency, many other such groups (e.g. women's organizations, elderly people, farmers) could demand an equal treatment, and often for good reason. The result will be that all these groups will gain extra seats in the parliament, and strengthening one might be balanced by strengthening another.

Several philosophers have raised yet another problem with Dobson's idea. They have argued that it is not unequivocal that we can describe future people and non-human species as 'having interests' (Steiner 1983). Some of the difficulties mentioned are: (*a*) if future people have interests, the first interest they have is to exist; this would put us contemporaries under an obligation to reproduce all these potential future people; (*b*) people who do not exist now cannot be said to have rights because somebody who does not exist cannot have anything; and (*c*) if non-human animals have interests then they have rights, and this, by so extending the notion of rights bearers, reduces the power of any theory of rights, and hence of what rights entail.

These difficulties, however, should not bother us too much here. Since I have discussed these objections elsewhere in depth (de-Shalit 1995*a*: 112–22), I will only say that we could distinguish between having an interest in the sense of having a desire that is congruent with other desires of the interest-holder, and having an interest in the sense that there is something that could contribute to the well-being of the interest-holder. If we relate to the latter, we could argue that future people, once they exist, will have interests for which we should cater. But it seems that Dobson's model raises too many difficulties, as we have seen.

2. Participatory democracy is good for the environment because it is more likely than any other regime to incorporate the interests of non-human entities or because it will fight the interests of developers better

Participatory democracy could mean either intensified participation in voting and referendums, or mechanisms such as public hearings, citizen panels, writing letters, and demonstrating, or all the above. It is important to note, however, that in the context of environmental policies participatory democracy is often mentioned as an alternative to a common tendency in the developed countries to rely too heavily on experts and scientists. Thus, participatory democracy is not only a claim against centralist government or against a system in which all that matters is that the majority supports the government, but also a claim in favour of submitting decisions and policies to scrutiny by the general public and by activists in particular.

Two main arguments have been suggested to support participatory democracy. First, Robert Goodin holds the view that it is participatory democracy that will cater for the interests of the non-human, or those who have interests but are unable to give voice to them. Goodin (1996) claims that these could be incorporated within the human sphere of interest. Indeed, the more participatory the democracy, and the larger and the more diverse the electorate, the greater the likelihood of developers, vivisectionists, etc., having to justify themselves, and of their being a group of people who have internalized the interests of nature. Also, the more participatory the regime, the more it will need to respond to such interests since they are expressed as aspects of human interest. (I elaborate on this below.)

Advocates of this model of democracy believe that, if people have not already internalized the interests of nature, there is a good chance that they will do so within the framework of participatory democracy. Indeed, it is claimed that the main advantage of participatory democracy is that it 'educates' and 'enlightens' citizens. In Carole Pateman's words, 'psychological qualities' are developed. Thus, 'the major function of participation . . . is . . . an educative one, educative in the very widest sense' (Pateman 1970: 42). This is an optimistic belief, which forms an inseparable element of participatory theory. It is based on the assumption that people know best what is good for themselves (Thompson 1970)— a rather controversial assumption. Two arguments can be raised against it. It can be argued that, while people may indeed know what is best for themselves, this nevertheless does not mean that their actions are moral. In a case in which setting up a new industry provides lots of jobs at the cost of irreversible damage to future generations, contemporary people 'know' what is best for themselves (more jobs), but they act immorally (inflicting harm on future generations). Another argument against this optimistic assumption is that environmental goods are public goods and securing them is a matter of collective action. In such cases people might assume that what is best for them is that everybody else should comply and they should have a free ride. The result —it is well known—is that each individual acts in order to maximize his own interest, assuming that he is the only one having a free ride, until the collective action fails and the public good is not achieved. Later in this chapter I shall suggest a way to argue for participatory democracy without relying on this assumption, and shall examine whether participatory democracy would indeed yield better environmental policies.

A different claim in favour of participatory democracy has been put forward by Alan Carter, though his assumption is that participatory democracy is also decentralist. (Below I discuss the different possible relations between direct, representative, participatory, and centralist democracy.) Carter contends that participatory democracy is a vital and crucial instrument in opposing dominance and inegalitarian policies. Opposing such policies, he claims, will break a vicious circle: centralized, pseudo-representative states form ways of selecting competitive and inegalitarian economic relations, which develop 'non-convivial' technologies, which in turn, support military and coercive forces, that empower the centralized state. 'Convivial', environment-friendly technologies are incompatible with authoritarian and centralist politics; they provide less surplus fuel and are therefore disliked by the coercive forces. So what must be done? According to Carter (1993), we should break the system by introducing decentralized, participatory democracy, which opts for self-sufficient, egalitarian economic relations that will develop 'convivial' technologies that are globally aware and hence non-violent, and therefore will empower the decentralized democracy. Carter's theory favours local political units. This therefore leads me to the third argument.

*3. Direct and local democracy is environment-friendly. First, it develops
an attitude of 'relational self', a category of relations to which the
'ecological self' belongs; the ecological self presupposes ecological perspectives, hence localism is more in line with ecology. Secondly, localism is the
basis for direct democracy, since the latter assumes activities on the local
level; it therefore ties direct democracy and local, environmental attitudes
together*

This theme is typical of several Australian philosophers, such as Robert Young (1995) and Freya Mathews (1995), although it could be a continuation of the participatory democracy approach, to the extent that it regards participation as taking place at the local level. While I do not mean to discuss this in any depth here because it has already been dealt with in Chapter 4, I will just reiterate that it might be a mistake to regard localism as a precondition for a working, environment-friendly democracy. The reasons for this are, first, because environmental problems are global in character and demand a solution extending beyond the local,[5] so that localism will yield only NIMBY solutions;[6] second, because more and more people nowadays tend to move from place to place, and do not develop strong attachments to a particular location (see Chapter 4 above); and third, because small, local communities may tend to be highly cohesive and therefore intolerant towards minorities and groups of 'others' (Kenny 1996). However, I do want to relate here to an interesting suggestion that has recently been intensively discussed, not necessarily with regard to environmental policies.

Several theorists of democracy have suggested that local activists be fostered by forming 'secondary associations' that act locally, e.g. neighbourhood associations, parent–teacher groups. For example, Joshua Cohen and Joel Rogers (1995) claim that people refrain from participating partly because they get lost in the large, state-level political bodies. Such associations would therefore mediate between individuals and the state in setting the political agenda, determining choices from that agenda, implementing those choices, and so on. Cohen and Rogers not only claim that more associations would improve democratic participation, they also ascribe many failures in the American democratic system to these secondary associations not being strong enough. Wouter Achterberg (1996) applied this idea to the environmental policies debate. He argues that associative democracy could help in overcoming impediments to sustainability. In order to achieve sustainability, Achterberg claims, we must increase social cooperation and coordination, improve the 'embeddedness' of the market in society, and reinforce the mutual identification of the citizens. These associations will contribute towards fulfilling these tasks by coordinating through negotiation, by being plural, and by helping to decentralize.

Others, however, have claimed that this interest group pluralism ends up in a bias towards the wealthier groups or the manipulation of the state by particularistic groups (Barber 1984). Moreover, while we foster local, secondary associations because we want citizens to be more engaged and active in general affairs, we may be achieving the opposite, i.e. fostering the very associations that will strengthen a tendency to give priority to local or particularistic issues. Thus, Michael Saward (1993: 72) quotes Andrez Gorz, expressing the fear that 'the more self-sufficient and numerically limited a community [or, for our purposes, an association] is, the smaller the range of activities and choices it can offer to its members. If it has no opening to an area of exogen-

---

[5] John Dryzek (1997: 33) points to the contradiction: some advocates of localism tend also to rely on the UN to do for all people what national governments cannot.

[6] Daniel Fiorino (1996: 194) points to the difficulty of government authorities in the USA to site waste disposal facilities because of intense *local* opposition.

ous activity, knowledge and production, the community becomes a prison.' People then concentrate on minor issues, ignoring the larger ones. This direct democracy, Saward argues, is in practice far from what its advocates claim it to be:

Face to face participation arguably gives rise to greater opportunities for manipulation of the assembly. . . . Breaking down politics/administration distinctions may open up sensitive posts and jobs to inexpertness and incompetence. . . . Not having a structure of representation in any consistent respect opens up the possibility that informal leaders will be able to impose themselves rather than be proposed by the subject population. (Saward 1993: 72)

One should, perhaps, distinguish between voluntary associations such as neighbourhood committees or parent–teacher associations, and government-sponsored associations running public institutions. While it might be said that the latter could reflect interest in general political issues, it seems to me that voluntary associations often concentrate on particularistic issues, and that their members invest a lot of energy in solving the problems their associations wish to address. Achterberg is aware of this problem and suggests that, if each person belongs to several such associations, she will develop a general outlook which is the aggregation of these particularistic attitudes. But this is conceptually wrong. A general attitude is not the sum of many particularistic attitudes, but a different type of attitude, one not based on self-interest. A person who belongs to a literature society, a chess group, and a stamp collection group is no more likely to internalize an environmental attitude than if she had been a member of only one of these groups. Moreover, Achterberg is right in saying that in order to solve environmental problems we need an attitude that is as remote as possible from self-interest; but he forgets that it must also be a *political* attitude. Most members of these voluntary associations develop *non*-political attitudes in such groups, both because these groups are not necessarily democratic in the way they conduct their internal affairs, and because they do not deal with political matters.

Thus, we are left with an incoherent picture of what this form of direct, local democracy would be. Would it really enhance democracy and encourage debate on environmental issues, or would it in fact become a retreat from politics? (I shall return to this question in Chapter 6, where I discuss the socialist vision of associations and their activity within the state.)

4. Deliberative democracy is the ultimate environmental discourse

An interesting version of this theory has been put forward by John Dryzek (1988; 1995; 1997).[7] Environmental matters are both serious and exceptionally

---

[7] It should be mentioned that Dryzek's and Goodin's theories share some points, to which I relate below when I discuss the deliberative participatory democracy.

complex. As such, they pose a challenge to many common conceptions of democracy. Often societies determine democratic collective action through the mechanism of 'social choice'. However, environmental problems differ from other political issues in terms of complexity, non-reducibility, uncertainty, and spontaneity (the partial ability of ecosystems to solve problems without human intervention). If social choice is to be applied in such cases, a high degree of coordination is needed. And yet, bureaucracy and government cannot cope efficiently enough with these matters, and the political agenda of formal institutions is too dense for serious debate to take place. Hence there is a need for wide deliberation among the general public. This goes hand in hand with what democracy should be anyhow: 'Democracy, if it is about anything, is about authentic communication' (Dryzek 1997: 200). For this, claims Dryzek, the politics that is required is discursive. All other coordinatory mechanisms (e.g. the market, administrative systems, law, etc.) have failed, because they all rely on instrumental reason. As an alternative, Dryzek suggests the idea of 'practical reason', which involves purposes as well as means, and is pedagogical and communal rather than instrumental. It involves the 'collective cultivation of virtuous behaviour rather than administration of people or things' (Dryzek 1988: 200). If such 'practical reason' is applied, then the action likely to be taken is the one supported by the best reason rather than by the majority.[8]

In what follows I argue similarly, although my argument is based on the public reflective equilibrium, rather than on pedagogical and communal reason. It is not that I disagree with the first three theories supporting democracy in the environmental context. On the contrary, I do accept many of the arguments raised by the authors reviewed. However, my proposition is to offer a straightforward, anthropocentric—though 'enlightened'—argument, namely, that a democracy that is both participatory and deliberative, through its effect on human beings, is more likely to cater for human interests through the medium of environment-friendly policies. (Readers can see that elements of both Goodin's and Drzyek's theories constitute the model of democracy I recommend; however, the rationale differs.) I would also argue with any sharp distinctions made between participatory and representative democracy. Some theorists have suggested that to some extent participatory democracy stands as an alternative to representative democracy (B. Hayward 1995). However, representative democracy and participatory democracy may be regarded as complementary, and participatory democracy as an improvement on representative democracy. Let me then elaborate on this.

In the popular literature on the subject of democracy and the environment—pamphlets, Green newsletters, etc.—we find several conceptions of democracy. Figure 5.1 puts some order into these theories by distinguishing two

---

[8] Dryzek's claim is that such deliberation will overcome the problem often occurring in democratic regimes, namely that political power and money determine the outcomes of any deliberation. Below I develop the discussion of the role of, and the legitimacy by, the 'majority'.

Direct democracy	Representative democracy
Participatory or deliberative democracy	Legitimacy derives from majority support

Fig. 5.1 Variety of democracies

questions the theories answer: (1) should decisions be made by just everyone, or by representatives? and (2) do policies enjoy legitimacy because of a majority that supports them or because of the process through which they were reached?[9] Of course, a system can be majoritarian and either direct or representative; it can be participatory and either direct or representative;[10] it can be direct and either participatory or majoritarian; it can be representative and either participatory or majoritarian.

A closer look reveals that direct democracy can be either *fully direct*, in that everything, including the agenda itself, is decided by all citizens, or *semi-direct*, whereby all citizens are engaged in some sort of public opinion polls, referenda or citizens' gatherings, or all the above; and yet, the agenda itself is decided by representatives, or elected leaders. The difference is that a fully direct democracy can be conducted only in small-scale communities which would entail 'localism'; whereas semi-direct democracy could be run in larger-scale bodies—and the larger these bodies, the more this system resembles participatory democracy.

Those advocating representative democracy, on the other hand, claim that many issues are far too complicated for the lay person, and that people actually should not devote all their energies and time to politics: rather, they should be involved in non-political activities as well. Therefore representatives should be elected; these will be subject to re-election and therefore will be motivated to act to the greatest advantage of their constituencies (or, another version would claim, to the fulfilment of the general interest).

The question of the source of legitimacy of democratic decisions and policies is reflected in the debate on whether democracy should be 'majoritarian' or 'participatory'. It is majoritarian to the extent that policies are decided by (in the case of direct democracy), or according to (in the case of representative democracy), the will of the majority. Democracy is 'participatory' if policies are decided only after the public has been furnished with the relevant information and the policies discussed in depth. These are two alternative ways of

---

[9] Notice that none of these theories claim what was claimed in ancient Greece: that legitimacy derives not from consent but from the fact that access to office was equally open to all citizens.

[10] As argued earlier, I do not see any reason why representative should be contradictory to participatory; one refers to the body that decides upon policies; the other to the decision's legitimacy. An assembly can decide upon policies, on condition that it has heard all voices.

legitimating decision-making. Here too there are two versions to this stand-point: one that regards participatory democracy as closely related to, and dependent on, decentralization, and the other which does not regard decentralization a necessary condition for participation.

Now let us look at the application of these distinctions to the questions of environmental policies. As to who decides with regard to environmental questions, it seems that direct and localized democracy is both too locally oriented (see Chapter 4) and too technically implausible in the modern world: most environmental issues are so complex, and affect such a wide population, that they need a macro, hence centralist, approach to deciding which solutions to adopt. When implementing these solutions, we often see that the problems are so great that they require vast sums of money—sums unlikely to be available at decentralized levels. Hence environmental decision-making should take place in central bodies. I therefore regard semi-direct or representative regimes as the only feasible alternatives for environmental decision-making, and I think that the differences between the two are marginal. Decisions should be taken by the public wherever possible, and by representatives when not (which is often the case).

However, this should not imply that legitimacy—the question I am more concerned with in this chapter—derives from the majority. I shall argue soon that it derives from active participation before and after decision-making. Participation, however, is not mainly in voting (in elections and/or on policies), because, as I have just claimed, the latter is often carried out by representatives. Therefore, at this point I would add the *deliberative* characteristic of democracy to its being participatory and as part of its legitimacy.[11]

Deliberation is important for another reason: if we prefer a centralist model when it comes to decision-making, we run the risk of the bodies that decide upon the solutions disregarding what people think, resulting in the public's alienation from the political process. To avoid this, some form of deliberative participation should be introduced.[12] Usually when environmental activists

---

[11] Deliberative democracy is defined by several authors. For example, following Joshua Cohen, Seyla Benhabib (1996: 69) writes: 'according to the deliberative model of democracy, it is a necessary condition for attaining legitimacy and rationality with regard to collective decision making processes in a polity, that the institutions of this polity are so arranged that what is considered in the common interest of all results from processes of collective deliberation conducted rational and fairly among free and equal individuals'. This definition does not distinguish between deliberative democracy and any other form of debate. Deliberation is more than simple arguments, because the latter may relate to arguments about interests, whereas deliberation involves debating values and moral principles. Of course, arguments about values can be a cover-up for interests and a process of bargaining. Still, they are distinguished by the way other people relate to them, and by the fact that, as Jon Elster argues, even when such debates are meant to deceive, and even when interests lie behind the arguments, the process has a 'powerful civilising influence' (see Elster 1998a: 97–123).

[12] Of course, one has to concede that participatory democracy is not always realistic: in the autumn of 1997, a debate regarding the extension of NATO to include Poland, Hungary, and the Czech Republic hotted up in the USA. According to one US poll, only 10% of the American public could name even one country that was scheduled for inclusion in the alliance. Reading

refer to 'participatory' democracy they mean participation in decision-making. However, if deliberation is added to participation, the focus shifts from the decisions to their justification, to the reasons for them and the way in which decisions were reached. The view that deliberative participation is the most significant component of democracy implies that decisions and policies, rather than being the result of a deliberation process, are part of it, and should also be debated. Thus, decisions are subordinated to re-evaluation by the public, which, as I shall argue below, is crucial in arriving at environment-friendly policies.

Also, I do not accept the artificial distinction between democracy as being good for the environment, and democracy as being good for human beings. I therefore first wish to defend deliberative participatory democracy in general.

Democracy, Participation and Majority Rule

Beside the attack on democracy from environmentalists who doubt its ability to cope with the need for environmental policies, democracy is also challenged by many in the general public. It is not uncommon these days for people to express a loss of interest in politics on the grounds that democracy, supposedly 'the rule of the people by the people', is no longer 'theirs'. As Joshua Cohen and Joel Rogers write, people complain that 'Government is part of the problem, not the solution' (Cohen and Rogers 1995: 7). In explaining these sentiments, it is sometimes suggested that the political system does not take the will of the people seriously. But is this really sufficient grounds for claiming that this or that regime is not democratic? Is it in fact necessary for politicians to relate primarily to the will of the people in order for a regime to be a good democratic one? I wish to argue that the most important criteria for a regime to be considered democratic is the practice of public deliberation—

these figures, one wonders what the point is of theorizing about participation if the public is not interested in participating in the discussion. And yet, philosophers should never lose hope. 'If cedars have caught fire, what will the moss on the wall do?' I should mention that deliberation is not about discovering truth or about constituting the correctness of policies. Several authors have attacked the idea of deliberative democracy on the grounds that deliberation cannot discover political truths, or that it is foolish to believe that the agreement of citizens constitutes the correctness of policies (see Gaus 1997 and Christiano 1997). However, supporting deliberative democracy does not entail the expectation that political agreement will replace metaphysical justifications about the truism of a policy. Deliberation is legitimate not because it leads to a discovery of the truth, but because it is sovereignty itself. Indeed, I think that suggestions such as those made by Maarten Hajer in his very influential and profound book (1995: 282)—namely, that society should introduce 'reflexive ecological modernisation' in order to 'make environmental politics a matter of deliberate and negotiated social choice for certain scenarios of societal modernization'—ignore the unfortunate fact that the public is not so enlightened. I therefore argue below that the role of the public is to raise doubts and serve as the watchdog, forcing experts and politicians to be as genuine and as serious as they can be.

and not the ensuing decisions. Hence a policy is democratic if it is both pre-ceded and followed by debate while remaining subject at all times to public scrutiny. It is these qualities, rather than 'the [majoritarian] will of the people', that provide the ultimate authorization in democratic policy-making.

As well as providing arguments to support my claim, I will discuss other models and theories of democracy, showing why they are inadequate for cap-turing the essence of the democratic experience. I shall also attempt to anti-cipate possible counter-arguments to my theory, and to outline their respective shortfalls. I shall then explain why this model of democracy should appeal to environmentalists. However, I wish to emphasize that the impor-tance of democracy lies not only in what it might achieve for the environ-ment, but also in that it is good in itself. I believe that the model put forward here should appeal to those concerned with the future of democracy because it can narrow the gap between the citizens and the state, a gap originating partly from the idea that majority rule is the essence of democracy, and the belief that majority rule will make politics simple to handle and efficient at ful-filling citizens' interests.[13] While the model I offer here does not promise a rose garden, and instead demands responsibility and participation, it never-theless affirms that democracy is genuinely different from, and superior to, any other regime. My claim is that this is generally so, and not just when it comes to environmental policies.

Politics and the People's Various Desires: Two Different Questions

Let me begin by addressing the scepticism voiced by people throughout the democratic world. The question asked regarding politics and the desires of the public is whether politics actually reflects these desires. This question treats politics as a *sphere of life*, distinguishable from other spheres in that it takes place in characteristic institutions—parliament, the government, parties, unions, political clubs, etc. The question, then, is simple: does this sphere of life, i.e. the kind of action that takes place within these institutions, reflect people's values, desires, and interests? (The question is illustrated in Figure 5.2.) It is assumed that there are two discourses. One forms the inputs to the political process: the moral debate and individuals' expressed interests. The other is political, since it takes place in political institutions. The question, then, is whether the political discourse is similar to the inputs, i.e. the moral discourse and/or the expressed interests. Such a similarity would arise if the

---

[13] It is possible that authors like Ophuls and Hardin have lost faith in democracy because they had in mind a narrow conception of democracy, namely majority rule.

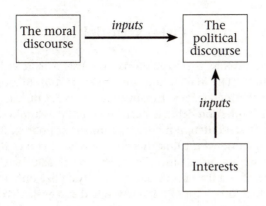

FIG. 5.2 Democracy: the *discourse* reflects interests and values

political discourse, on the one hand, and the moral discourse and discourse concerning interests on the other, use the same conceptualization and language, or if the political discourse contains arguments similar to those expressed by the inputs.

When many people complain about the 'alienated' nature of politics, however, they are actually asking a different question: they wish to know whether or not politics fulfils the desires of the citizens, or, more precisely, whether politics corresponds to the desires of a significant majority. This question, then, refers to politics as a process of decision-making. In other words, these people suggest that, when politics does not fulfil the people's (or the majority's) will, it is undemocratic. In the terms depicted in Figure 5.3, the question would be whether the outputs 'meet' or answer the demands of the inputs. In practice, the public's attitude is often one of 'why bother with politics if politicians do whatever *they* want rather than what *we* want?'

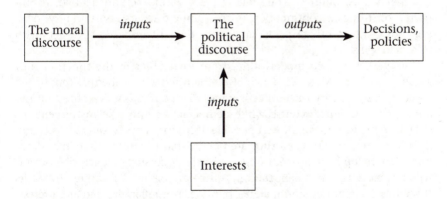

FIG. 5.3 Democracy: the *decisions* reflect interests and values

Elster's Model

In attempting to address these questions, it is useful to refer to Jon Elster's well-known article, 'The Market and the Forum' (1986). By doing this I also want to expose the inadequacyof mainstream theories of democracy. Let us start with the first question—that concerning politics as a sphere of life. Elster distinguishes between different models of democratic politics. First, he distinguishes between those who think that the individual comes to the political arena equipped with a precise list of interests and remains faithful to it, and those who think that a list of preferences can crystallize only through public discussion in which others' opinions are weighed and evaluated in the light of one's own interests.

Thus, Elster's first model sees politics as a market for trading *interests*. A person (or a party, or some other political body) declares an interest, specifies how important it is to him (for example, by providing a list of preferences), and is then ready to bargain and eventually to compromise by accepting others' interests in return for their acknowledgement of his own. There is no problem in this model with regard to representation of the citizens' desires and/or interests: they are present in the sense that they are discussed and considered (in one way or another) by all participants in the political bargaining process. Thus, this model—let us call it Model I—views democracy as a market of interests. The main difficulty with Model I is that it fails to distinguish between the citizens' wills, which can be described as 'temporary' and 'deriving from certain circumstances' (i.e. interests expressed as desires), and the wills of the citizens had they been well informed and equipped to analyse the relevant information. It is at this point that Elster's other two models come into play.

These two models share a way of looking at politics as if it were a *forum*. In other words, politics, while taking place within certain defined institutions, constitutes a continuation of the public discourse on morality, dealing not with temporary or circumstantial interests, but rather with informed wills.

However, these two models differ from each other in the function they ascribe to politics. Model II, which Elster identifies with Habermas (but which we could also identify with others), argues that politics is indeed the continuation of the moral discourse while democracy is only the instrument. Its objectives are to achieve the best possible decisions, namely *rational* decisions. Decisions are rational when they are public; that is, after matters have been subjected to open, reasoned, and in-depth discussion. Hence democracy, which is based on open deliberation, is the best regime. To sum up, in Model II politics is about decision-making, but does not reflect immediate interests and expressed desires as in Model I; instead, it reflects the wills that well informed and rational persons would have (Habermas 1994; J. Cohen 1989; Miller 1992; Benhabib 1994).[14]

A different theory, but of the same category and model, is Giddens's 'Dialogic democracy'. According to this, democracy is not about consensus, but is rather the aggregation of a variety of activities which together constitute a dialogue in a public space which allows us to live alongside one another. In other words, democracy is instrumental to developing mutual tolerance, rather than achieving agreement. It is the 'capability to create active trust through an appreciation of the integrity of the other' (Giddens 1995: 113–24).

Now, while Models I and II regard politics instrumentally, as a means of reaching decisions (the former regards politics as producing and grading a list of public priorities based on individuals' lists of priorities, and Habermas's model regards politics as a means of reaching decisions through a rational public debate; Giddens regards democracy as a means of achieving tolerance), there is a third model, which differs in that it does not assume that the only purpose of politics is to arrive at decisions. Rather, it claims, the main point in politics is participation and the discourse itself. Whether interests and desires are reflected or fulfilled in this process is less important than in the other models, since democratic politics is valuable in itself.

This third model is often attributed to Mill and Arendt (Elster 1986). Both, however, may still be seen as regarding politics as partly instrumental, inasmuch as they regard politics as enjoyable and as a means of exercising one's power of agency (Arendt), or as a means of self-education (Mill). And yet, there is a significant and interesting difference: unlike Elster, Miller, Benhabib, and Habermas, whose instrumentalism in politics is external, or other-regarding (obtaining the agreements and actions of other people, leading to collective actions),[15] Mill and Arendt are concerned with internal, or self-regarding, instrumentalism (achieving something with regard to one's own personality). Below I shall propose a more radical version of this model which claims that in addition democratic activities are good in themselves.

---

[14] Miller argues that deliberative democracy is a decision-making system, which, compared with liberal democracy, is less vulnerable to the arbitrariness of decision-making rules and strategic voting. Benhabib can sometimes be read as if she considers the discourse rather than the decision-making to be the main point of democracy; on the other hand, she claims that the deliberative model of democracy is procedural, and therefore I believe she regards it as instrumental—'The more conflicts of interests there are, the more it is important to have procedural solutions' (Benhabib 1994: 34)—so the deliberation is a procedure for reaching a decision that allows cooperation: it is not a good in itself.

[15] Elsewhere David Miller argues in support of the internal instrumentalism (what Chan and Miller 1991, call 'side-effects'), i.e. educative potential and the status that democracy confers on participants.

Politics and Fulfilling the Different Wills: A Critique of Majoritarianism

Let us return to the proposition that politics is a means of fulfilling the people's will. I wish to begin by arguing that democratic politics *cannot* fulfil all the desires of a society's citizens. I shall then go on to demonstrate that, although this is the case, this observation should harm neither the basis nor the legitimacy of the democratic system.

While politics is about how we live together, unlike law, it benefits from the luxury of not having to decide unequivocally. Decisions may be shaped so that they satisfy more than one side. Nevertheless, whenever there are more than two or three people, it is assumed that there will be a variety of political wills, the relations between which may vary. In fact, there can be four types of relations between different wills:[16]

1. *Indifferent wills.* My desire that the government should support students who cannot pay their fees has nothing to do with George's desire that the national anthem should be played at every international football match. The fulfilment of one desire is not related to or parasitic upon the other desire and its realization.

2. *Complementary wills.* One desire needs the other to be fulfilled. Naturally, if both exist at the same time they can be fulfilled together; e.g. if Helen wants to open a business that requires an employee and Joy wants to work in that business.

3. *Rival wills.* Here the desires reflect different outlooks, but they can nevertheless coexist, for example, if Melissa wants her village to remain rural and Charles wants his town to become more urban, these desires can both be fulfilled without harming each other, even though they reflect two rival attitudes.

4. *Contradictory wills.* Until now I have mentioned desires that are self-regarding: Helen, Joy, George, Melissa, and Charles all desire something with regard to their own lives without requiring anyone else to abandon their own desires. The fourth kind of relationship between wills is what may be called contradictory wills: here, the fulfilment of one desire is dependent on preventing the fulfilment of another. Often the other desire is someone else's, but not necessarily, because two or more contradictory wills may sometimes coexist in the same person.

---

[16] Notice that I am *not* concerned with how preferences are shaped and whether they are manipulated, nor with how one measures preferences. For these two questions one may consult Ajzen and Fishbein (1980). For the first question see Ingelhart (1977). For a rather conservative answer to the second question see Riker (1982) and his critics, MacLean (1987: 187 f.) and Weale (1984).

Let me offer two examples. In Jerusalem there is a large group of people seeking to develop and modernize the city—to bring in industry, build motorways and skyscrapers, and transform Jerusalem from a relatively poor city into a rich and affluent one. This group's desire opposes the desire of the conservationists and many others to conserve the special atmosphere and unique character of the city. But the conservationists must enforce their desires on the developers if they wish to conserve the city's special atmosphere, and vice versa. These are contradictory wills: the fulfilment of one depends on the rejection of the other. This is because these desires include other-regarding preferences: preferences that indicate how others should act and live. The most we can hope politics to achieve regarding to these contradictory, 'other-regarding', desires is to downgrade them to rival wills by redefining them in such a way that they are no longer mutually exclusive (for example, by persuading the developers to request development and industrialization only in suburbs). In so doing, however, none of the *original* wills will be fulfilled. In the final analysis, each is other-regarding, and fulfilling one invariably frustrates the other.

The other example refers to conflicting wills within a single person. Benjamin may desire the environment of his country to be preserved, and so may oppose an unrestrictive planning permission policy in the countryside; at the same time, however, Benjamin may wish to have inexpensive housing, in the knowledge that low prices for housing can be sustained only by massive building, in turn necessitating a permissive planning policy. Other examples are current concerns with creating employment in the industrial sector, coexisting with the contemporary wish to preserve the environment for future generations, the right of so many ethnic groups and nations in Eastern Europe to national self-determination alongside fear of instability and Balkanization; or we may cite the more basic conflict often said to exist between the wish to allow more freedom and the desire for greater equality.

We are drawn to the conclusion that politics cannot fulfil many of the citizens' desires. At best, it can satisfy the will of a certain majority, but in doing so, it often seems illiberal and intolerant, or even arbitrary. Who says the majority is right? Why shouldn't the state, faced with the clash of wills, adopt a neutral position, or even decide which desire to prefer, in which case it may be that of the minority? Indeed, *should* democratic politics concentrate on fulfilling the wishes of citizens (see Brecher 1998)? Assuming that the answer is positive, a politician's first priority would be to satisfy the desires of all who turn to her, and therefore would be open to criticism for failing to abide by this principle. However, while politics in general clearly involves decision-making, it is not just instrumental; i.e., it is not only a means to specific ends. In so far as it serves, albeit at a highly abstract level, as a tool for overcoming differences, politics in turn constitutes a distinctive, though not autonomous, sphere of life. As such, it takes on characteristics that are intrinsic and not purely instrumental, the chief among these being the act of deliberation. I shall now proceed to defend this position.

Deliberative Participatory Democracy: Subjecting Policies to Critical Scrutiny

First, I would like to distinguish between the views of Arendt and Mill and my own suggestion. Mill believes that politics is good in itself, because by participating in political deliberation people realize, express, and manifest their social character, learn to become social, and find out a great deal about themselves. But if so, Mill is actually referring to what I have defined earlier as 'internal' instrumentalism, i.e. a psychological change in personality.[17] The same goes for Hannah Arendt. She argues that politics is good in itself because it is enjoyable. To support her position, she describes the citizens of Athens as having enjoyed their political activities (Arendt 1958). And indeed, if we examine diaries written by politicians and semi-professional politicians, or the literature on the political experience, we immediately notice that they are incredibly enthusiastic about politics and the political world, either as a social or collective experience or on a personal level. But this too is a kind of 'internal' instrumentalism. If one reads Arendt on another level, one might claim that politics is good because it makes people who participate more 'whole',[18] a term that reminds us of many Green theories. Again, politics is seen as internally instrumental: those who participate in politics develop their capacity for judgement and their 'power of agency' by being confronted with other opinions (d'Entreves 1992: 146; Arendt 1968: 220).

At this point, however, I would like to stress that, in addition, politics has certain other qualities that are no less important. For instance, it has an aesthetic dimension. Disharmonies are resolved and tensions relieved, just as in the most common models of music, especially popular music. If we think of blues or the Greek *Rambatiko*, or even classical music, we often think of a

---

[17] Mill actually thought that this internal instrumentalism—the educative effect—would tend to make people more altruistic, and therefore attain a more moral type of participation and make better decisions. For a similar view, see Barber (1984: 42): 'In a strong democratic community . . . the individual members are transformed, through their participation in common seeing and common work, into citizens.' It is interesting to compare Mill and Rudolf Bahro: Mill thinks that liberal democracy will transform the individual; Bahro believes that the transformation must emancipate the person from liberal democracy.

[18] Chan and Miller's argument is perhaps more sophisticated because they distinguish between the level at which one decides to join the political process and the present level of involvement. The motivation for political activities in the latter is instrumental, they argue, whereas 'in the context of constitutional debate, where citizens ask themselves what institutions to adopt or what changes ought to be made to their present institutions . . . it would be relevant to cite psychological by-products . . . [for choosing A rather than B]' (Chan and Miller 1991: 97).

development in which there is a 'climax', a 'tension', and then 'relief'. The same goes for politics. Sometimes, however, as in modern music, it is the lingering tension that makes politics exciting. Clearly, aesthetics, tensions, and relief are not all that politics is about! Neither do I wish to overlook the instrumental value of the political debate. This value, however, is not limited to the ability of the debate to produce a more rational decision. Rather, the value is located in subordinating the decision to the debate, and in considering decisions and policies as *new inputs* to this debate, and therefore subjecting them to new critical scrutiny. (This is illustrated in Figure 5.4.) In this model, democracy is viewed as a regime that, in the long run, offers a better chance of correcting a mistaken decision. So, while some may hold that democracy is a system of rational decisions, my claim is that it is distinguishable from other regimes in that it gives priority to the deliberation itself. Democracy does not always yield rational decisions, and other regimes can also arrive at rational decisions; for example, a militaristic dictatorship could form a group of experts who would decide on policies using a careful procedure of reasoning. But no other regime regards deliberation as part of popular participation or as having priority over decisions.

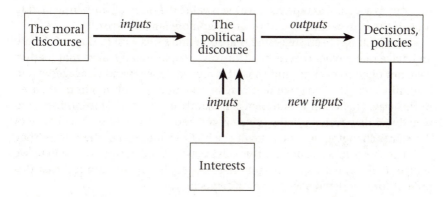

Fig. 5.4 Democracy: participatory and deliberative

Now, subordinating decision to the debate as new inputs also increases the aesthetic value of the debate, because it intensifies it, and makes it more vivid and profound. Notice that I say it is 'profound' rather than 'rational', because it is not necessarily solely rational: it may also be emotional and full of mistakes. But it is more profound, or serious, because the policies are discussed not only theoretically, prior to their exercise, but also *after implementation*, and *on empirical grounds*. So I want to emphasize these aspects of politics because they are so often disregarded by theorists of democracy. Bearing these and the theories of Arendt and Mill in mind, we may then see the deliberation itself as the most significant component of democratic politics, and reshape our expectations of politics accordingly. We must hope, therefore, not that policies and decisions will fulfil certain (the majority's?) desires, but rather that the deliberation will be open and public.

Let me immediately counter two arguments that may be raised against my claim that politics should be open and public. First, it can be said that, if one cares about the beauty and intensity of the political deliberation, one should not aim to increase the circle of participants, but rather should leave the debate to the 'professionals', e.g. political theorists. In this way, the argument goes, the debate will be more sophisticated. In response to this, I would say that, unlike many other spheres of life, the beauty of the political debate derives not from a 'professional' performance but rather from an 'authentic' one. In other words, members of the public (not necessarily the professionals) put their varied ideas on the political agenda in their own, self-created, and personal manner. In any case, the 'professionals' are already part of the deliberation. It would be far more intense and profound if more people with different outlooks were to take part and thereby reflect a greater number of ideas. Authenticity is an advantage of democracy because authenticity implies value. For instance, we value the original picture rather than the copy even though the copy is accurate and perfect; we even value the original, authentic picture more if the copy was produced by an even more famous artist.[19]

Secondly, it has been suggested that sometimes it is wise to skip the debate and make unequivocal decisions. This way, people would realize that matters were not open to change, and thus, it is argued, tension and cleavages would be diminished. However, while it may be true that tension might be reduced in this way, alienation would increase, mainly on the part of minorities who would feel they weren't being 'given a say' and who would see no chance of decisions changing in their favour which would make them feel they 'belonged'. So if we followed this advice we would arrive back where we started, namely, with a growing number of people who did not feel that this present form of democracy was *their* democracy.

I will now develop the view that democracy's main value lies in its deliberation and discuss its implications, by first stating and then dismissing a few arguments that may be raised against it. There are two main categories of counter arguments: (1) that I am wrong and that democratic politics is in fact

[19] Interesting comments about the 'professionals' in the history of politics can be found in Castoriadis (1991: 108–9). As for 'authentic' democratic discourse, John Dryzek beautifully describes it: '[It is a discussion] open to all interests, under which political power, money, and strategizing do not determine outcomes' (Dryzek 1997: 199). I would like to draw readers' attention to the correlation between this priority of authenticity over professionality and the model of *public reflective equilibrium*, which I have put forward in Chapter 1. Since authenticity is important in the democratic deliberation, and since both the democratic deliberation and the philosophical one are of the same category of discourse, i.e. the social one, public reflective equilibrium should be applied to the academic deliberation about environmental policies.

instrumental and policy-oriented; and (2) that the normative and moral implications of the position I have advanced are objectionable, and therefore my position is morally wrong.

The first counter-argument would go as follows (see Elster 1986: 126–7). The claim that democratic politics is good regardless of its instrumental value (towards decisions) is as ridiculous as the claim that sport is good in itself and is not engaged in for the sake of winning. Such a claim, the argument goes, ignores the psychological motivation of most people to participate: namely winning. My response is simple. Yes, democratic politics and sport are alike (though it must be said that politics makes a lot more difference), but this is precisely because sport is also good regardless of whether one wins or not. Admittedly, sport is about winning, but the competitive aspect is only part of it. In fact, many teams are praised for playing attractively and with elegance, whereas other teams, in spite of winning their games, lose fans because their performances are dull and uninspiring. Moreover, the whole purpose of the Olympic games is to participate. Contestants come to take part, even though it is crystal-clear that most will not even reach the finals.

The same goes for politics. Many people value participation in politics itself: they want their voice to be heard and they think it is important that their views are expressed, even if they do not make an impact on policies.[20] Indeed, although some parties never achieve enough votes to become eligible for a seat in parliament, they still keep trying. Moreover, people vote for them even though the polls indicate that they are wasting their vote. For example, under the British electoral system it makes no sense to vote for the Greens if voting is only instrumental, and yet in every election the Greens get their share of the vote. We may learn, then, that even in voting—the most instrumental of political actions—there are non-instrumental motivations.

To conclude my answer to this point, notice that I am not claiming that democracy is good regardless of whether people or not exist. Rather, it is good that people behave democratically and engage in democratic activities even if by so doing they do not gain extra happiness or welfare. In other words, it is better if political relations are democratic even if the impact of the democratic relations on people's welfare is similar to the impact that non-democratic relations would have.

The second possible argument (still in the same category of arguments) against my claim stems from the rational deliberation model: admittedly, it states that the goal of politics is not to enforce a certain interest or to transform interests into policies, but to engage in rational decision-making.

---

[20] The parallel is therefore not the Olympics but rather a village sports day, where everyone is encouraged to take part, while winning does not form the essence of the event. As for my claim that people enjoy participation in politics, there is empirical and theoretical literature about this. For example, Robert Dahl (1989: 98–9, 104–6) relates this to enjoying a sense of *equality and of self-fulfilment*. See also Wolfsfeld (1988).

Accordingly, it is the democratic system that maximizes, via public debate, the chances of reaching rational decisions. Hence we choose democracy, since it is the most rational form of politics (Habermas 1994).

But this claim assumes that what people decide is always rational, and therefore this claim may contradict one of the basic assumptions of democracy: namely that we cannot make ourselves flawless. In fact, this is a psychological premiss regarding the nature of human beings that democracy and democratic theory imply. People are not perfect: they have conflicts both between and within themselves; and they cannot claim to be absolutely rational, at least because they must admit that they cannot always imagine the consequences of their actions.

Even more importantly, while it may well be that the *deliberation* improves if it is open and involves as many people, and hence as wide a variety of ideas, as possible, it cannot be concluded that the *decisions* will therefore also be better. The deliberation may improve, but the decisions are the product of a majority vote (even if, as I claim, the majority is not sacred, it is the mechanism of decisions), and we have no guarantee that the majority (whether it exists prior to or emerges during the course of the debate) will be more rational than the minority, or that the majority will become more rational by discussing things, or that the majority has chosen the most rational alternative. Are we indeed ever likely to get better decisions by enlarging the circle of those who decide? If by 'better' we mean more rational, and especially better informed and less hasty, it seems unfortunately that enlarging the circle of those participating in the decision-making is not necessarily a good strategy. This, I should emphasize, should not be read as support for elitist politics. On the contrary, I oppose elitist politics mainly because it does not allow, let alone encourage, deliberation, and because at the end of the day, when decisions reflect the interests of small groups, others cannot be expected to follow blindly. (See also the discussion below of risk evaluation, where I analyse the advantages of enlarging the circle of participants in the evaluation process.)

So is there nothing valid or true in the claim that democracy is more rational than other regimes? Of course there is. But the reason is not the one appearing in the above challenge to my theory. I elaborate on this below in my discussion on risk evaluation. At this moment, though, I would like to explain that the model I put forward seems better to me because it admits that politics involves a long process of trial and error. Ideally, of course, we should minimize the error factor. While we cannot get rid of errors altogether, we could try to reduce those caused by politicians' tendency to think in terms of political self-interest and individuals' tendency to vote according to short-run self-interest. The way to achieve this is to subject each decision and policy to a process of re-evaluation and open, public scrutiny.

There is a third argument against my claim that politics is not merely instrumental. This is that, although people profess to enjoying political activities, they enjoy them only because such activities eventually lead to decision-making, and it is decision-making that provides the real source of pleasure. A similar argument is that, while the democratic process is admittedly beneficial, since people become political animals by playing the political game, its value lies in teaching them to succeed in politics, i.e. to realize their goals through the political process (Elster 1985).[21]

Is this really the case? If it were, we would not witness the large numbers of people participating in debates, marches, demonstrations, etc., in the knowledge that their actions have no immediate effect on political decisions. In many cases participation does have an effect. For example, such participation often prevents politicians from committing immoral acts or deceiving the public, especially when participation takes the form of a watchdog, and it often corrects wrong decisions, especially when it takes the form of a public critique. (I elaborate on this below.) However, in many other cases people participate even though they know they have little chance of changing decisions. In these cases they participate because that is their way of expressing their ideas, which, in turn, are extensions of their own identities. In doing so, they 'create' politics.

Once again, I would like to compare this with the arts. It seems to me that politics in this respect is similar to a good detective film. The film works not only because of the result, i.e. the moment when the detective solves the problem, but because of the tension itself, the story, and all those moments that lead, finally, to the resolution of a complicated case. These moments are 'good' in themselves, rather than because they lead up to the final moment. The story is thought to be good not because the murderer is found. (Some people even think that detective stories in which the crimes are partly or wholly unsolved may be better.) The same may be said about politics: cases where there are no 'results' or collective decisions form part of politics and constitute what good democracy is all about. Indeed, there are political events—especially ceremonies—that are symbolic, and do not end up in decision-making. The legislative process itself is very long (in many countries it involves several stages through parliament in addition to public debate, and sometimes judicial scrutiny), and on many occasions does not produce any decision at all, but simply fades away. And yet, such processes are not regarded as useless or pointless. On the contrary: even though many legislative initiatives do not result in new legislation, we value the fact that they occur in our society.

Had Elster been right in saying that in the final analysis all political events lead to decision-making, there would be no problem in defining the 'political'

---

[21] Elster (1985) argues that the enjoyment of politics is simply a byproduct of decision-making, and that, finally, one enjoys politics more when one is successful (p. 147). For this reason, I believe, he defines deliberative democracy as 'collective *decision making* with the participation of all who will be affected by the decision or their representatives' (Elster 1998*a*: 8; my emphasis).

as 'that which leads to public decision-making'. In fact, there are many other criteria by which action is judged as 'political'. It is often thought that the sole criterion for deciding whether or not an issue is 'political' concerns the type of subject matter involved rather than whether or not it leads to decision-making.

Furthermore, were politics merely instrumental—the sole goal being decision-making—we would no doubt be very satisfied with the following hypothetical regime scenario. In the capital city there would be a huge computer, connected to personal computers in homes or public centres. Whenever the need arose to decide upon some issue, the central computer would send a question to all the connected computers, and citizens would vote 'for' or 'against'. The main computer would then analyse the results and recommend a policy. But there would be no debate, and people would not demonstrate, engage in party activities, etc. There must be reasons why most of us would reject such a regime, one of which is that we value participation not as a means of reaching decisions (as in Schumpeter's theory), or even as means of reaching the *right* decision (Habermas, Benhabib, Miller), but rather for itself.[22]

'But then,' you might ask, 'do you really mean to suggest that decision-making is of only marginal significance?' Well, of course I do not. Clearly, political decisions play a part in determining the way we live, and are therefore of the utmost importance. My aim, however, is not to dismiss the importance of decisions, but to reinterpret the relationships between decisions and deliberation. In contrast to the proposition that the deliberation and the debate are nothing but a means of achieving better decisions, I would argue that decisions and decision-making, *as well as* providing guide lines for public life, are a means of achieving a better quality of deliberation. Were there no decisions at the end of the deliberation, the deliberation itself would be less intense and less serious. Thus, decision-making (including legislation) is often a kind of façade which enhances dramatization and makes the debate lively and real. Politics as deliberative participation is politics as ongoing debate, inspired and stimulated by the idea of decision-making. The need to decide, and sometimes to legislate (which in itself is highly important), also causes the debate to be limited in time, and thus more intensive, more exciting, and hence much better (not only in instrumental terms) than it would have been had there been no prospect of a decision. (Notably, ceremonial debates in parliament, and those that do not involve a decision, tend to be less lively, although we may still enjoy them.)

---

[22] Habermas, Benhabib, and Miller may still reply that the computer example does not apply to their model, which is concerned with reaching the best decision through deliberation. But to see why it does, imagine a more sophisticated computer which weighs the different arguments and even develops by itself the various possible answers each side can raise to the other's arguments, in such a way that eventually it reaches the best decisions. It seems to me that we would still resent a regime such as this, because what we value is our own active participation in the democratic game.

Now for the second set of counter-arguments. What, then, are the moral implications of my argument? First, it may be argued that my position reduces everything to games. Politics, however, is not a game; it is far more important. And what, the argument would go, if elegant debates lead to dreadful decisions? What value do such debates have then? In response, I would first like to clarify an important difference between games and politics. A game is just a game, and would be a pointless activity were it not a game. Politics, however, makes a difference. People literally live or die because of policies.

And yet, why should it make a difference if a policy is a *democratic* one? Why is a policy more legitimate when it is democratic? The reason, I argue, is the process of debating, which involves as many people and ideas as possible, and a re-evaluation of the chosen policy some point after its implementation. This does not guarantee that some decisions will not be dreadful, but what model of democracy can promise that? The lack of a guarantee is not a challenge to the specific theory advanced here, but rather to democratic theory in general. So one must first admit that democracy is in no way immunized against immoral or inefficient decisions. Deliberative participatory democracy, however, can correct such decisions because it comprises critical scrutiny by the public—in other words, deliberation. Now, the first round of this deliberation, the one preceding the first series of decisions, may not be sufficient to rule out immoral, or simply bad, decisions. (Notice that I do not assume that people are always rational.) However, the model put forward here is less vulnerable to this critique, since all decisions have to be *re-debated*; the public can therefore reflect again, taking into account newly entered voices of individuals and minorities harmed by that decision.

One may also argue that my position opens the door to paternalism: 'Let the people *talk* and have debates,' the politicians may say, 'eventually it is we who make the decisions.' But I do not argue that decisions and majority rule are not important: instead, I claim that, while democratic decision-making is an important procedure, its special value derives from the more fundamental value of deliberative participation in self-government. So my argument does not imply that I am indifferent to people's wills. On the contrary, I maintain that a decision reached by a majority vote without open debate is not more democratic (and perhaps less so) than a decision that does not necessarily reflect the majority, yet has been, is, and will be, open to public debate. [23]

---

[23] If we bear in mind that democracy is historically concerned with promoting the sovereignty of the people, then the shortfalls of majoritarianism become clear. All majoritarianism leaves for the 'people' is the task of asserting whether they are in favour of this or that candidate or policy. This is not majority *rule* but majority *consent* (see Crick 1993: 56). Taking the idea of popular sovereignty seriously would instead imply encouraging the people to take part in the debate and allowing this debate to inspire (and re-examine) the policy. In this respect, even voting itself can be counted as part of the deliberation in so far as it is seen as a statement about the common good or policy (see J. Cohen 1986; for a critique of this position see Christiano 1995). Thus, politics would be considered democratic not when it fulfils the wills of the majority, but rather when it is subordinated to continuous reflection and critical

The third counter-argument relating to the moral implications of the theory that I have advanced is that, if decisions are relegated to the status of new inputs to the process of political deliberation, then politicians may simply abdicate their public responsibilities, and seek to advance their own interests, just like any other group in society (because these politicians will consider their decisions as nothing but new inputs). There are two parts to my response. One is that the politicians must stand for re-election, and therefore will not decide upon very selfish policies. In reply, it may then be argued that this response ignores the possibility that politicians will indiscriminately produce very populist policies, precisely because they seek re-election. Thus, the second part of my response is that, precisely because these policies are considered to be new inputs, they are subject to ongoing critical scrutiny; this process should involve a serious consideration of the policies, a consideration that benefits from the fact that it is initiated after some time has lapsed, allowing the consequences of these policies to emerge. The public is then in a position to consider the policy in light of these new data. In other words, this model is realistic. It may be that some politicians would act irresponsibly because their decisions are regarded as new inputs to the deliberation, but the resulting policies would be reconsidered by the public, and can therefore be corrected. Hopefully, politicians interested in re-election would take this into account when making decisions, and would refrain from acting irresponsibly. The condition, though, for such behaviour is that we look at democracy as I suggest: rather than regarding the debate as preceding the decisions and ceasing after decisions, we should regard the debate as an ongoing process, in the midst of which there is a stage of decision-making; the latter is only a new input to the debate, and therefore decisions can change following new reflections on them.

Finally, it may be claimed that only majoritarianism can prevent despotic rule by one person. This is a popular belief, but is not necessarily true (Dahl 1989: 135–53); rather, it is open and free deliberation that ensures no individual will enforce her will on the others. With such deliberation, there is an equal chance for every citizen to raise an issue and place it on the political agenda, without any one individual imposing her preferences for discussion upon others.

A good example is the minimum wage debate which never took place at the British Labour party conference in September 1995. Everyone anticipated a lively debate; the trade unions and the Left believed a decision in favour of a minimum wage was imminent. The leadership however wavered. Above all, the leadership was eager to prevent its defeat in the vote. Accordingly, Tony Blair met with union leaders and made it clear that he would not accept a different position from his own. Eventually the vote was a majoritarian one. But there was no debate at all: in fact, the will of one person was enforced through

scrutiny by the people, i.e. when there has been a political process of free, open, and egalitarian public deliberation.

a majoritarian vote and with no open discussion. Had the union leadership insisted on an open debate, others could have voiced their doubts or challenged the leadership's position. The position I am putting forward here is that without debate this could hardly be called a democratic decision, even though it was majoritarian.

Think of the many majoritarian decisions taken in non-democratic regimes, and of the many decisions made in democratic regimes without any voting taking place. First, what is the difference between a majoritarian decision in a totalitarian parliament and one in a democratic parliament? It is widely—but wrongly—believed by the general public that totalitarian regimes do not care about legitimacy. This is not true. Both systems seek a majoritarian legitimization, but the totalitarian regime manipulates public opinion by varied means to gain support; the majority supporting the policy, in turn, legitimizes the regime. In a democracy, however, manipulated public opinion may support a certain policy in the short term, but will, in the long run, weaken the legitimacy of the system. Thus, democracy receives its legitimacy from autonomous individuals.

It follows that what really matters in democracy is that debate is *genuine*. Indeed, not always is there a majority decision. Think, for example, of a bureaucratic decision to build a certain bridge one year and a different one the year after, or the decision to broaden economic relationships with a neighbouring country, or to forbid the use of a new medicine.[24] Why do we distinguish between such decisions in a democratic regime and similar ones in a non-democratic regime? What difference is there if, in any case, these decisions are not taken by votes and only reflect the opinion of a tiny minority of experts?

The difference lies in the quality of the deliberation that precedes and follows the decision. As long as every citizen can freely, openly, and equally contribute to the ordering of the agenda and criticize a decision, then that decision is democratic. This is the reason why most of us consider decisions and policies in a democratic regime to be temporary, circumstantial, and always open to question, whereas the principle of deliberation and argumentation itself is regarded as eternal. Perhaps therefore we should conclude that democratic theory ought to shift to a model that encourages deliberation, rather than letting the majority determine and constitute the way we live—a model emphasizing participation rather than majority rule, and debate rather than decision. This is not to say that going by the majority is not important, or has no place in a democratic regime; rather, that in the absence of genuine deliberation, theorists and the public have come to emphasize the majority

[24] On the face of it, these decisions are indeed bureaucratic, and hence the question of whether or not they are democratic is irrelevant. But, in fact, these decisions affect or are based on the budget, which is debated and voted on in parliament, and has the status of legislation.

aspect of democracy as if this were the essence of the regime. However, as I have suggested, the main point of democracy is in fact deliberation.

However, deliberation in itself is not enough. It must be subject to three conditions:

1. It has to be free: everyone must be able to take part, at any time, even after decisions have been taken, and it must not be controlled or directed by government.

2. It has to be open: every issue must be legitimate and may be placed on the agenda, as long as it does not harm anyone else or limit another's chance to put his own issues on the agenda. If the debate is not open, and if people assume that they know best and need not listen to anyone else, the debate is pointless.[25]

3. At the same time, the debate must be egalitarian. This not only means that everybody must enjoy the same initial position and the same right to raise issues, but also that one may not raise the same issue endlessly, because, assuming time is limited, this would prevent others from raising their own issues. So citizens are expected to be reasonable in repeating their demands to discuss issues that have already been raised. This condition meets one possible challenge, namely that condition 2 makes deliberative participatory democracy terribly inefficient since people may maintain their standpoints and bother others with their ideas, thus preventing society from even making decisions.[26]

'Even so,' one may still insist, 'what is the significance of politics if it is all about debating rather than deciding? If politics is just a matter of harmony, tension and aesthetics, why isn't a piece of music by Bach or a good movie just as satisfying? Why bother with politics at all?' My answer to is that by no means have I argued that politics is only about debate and aesthetics. Indeed, societies often have to take decisions, sometimes urgently, in which case there is no time for a profound deliberation. But clearly, a political process is required if we wish to live together. Now, the reason why democratic politics is better than any other system resides at least partly in its non-instrumental (towards decisions) qualities. For this reason, democratic theorists should emphasize participation in the deliberation rather than stressing majoritarian decision-making.

It goes without saying that, if implemented, such a model of democracy would require radical reform of our current institutions. For example, there would need to be easier excess to parliament and its members, and a reduction in the elite's domination of the political discourse by introducing institutional incentives to encourage participation (subsidies to parties and local branches,

[25] Reviewing several cases, Diego Gambeta (1998) argues that, in cases where people have too strong opinions on 'virtually everything', deliberation is never efficient.

[26] When this occurs in a parliament it is called a 'filibuster'. However, although legitimate, even filibusters are limited in time.

for example). There would have to be protective measures to ensure pluralism in communication, e.g. laws that do not allow a single body to control several newspapers, television networks, and/or internet communication, and by doing everything else needed to encourage individuals to become more politically involved. We should also take into account psychological elements in debates. For example, for many people it is important that they do not lose their face in debates. They will be ready to be persuaded if their dignity can be maintained. This will need to be kept in mind when people are engaged in such debates and when the community conducts them. (Compromises can sometimes be a good solution.) It seems to me, however, that all these changes are compatible with environmentalists' goals. So I now turn to this point.

Why Should Environmentalists Find Deliberative Participatory Democracy Appealing?

Earlier I mentioned 'survivalism' and 'eco-authoriatarianism', two schools of thought that regard democracy as an obstacle to environmental policies. To some people it is not surprising that some environmentalists attack democracy: if what we have in mind is a highly important, crucial, and urgent goal (defending the Earth), based on a metaphysical assumption about the existence of 'values that transcend the individual' (Dobson 1993), then it is likely that some environmentalists would prefer a goal-based theory which evaluates policies according to their consequences, rather than according to their paths. According to this view, democracy, being hesitant and rights-oriented, could be seen as an impediment to the environmentalist efforts to save the Earth. However, it would not be wrong to generalize that the vast majority of environmental activists are committed to democracy. The reasons for this relate not to environmental matters in particular, but rather to a general attitude towards politics. However, I would like to claim that, in addition, environmentalists have sound environmental reasons for adhering to democracy—more precisely, to *deliberative participatory democracy*.

So now I would like to discuss an example with bearings on my claim that deliberative participatory democracy is good for environmental policies. I do this by relating to the question of risk management, or, more specifically, to information, rationality, and risk. My argument is that, in addition to legislation, deliberative participatory democracy is needed to force governments to disclose to their citizens all they know about hazardous waste, radioactive power, ecological disasters, plans for development, etc. It also forces governments to execute environmental impact assessments whenever they decide on a development programme. This may seem trivial, but in most cases it is not practised properly, even in the democratic world. It may be argued that governments get away without executing environmental impact assessments properly partly because democracy is not deliberative and participatory enough. Instead, citizens count on their representatives to ensure that environmental impact assessment is carried out on their behalf. But these representatives fail to do this for various reasons, among them their dependence on developers who finance politicians and the political system, their mystical belief in development, and the popular belief that development means more jobs (hence more votes for these representatives). Consequently, the environmental voice is not loud enough, and governments tend to prefer the interests of developers on environmental perspectives.

The model of deliberative participatory democracy should solve these problems because it overcomes the two most important difficulties. First, in order for people to act and have an impact on policies, they need to have what I called 'environmental consciousness' (see Chapter 3). However, outside the democratic deliberation, most people have very romantic (ruralist) perceptions of the environmental issue.[27] According to experts' and activists' reports, such perceptions prevent people from grasping the real issues at stake, or at least from sharing and understanding the experts' positions and their professional approach to complicated environmental problems (Fiorino 1990).

The second difficulty is that, when people make up their minds whether or not to participate in a political debate or campaign, the key factor determining their decisions is whether they understand enough about the problem and its alternative solutions. This observation is a rather uncommon view: many people think that one would tend to participate when one feels that the controversy is a serious matter, a 'big issue', and that one tends to ignore the marginal, small issues. However, there is sociological evidence that the scale of the problem or its importance is not a key factor in determining the percentage and intensity of participation. Rather, participation is a function of the information available, a knowledge of the issues and the subjective sense of being able to grasp the problem.

The best example of this is the kibbutz democracy. This is a good example because many external factors (i.e. ones not having to do with the issue at stake) which could have had an impact on the decision of whether or not to participate, such as economic circumstances or wide gaps in political skills, are irrelevant in the kibbutz: there is an equality of political power and economic status in the kibbutz's weekly assembly. And yet, decisions on 'big issues', e.g. setting up a new industry, the optimal number of members, etc., are reached rapidly and with very little discussion, whereas decisions on issues about which members feel that they know a lot—and these could either be 'big

---

[27] These people glorify rural life; they love and admire nature, are fond of wild animals, and 'care' about the environment. However, they lack a scientific, systematic understanding of the way ecosystems work, how urban pollution and sewage affect their lives, etc.; and therefore they fail to relate such questions to political, collective action and questions (de-Shalit 1995*a*).

issues' such as the recent abolition of collective child raising, or 'small issues' such as purchasing a new television for the communal dining room—are reached only after lengthy debate.

So the two difficulties are that people tend to have romantic perceptions of environmental issues, and that, moreover, since they know very little about these issues, they tend to disregard them. As a result, it is difficult to treat environmental issues democratically and to organize the environmental voice. The model of deliberative participatory democracy relies on a flow of information from the centre to the citizens and vice versa, as well as between the citizens. It is therefore more likely that people will be able to understand the problems, the professional terms that are used, the attitudes of experts, and the various solutions offered under such a political system. The more information about an issue that is readily available, the more people are likely to know and understand, and therefore the more they will be likely to participate in the deliberation. This in turn will expose people to even more information and knowledge, re-encouraging them to participate.

As an example for my argument, I wish to discuss a current attitude to risk—risk perception and risk acceptability—and how deliberative participatory democracy might change our attitudes to risk evaluation. (I should emphasize that this is not a comprehensive discussion of risk or attitudes to risk: rather, the issue is raised as an example for my argument.) At the moment, the rationale of risk-taking with regard to the environment is this: the public votes for its leaders, who in turn choose and nominate experts, the latter taking upon themselves all risk assessment: (1) identification of public hazard; (2) estimation of potential associated harm; (3) risk evaluation (Shrader-Frechette 1985; 1991: ch. 4). However, it seems that the experts also take upon themselves (4) the decision as to whether the public should be informed of the risk. My main argument in this section is that, instead of leaving the last decision to the experts or politicians, society must be equipped with the information to decide for itself whether and how it wishes to accept the risk. It is reasonable to believe that, if individuals (and society as a whole) know more about the risk, they will also learn to evaluate risks rationally.

To get this discussion rolling, we first need to distinguish between risk and danger. Risk is a notion that incorporates a willingness to accept the danger. For example, suppose I want to go trekking in the Himalayas. I know that the safer seasons are spring or autumn. But it's winter now, and the weather experts tell me there is a 30 per cent chance of snow, and that half the time it snows, avalanches occur. I therefore know that I have a 15 per cent chance of ending up in an avalanche. This is a danger associated with my journey. But my journey bears other values: for instance, it has a social value for me, a value associated with my enjoyment, or with the idea of me being a hero when I return, or with the fact that I promised my grandfather I would do this because he always wanted to but could not, or what have you. I am therefore ready to 'take the risk'. Risk, then, involves weighing the possibility that a certain danger will occur against certain advantages (or values).[28]

Thus, unlike danger, risk is a concept already loaded with values and value judgements. This carries two implications. First, activists should be sophisticated when discussing risks. To see what I mean by this, consider, for example, the following statements by two members of the Green Party in Britain, Sandy Irvine and Alec Ponton:

Human society . . . is threatening not only itself but all of the rest as well. . . . Human activity has become a malignant cancer draining the vitality of the Earth. . . . Unless we change course human society faces self-destruction, taking many other life-forms with it. . . . Prophecies of doom have been proved wrong many times before, yet some societies in the past *have* committed ecological suicide. (Irvine and Ponton 1998: 5–6)

Such statements, I am afraid, do not serve the environmental case. If people are faced with very broad talk of abstract—but total—destruction, they are very unlikely to do anything to prevent this 'destruction', and with quite a good reason. Remember that risk is a concept loaded with value judgements; thus, people evaluate the likelihood of a certain danger *vis-à-vis* the values of welfare, more jobs, and so on. Now, if people are told that the danger is total and abstract destruction, they will fail to evaluate the risk: first, because the danger is so abstract that there is no way to grasp it and its likelihood, and second, because of the competing value—having more jobs and higher welfare—which is very tempting. One should be able to sense a great danger that is very likely to occur in order to give up opportunities for jobs and welfare. Thus, activists should point to specific, not abstract, dangers. People would then realize that if X is done Y might happen. For example, if a particular forest is cut down to build a new motorway, there will be no countryside nearby and owing to the increase in traffic there will be much more noise (and, perhaps, psychological effects on the town's inhabitants). Only then will people think again about whether this motorway is worth it. Or, activists could explain that, if we fail to reduce 'producing' certain hazardous wastes because we are so eager to have more industries regardless of the ecological cost, and if we continue storing the waste carelessly, there is a high chance (percentage of likelihood can be specified according to previous cases) of fires in which dioxin will be released, causing many childhood diseases in the area.

---

[28] This 'weighing' of possibilities *vis-à-vis* other values may sound easy, but it is not. Often we err, and often those who calculate risks are not those likely to get hurt; therefore they tend to be too tolerant of the dangers, and to ignore the likelihood of the danger occurring. The terrible tragedy in Bhopal in December 1984, in which thousands died when 40 tons of gas from the Union Carbide factory escaped into the atmosphere, could perhaps have been prevented if more attention had been paid to local experts who disagreed with and criticized the evaluations of the American experts with their optimistic calculations (Jaising and Sathyamala 1993).

The second implication of risk being loaded with value judgements, however, is controversial. Some people imply that risk is relative, or that there is no way of conducting a rational evaluation of risks. I would like to argue that this is a wrong conclusion. The fact that risk involves value judgements does not mean it is relative: it only implies that these rational evaluations should be public because they involve balancing dangers with *public* values or *political* goals, which the public has to decide upon. So it is possible for risk evaluation, an important element of environmental policies and environmental impact assessment, to be rational even though it is not value-free.

As I have mentioned, some people hold another view. For example, Mary Douglas and Aaron Wildawsky claim that risks are 'nothing but social constraints'. Risk is always perceived, not objective—for example, it is influenced by the type and size of the organization within which one works, by the duration of time one has been aware of the specific dangers (the longer it is, the less one is concerned) and by the cultural background of the person involved (Douglas 1985)—and therefore all its evaluations are relative (Douglas 1966; Douglas and Wildawsky 1982; Renn 1992). I tend to disagree. There are two reasons why these evaluations are not necessarily relative. The first is offered by Shrader-Frechette, although her answer is not full:

Even though all risks are perceived, many of them are also real. The risk of death, for instance, is real. But it is also, in part, a probability, and such probabilities can rarely be known with certainty. Until death becomes a certainty, the risk of death is purely perceived, theoretical, or estimated. Indeed, the occurrence of death, in a particular case, reveals how accurate our perceptions or estimates of the risk of death were. More generally, although the risk that some X will occur is real, the exact degree and nature of the risk are not, in principle, confirmable until X actually occurs. Prior to this occurrence, risk perspectives can be judged as more or less accurate only on the basis of non-empirical and theoretical criteria such as explanatory power, simplicity, or internal coherence. Nevertheless, risks perceptions are often *real and objective* at least in the sense that *empirical evidence is relevant to them and is capable of providing grounds for amending them*. All risks . . . then are both perceived and real. Their exact nature and magnitude become more fully knowable, however, insofar as more instances of X occur. The relativists erred in believing that, because all risks are perceived, all risks are therefore relative. (Shrader-Frechette 1991: 80; my emphasis)

I have said that this answer is not full. The reason is that it may imply—though I do not think this is what Shrader-Frechette meant it to imply—that risk is 'only hypothetical' until it happens. Indeed, developers often claim that society should not worry about risks because they are 'only hypothetical'. But the concept of 'hypothetical risk' is meaningless. Yes, every risk is hypothetical until it happens. (Even if we do have enough statistical information, one could say that our calculation is hypothetical.) But this does not make the risk less riskier (not to mention less objective and real, as Shrader-Frechette argues).

The other reason why risk evaluation is not relative is that public deliberation may prevent the evaluation from becoming relativist. Or at least, it can
be said that the evaluation will become more rational the more deliberative
and public it is. At first sight, this claim of mine may seem to contradict an earlier claim in this chapter, when I dismissed the argument whereby the greater
the number of participants, the 'better' or more rational the decision will be.
Indeed, the public is not better informed than the experts of an outcome's
probabilities. Moreover, the public tends to overestimate the risks involved in
low-probability catastrophic events, and to be too tolerant of risks borne voluntarily or risks that seem familiar (Fiorino 1996: 196; Dryzek 1997: 72).
Perhaps the best example of discounting risks borne voluntarily is gambling,
which, despite being very risky, is nevertheless popular. Driving cars is another
example. Yet another good example is the discrepancy between the equanim-
ity with which Israelis accept the existence of nuclear waste (its burial locations are not known to the general public because it is still an official security
secret that Israel has atomic weapons) and the exaggerated reactions to the
possibility that Iraq might attack Israel with chemical missiles. The former is
voluntarily accepted, since many Israelis regard the atomic weapon as a deter-
rent capable of forcing the Arab countries to accept Israel's existence; whereas
the latter is a case of a low-probability catastrophic event, the risk of which is
not voluntarily taken. So if the public reacts in this exaggerated way, and if
indeed it does not have the relevant data, it seems, prima facie, that there is
no reason to believe the evaluation would be more rational if it were more
deliberative. Shouldn't we leave it in the hands of the experts?

No, we should not, and if we do not the evaluation does not become relativist. Why? Because, interestingly, the public serves as the watchdog for these
experts. If the experts are forced to disclose the probabilities to the public, and
if they know that they will have to face the public and explain their information and justify their recommendations, they will be more careful and will also
refrain from certain ideological biases. These biases may occur if and when
experts, with or without intention, maliciously or not, ignore a certain probability, or a certain public value, which should be weighed against this probability.

For example, in the early 1950s experts in the USA allowed the army to use
soldiers as guinea pigs in radioactive experiments, exposing them to radioactive radiation during atom bomb tests—not because they did not *know* (or
anticipate) the dangers, but rather because they ignored the values and considerations they needed to weigh against the benefit of the information they
obtained. The price paid was human misery and death, and an abdication of
respect for people as equals. Had there been public deliberation regarding
these tests, based on full access to information, and had the experts known
that there would be such a debate, they probably would have recommended
against exposing the soldiers to radioactive radiation, out of a sense of respect

and fear of public criticism; or, at least, if they had decided to carry out the test but to inform the public about it in advance, the debate would have forced them to change their minds.

Moreover, democratizing the deliberation on risk is a way of changing the attitude that sees the risk to individuals as a matter of luck (society accepts a certain risk, but who is ultimately affected is down to chance) to an attitude based on an assumption that it is within human control to conduct and distribute risk. So democratizing the deliberation implies that risks will be avoided unless they are crucial to a much needed public good. If risk is discussed in such a way, individuals will understand that they have an equal chance of being exposed to the danger, and therefore will refrain from accepting danger off-hand; whereas often, when risks are discussed within closed circles of experts and politicians, dangers are too easily accepted as a means of achieving some political goal, owing to the fact that those involved in the discussion are less likely to be exposed to, or harmed by, the danger. So the rationality of risk evaluation may be increased if, in the process of evaluation, people are committed to the criterion of equity of risk distribution.

Notice that I do not claim that decisions related to risk will be 'better', in the sense that deliberative participatory democracy leads to more efficient policies or that the process of decision-making becomes more efficient. Risk decisions must involve value judgements; hence they are moral decisions. So, when I claim that decisions would be more rational, I do not mean that they become more efficient, but rather that the relevant values will indeed be incorporated into the decision-making process.[29]

I can now summarize my discussion of the example of risk evaluation:

1. Risk is perceived, but there is always some chance that the danger will occur.
2. Deciding whether or not to accept the risk of danger occurring involves weighing the danger and its likelihood *vis-à-vis* social and political goals and other values.
3. Since political goals and values enter the picture, the public is entitled to participate in this deliberation, and to be able to base their participation in the debate on the most accurate and full information available. This is

---

[29] Admittedly, when risk is discussed in public, it may produce a wave of national paranoia. The Beef Scare or the Salmonella Scare in Britain are prime examples, of how issues involving far less damage, misery or death than traffic accidents, or drugs, became the most important issues on the public agenda for quite a time. And yet, these 'paranoia' events fulfil a role in raising politicians' and governments' awareness of certain problems. Historically, it can be said that even the debate about toxic pesticides, following the first publication of Rachel Carson's *Silent Spring* as a three-part serial in *The New Yorker* in 1962, was perhaps paranoid. And yet it was crucial in shattering the absolute belief in technology and in the development of public and political awareness of environmental issues. As Charles Secrett, director of *Friends of the Earth* wrote recently in the BBC Wildlife Magazine (June 1998, p. 77): 'Name me an environmentalist who claims to be neither profoundly influenced nor moved by Rachel Carson's *Silent Spring* and I'll show you a liar'.

so even though, admittedly, laypeople tend to overestimate low-probability catastrophic events and underestimate voluntarily borne risks. The public is, therefore, entitled to be informed, and this entitlement is more likely to be respected in a deliberative participatory regime.

Moreover:

4. Risk is always perceived, but it is always at least partially real. If it is democratically discussed according to the model suggested here, so that every decision is exposed to public scrutiny and revision, then there is a greater possibility that the experts—who know that they would have to face the public whatever they recommend—will take the trouble to measure dangers carefully, will genuinely refrain from any (ideological) bias, and will openly inform the public so that people can weigh the danger against the relevant values.

5. The more participatory the deliberation, the more egalitarian it will be, and hence the more likely the decision is to be rational, in the sense that all relevant values will be incorporated in the decision-making process.

Thus, we, as a society need more than merely information (*environmental literacy*), or the philosopher teaching us about the morality of these decisions (*environmental awareness*). We need *environmental consciousness*. We have to realize that risk management is a political issue, involving a process of collective (i.e. in a community) rational reflection on the evaluation of dangers *vis-à-vis* the values we hold. We therefore have to discuss these values as well, and this should also be done within the community. In that sense we see how democracy as characterized here ties in with the model of the community of collective rational reflection, described in Chapter 4. And thus, when environmental and political philosophers engage in this public reflection, they should relate to the public, its values, and its theories, and therefore should apply the mechanism of *public reflective equilibrium*.[30] Interestingly, the more governments seek to prevent this public reflective equilibrium and rely on experts only, the more the theories of risk are likely to differ from the public's perception of risk—which, as explained above, is very likely to be based on different values from those of the experts. Hence, if the government wants its risk policies to be legitimate, it should include the public's perceptions of risk by a process of public reflective equilibrium.

At this point a problem may arise: namely, that individuals within the public differ in their views of risk, according to their own likelihood to be exposed to it. This, naturally, leads us to a discussion of the distribution of risk. It is noted, for example, that below a certain level income is a good predictor of relative exposure to risks of most kinds (Douglas 1985: 6). Indeed, if we now turn from my example of risk to the issue of environmental policies in general, we

---

[30] I take it that this is what Shrader-Frechette means when she calls for 'negotiated accounts of risk and rationality' (1991: 77–89).

must not ignore the very nature of environmental policies. Though they protect the environment and humans, they are often very expensive, therefore require that someone or some group pays for them. They are also likely to protect some more than others. Thus, environmental policies redistribute costs and benefits. No matter how democratic they are, and how communitarian the society is, environmental policies call for a theory of the distribution of access to goods and services. It is to this matter that I now turn.

6

Socialism and the Environment

I would like to begin this chapter by mentioning the questions *not* raised. First, there is the interesting question of whether or not a socialist theory must be 'green' to be socialist. The answer, I tend to think, is negative. Second, it is often asked whether Greens must be socialist to be green. The answer this time, I tend to think, is positive. However, while these are two important and no doubt interesting questions, they belong to a different group of issues. In fact, they are very useful if one is interested in the relationships between the parties that lead the environmental campaign, namely, the socialist or social democratic parties on the one hand, and the Greens on the other. In this book, however, I am more interested in the ideas or ideologies behind the parties. So my question is, What makes socialism an economic, social, and political system, one that is good rather than harmful to the environment? To put it another way, Why is socialism better for the environment than other, rival or alternative, political systems?

Notice that I have phrased the last question rather hesitantly. Indeed, I do not ask why socialism is perfect for the environment, simply because it is not. Rather, I ask about elements within socialism which make it more attractive than other systems or theories from the environmentalist's perspective. I do not therefore put forward what is, in my view, a pretentious argument, namely that 'socialism is wonderful for the environment'. Indeed, I subscribe to the view that the 'environment' as a political issue poses a challenge to all political theories and to their claim of being able to solve all political problems, hence it calls for a combination of theories. Thus, I would prefer to offer a far more modest thesis: namely that many elements in socialism make it a preferable theory and system in terms of the effect on the environment.

But what is socialism?[1] This is indeed a difficult question. It is difficult not

[1] Since in my discussion of socialists' ideas I shall be applying the public reflective equilibrium mechanism and referring to standpoints of NGOs and activists, I feel I ought to distinguish here between eco-socialists (to whose works I mean to refer often) and social ecologists. The latter, e.g. Bookchin, are often classified as 'anarchists' (see e.g. Pepper 1993). I should also emphasize that I will not relate to a group of socialist writers whose position, though interesting, is on the verge of a 'conspiracy theory'. For example, Faber and O'Connor (1989) argue that American industry 'bought' Ronald Reagan the presidency to balance the effects of earlier environmental legislation on industry. I find such positions often far-fetched and lacking sufficient empirical ground.

only because of the variety of socialist theories (Wright 1987), but also because the world has experienced so many different regimes that call themselves 'socialist'. Many people think that, whatever socialism is, it is not relevant any more. Indeed, since the destruction of the Berlin Wall, which symbolized more than anything else the collapse of East European 'socialist' regimes, many have claimed, some with sadness and some with joy, that 'socialism is dead'. But we need to ask whether this is in fact true. Is the socialist *idea* dead, or is what was buried beneath the ruins of the Berlin Wall simply a deviant totalitarian system?

It seems, at least among academics and philosophers, that socialism as an idea is enjoying something of a comeback.[2] So, in this chapter I would like to join those who believe that, as long as capitalistic individualism is alive, then so should socialism be, as the main and most important alternative. I will not be defending this claim here,[3] but rather wish to defend the relevance of socialism with regard to environmental policies. However, it should be emphasized from the start that when I refer to 'socialism' I do not mean the communist regimes of Eastern Europe. At least prima facie, if these regimes were socialist, then socialism cannot be said to be good for the environment, because in those countries we found evidence of the worst examples of irrational human exploitation of the environment—ecological disasters, contaminated rivers that look more brown than blue, etc. (Podgorodinkov 1993; Tickle and Welsh 1998; Gille 1997). This evidence, however, does not prove that socialism is bad for the environment, for two reasons. First, as I say, these were not necessarily 'socialist' regimes. Second, the poor quality of the environment could be due to another characteristic of these regimes: that they were extremely totalitarian and dictatorial. So it now remains to be proved that the poor state of the environment was due to the anti-market economy (or any other socialist policy), rather than to the totalitarian characteristics of the regime. It seems to me that the totalitarian atmosphere bred a lack of information, and hence an ignorance of ecological and environmental processes, as well as an attitude of fear of opposing irresponsible environmental policies, and a recklessness regarding the public and the common good, which contributed more than anything else to the neglect and misuse of the environment in those countries. In the terms I used in the previous chapters, there was no environmental literacy and environmental awareness. In their absence, there could be no environmental consciousness, and therefore no proper environmental policies.

The other notion I wish to distance myself from is that there should be a single, monolithic theory of socialism. So I will be looking for foundational

---

[2] Many people claim that, since capitalism is moderate and not too aggressive, no place exists for socialism any more. But, as David Marquand argues in his recent book (1997: 62–3), capitalism today is not very different in form and substance from capitalism 100 years ago. He claims, in particular, that this is true with regard to structural unemployment.

[3] Interested readers may refer to the works of Barry and Miller quoted below.

socialist values and practices[4] while refraining from making any claims as to the ultimate socialist theory. In doing so I run the risk of being vague, besides laying myself open to the charge of misrepresenting socialism. To this my answer is twofold.

First, it seems that one cannot draw a line between socialism and non-socialism. Socialism is a matter of degree. The more we have of certain values or practices X, Y, and Z, the more socialist a system will be. Of course, 'the more' should be read 'up to a certain limit'. For example, the claim that the more public direction of the economy and the less competition there is, the more socialist the system will be should not imply that the total abolition of private initiative is more socialist, because the price for this could be less political equality or self-realization. In other words, we are looking for an optimal balance of policies, so that the more we have of X without limiting Y and/or Z, or the more we have of X up to the point where adding X limits Y and/or Z, the more socialist the system is.

Second, there is, in fact a need for new, innovative theories of socialism since, as G. A. Cohen (1995: introduction), John Roemer (1994), and the Red–Green Study Group (1995: 15) point out, it is no longer the case that the working class constitutes the majority of society and produces its wealth, and it is no longer the case that workers stand to lose nothing in the event of revolution.[5] However, it is also true that the gradual disappearance of the working class is 'achieved' by paying the price of higher levels of consumption and other devastating consequences for the environment. Socialists should therefore revise and modify their theory in face of these new circumstances. Thus, for example, both Tim Hayward (1994) and Ted Benton (1989) point to the fact that Marxist socialism lacks genuine recognition for what constitutes a crucial element of environmental attitudes, namely 'natural limits to growth', or the recognition that the world has finite resources.[6] It is actually interesting to note that, while many scholars have been engaged in the debate about what socialism is (e.g. whether its main idea is the abolition of private property or whether it is an egalitarian theory), they all seem to be asking not what is *socialism*, but rather what is *feasible* socialism.[7] So here is another question I

---

[4] Foundational values are values that characterize only a particular theory or ideology. Derivative values are values that may form part of this theory, but nevertheless derive from the more fundamental values, and may form parts of other theories or ideologies as well (Dworkin 1986: 181–205).

[5] The 'Red–Green Study Group' write that many of the concerns of the newer social movements lie outside the labour process—they often focus either on the needs of groups who have been excluded from the labour process or on groups such as travellers, 'New Agers . . . who have rejected wage labour'.

[6] But see M. O'Connor (1994), who claims that a proper reading of Marx leads one to acknowledge that human exploitation is closely related to the exploitation of nature. For an interesting analysis of industrial exploitation in domains that on first appearance seem external to the capitalist workplace, see Salleh (1994; 1997).

[7] Some of them are motivated by the very interesting philosophical and practical question of what it is that egalitarians should be trying to equalize: is it equality of opportunity to

will not be asking: What is socialism in both its theoretical and practical historical manifestations? Rather, I will be looking for those elements of socialism that construct feasible socialism in contemporary society, feasible in terms both of the theory (i.e. that it is consistent and coherent) and the practice (that it is likely to work). However, I am not talking about the theory that is likely to be most attractive in the populist sense. The reason is that sometimes well structured theories and systems are capable of creating new circumstances which will expose latent positive, altruistic, and optimistic human qualities, all of which are depressed under capitalism by the constraints imposed by extreme inequality, poverty, non-participatory regimes, and competitiveness. So a socialist theory—even that of democratic socialism—need not be a populist one. (I elaborate on this in the book's summary.)

Notice that this conceptualization of socialism is not about changing attitudes directly, but rather about changing circumstances so that the right attitudes, which are believed to be latent in people, may emerge. It seems to me rather incomprehensible that socialists, who often accept materialism—that is, the theory that consciousness is a function of circumstances—would try to manipulate or even brainwash. Socialism must be non-compulsory and non-coercive, because if its goal is to change attitudes it must do so by changing circumstances rather than by direct manipulation and indoctrination. (This is one of the sources for the ideological tension between eco-socialists and Deep Ecology.) I therefore have in mind a *democratic* form of socialism, and I rule out any form of non-democratic socialism as being both immoral and inadequate for bringing about environmental change, which, in order to be significant, must be accompanied by a change in attitude towards the environment, and therefore needs democratic deliberation.[8] But unlike those who argue about whether democracy is a precondition for socialism or, vice versa, whether socialism is a precondition for democracy, I think that it suffices to say that the two are inseparable: democratic socialism should mean that democracy is an adjective describing socialism and socialism is an adjective describing democracy. Now the term 'democratic socialism' does not mean only socialism that is conducted via democratic institutions. It implies a socialism that goes along with, rather than against, people. It is the *people*

welfare, or what? See Roemer (1996), Arneson (1989), and G. A. Cohen (1995). But this is another question beyond the scope of this chapter, because it looks not at socialism as such but rather at egalitarianism in general. Many of these works are debates with Ronald Dworkin's concepts of 'equality of resources' and 'equality of welfare' (1981*b*, *c*).

[8] The differences between socialist and non-democratic socialism (e.g. anarchism) are further explored by David Pepper (1993: 106–7). The emphasis on democratic forms of socialism is related also to the acceptance of the state. Indeed, argues Pepper, if we relate to the environmental issue in its broad meaning, local activities and communalities cannot solve the problems and a state is therefore needed (Pepper 1993: 215). Of course, the aim is to democratise the state, which is possible because the current state is far from being unresponsive and bureaucratic. Such a description of the state as unresponsive would be a 'flat' description, ignoring many features of the modern state; see Ryle (1988) and Frankel (1988).

that count: it is they who are the goal of politics, rather than the ideas or the system. While this may sound like a slogan, it is not. For example, the social-ist environmentalist David Pepper (1993; 1996) has launched a powerful cri-tique of some of the extremely radical green organizations such as *Earth First!* (see Foreman 1991). He claims that they have become misanthropic in their impatience, and that they seem loyal to ideas rather than people.

But is this achievable? How can one both be paternalistic to a great extent, as socialists are, and refrain from enforcing a particular position? I suggest that the way to do this is to practise deliberative democracy in politics and 'public reflective equilibrium' in philosophy (see Chapter 1). A democratic form of socialism supports—indeed, must rest upon—intensive deliberation and pub-lic reflective equilibrium because there is a strong need to reach agreement between citizens regarding the principles of justice, and the values and policies related to justice, e.g. what constitutes lack of exploitation, toleration, liberty, and equality and the institutions needed for their implementation. Thus, democratic socialism is open to internal as well as external criticism. This, of course, differentiates between the type of socialism discussed here and that practised by the Eastern European communist states, where internal criticism was regarded as treason or betrayal and external criticism as subversion.

Now readers may notice that the kind of socialism I have in mind is com-patible with the theory of democracy developed in the previous chapter, in so far as any change is controlled and re-examined by the public. It is also com-patible with the role of the philosopher as described in Chapter 1. The social-ist theory should point to necessary changes in policies, e.g. the need to reduce private car use and increase public transportation, and then socialism, while respecting people's intuitions, should introduce new measures in a gradual way; for example rather than banning the use of private cars, it should raise taxes on petrol and subsidize public transportation. Then again, the theorist should point to what is needed, for example banning car use in city centres at midday. Since by this stage people will have revised their attitudes and prac-tices with regard to public transportation (the economizing on petrol and the benefit to the environment will be a good enough incentive to use public transport, and the public will begin to acknowledge this), they will be pre-pared to consider something like a ban on private cars in city centres during rush hour. This, I should add, reflects suggestions already put forward by sym-pathizers of socialist environmentalism. For example, John O'Neill thinks that more ecologically sound behaviour is not contradictory to freedom (and see Chapter 3, where I argue that liberal freedoms have contributed to the emer-gence of the environmental discourse), and that therefore policies should not be imposed but should derive from debate and consensual decisions based on the question of the good life (O'Neill 1993, 1994; de-Shalit 1995*a*).

Possible Tensions: Changing Forces of Production or Relations of Production

If we are to apply the public reflective equilibrium mechanism, and relate to activists' intuitions and theories, we should relate to common arguments often raised by socialists themselves, who tend to be suspicious of environmental standpoints.

First, socialists claim that the environment is a challenge to socialism, since they have always been in favour of growth as a solution to 'structural unemployment', whereas environmental protection looks to ecological carrying capacity to limit growth. In this respect, socialists have not differed from capitalists; they have both taken issue with regard to who is to benefit from the fruits of growth, but not with regard to whether or not there should be growth. Conservation policies are likely to reduce the number of jobs, they claim, or to hurt the least advantaged:

Environmental improvement costs money, and this inevitably raises prices; often for basic needs, such as water and food. In other cases higher prices are specifically the means by which environmentalists seek to reduce environmental consumption—the case of VAT on domestic fuel being a pertinent example. In both cases this is inequitable, not to say politically damaging, and cannot be countenanced by a government of the left. (Jacobs 1995b: 6)[9]

But socialists' reservations regarding environmentalism are founded on a misconception of environmentalism: on the belief that environmentalism entails no growth. This is wrong. Environmentalism could entail sustainable development—admittedly, a vague concept—which involves a moderate form of growth limited by ecological carrying capacity. Not all environmentalists oppose development, growth and progress (e.g. Porritt 1984: 215). Rather, many accept the inevitability of development and growth, provided they are sustainable, that is, limited by obligations to future generations and (some add) to the non-human world. For example, with regard to the limitations on production that have resulted from environmental concern , this could affect the amount of production jobs available; however, rather than implying that, strictly speaking, we should cut jobs, many environmentalists and socialists (Gorz 1980; 1982) claim that we should redistribute access to jobs and leisure time.

Second, and following on this first objection, socialists often suspect the idea that a redistribution of goods and access to them should be limited by

---

[9] It should be noted that Jacobs is here referring to what other socialists claim. He himself goes on to reconcile socialists with environmentalists. Such positions as quoted by Jacobs are 'fuelled' by theories of post-materialism (e.g. by Ingelhart) that suggest that the environment is a *petit bourgeois* issue, as if only those who enjoy affluence can worry about the welfare of antelopes.

considerations that have to do with non-human entities (species, individual animals, ecosystems, etc.). The poor do not care about the environment, they claim. To this my answer is straightforward: it is empirically simply not true that the poor care less about the environment.[10] Moreover, as I shall show below, it is the poorer section of society that suffers most from environmental problems. Hence it makes sense that they should be concerned. It is probably true that poorer populations fail to demonstrate and express their interest in environmental matters; but this could be said about any matter—e.g. education, unemployment, or foreign policies: poorer people, who often suffer more, participate less. So the fact that the poor do not express environmental concern, if this is true at all, should not imply that those in favour of improving the well-being of the poor should take a stand against environmental policies.

At this point another reservation about environmentalism is raised by socialists, i.e. that many environmental activists and theorists claim that the tension between humans and nature is nowadays greater and more important than the tension between capital and the working class. For example, Ulrich Beck has been arguing that the conflicts that contemporary societies experience are about the distribution of 'bads' such as environmental costs, rather than the distribution of 'goods' such as money, leisure time, and so on. Therefore, new coalitions should be formed, and environmentalists should position themselves on 'neither the left nor the right' (see Beck 1992, and the response by Benton 1997). 'Such standpoints', argue these socialists, 'are beyond what socialists can accept. If this is the environmentalists' claim, then it weakens and undermines the socialist message. Why should they go hand in hand?' For the moment I will leave this question open, though it will be answered below.

A third argument put forward by socialists who are sceptical about environmentalism relates to the former two. Marxist socialists have always relied on the ability of humans to transform nature in their quest for social justice. For there to be justice, greater productivity is needed, and, given the ability of human beings to transform nature, this could be achieved through industry. At least prima facie, there is a contradiction here between this theory and the environmentalists' claim that all beings should be left to develop 'naturally', in their own way. If we adopt the socialist approach, humans will be allowed to transform nature; but this, environmentalists would claim, is actually damaging nature. If we follow the environmentalist track, humans would be asked to limit the transformation of nature; but the socialists would then say that

---

[10] This has also been suggested by a group of my students who studied attitudes to environmental issues among poorer populations in Israel. Many were disinterested in those issues because they lacked the relevant information and knowledge; however, when introduced to this information, they showed concern and care. The conclusion of this study was that lack of concern was a function not of a socioeconomic background *per se* but rather of a lack of information and knowledge.

humans would not be allowed to act 'naturally': they would be prevented from transforming nature through industry.

Eco-socialists and environmental theorists have reacted to this claim in three ways. Some (e.g. Pepper 1993: 223–4) imply that non-anthropocentrism (and its principle that all beings should be allowed to develop in their own way) is wrong. Others (e.g. Eckersley 1992a) attack the Marxist conception of human nature as wrong because it is based on anthropocentric (often specieist) assumptions. However, several theorists (e.g. J. Barry 1998; Benton 1988) have tried to tie the two—Marxist conception of human nature and non-anthropocentrism—in with each other. Indeed, it seems to me that the idea that humans should transform nature does not have to be interpreted as a description of human obsession. Rather we could look at it this way: human beings cooperate with nature; they depend on nature; and yet, they differ from other animals in that their intellectual abilities allow them to cooperate with nature in a sophisticated manner, to take whatever they want from nature and reshape it to suit their own needs. Rather than seeing only the manipulative potential in this human interaction with nature, we should look on the bright side: this ability allows human beings to be economical in how much they take from nature because they can use different parts of natural products to answer different human needs: they can peel the fruit's skin and use it for organic fertilizers, eat the fruit, and use its seeds to make dyes, medicines, etc. In other words, by transforming parts of nature, waste of natural 'resources' can be reduced or prevented.

Another way to overcome the difficulty of the Marxist emphasis on the human ability to transform nature as part of the definition of being human is suggested by Grundmann (1991: 58–61), who writes that nature is harnessed by obedience to its laws. In a way this is true, both if we think of 'conquering' Everest—it is only by being extremely modest *vis-à-vis* nature and obeying its laws that people have been able to climb such mountains—and if we think of science in general—its quest is to learn to survive in nature. Thus it seems that, while science seems to be interested in conquering nature, it in fact is seeking to understand it in order to obey its laws, because that is the path of human survival.[11]

In fact, the claim that any transformation of nature is 'bad' or anti-environmental is simply wrong. As I explained in Chapter 2, an ecological perspective should not imply that ecosystems should never change. They will inevitably do so, even when humans are not part of the system. Hence the ecological perspective is one that seeks to ensure that ecosystems remain stable, not unchanged. Thus, Tim Hayward distinguishes between transforming nature in the sense of overcoming necessity by meeting 'human needs for

---

[11] For more about knowing nature in this sense see T. Hayward (1994; 1998) and the activist Sara Parkin (1991, 29), who claims that science is not there to triumph over nature but to 'make peace with nature'.

food, shelter, good health and so on'—a case that need not be ecologically objectionable—and transforming nature in the sense of 'transcending natural limits'. The latter is what he refers to critically as the 'Promethean aim' (T. Hayward 1994: 74).

So much for the possible tensions between socialism and environmentalism. There may be additional tensions, but, as I declared in this chapter's opening paragraph, I do not pretend to claim that socialism is perfect for the environment: this is simply not true. Instead, I want to examine the main elements of 'feasible' democratic socialism, and to analyse the advantages and disadvantages of these elements in terms of the environment and environmental policies. I shall discuss socialist egalitarianism, rationality in politics, the abolition of alienation (and in relation to this, the options of restricting or controlling competition and of fostering community), the fostering of equal citizenship, and finally the question of property relationships—whether they need be in the form of public ownership. The reason I discuss these (rather than other) values is that they commonly appear in works by socialist and eco-socialist theorists and activists. It is interesting to note, however, that these elements of socialism are raised during a process of deliberation as described in the previous chapter (Chapter 5). The deliberation shifts the focus of democracy from liberal values, mostly individual freedoms, to these social values. This occurs because of the characteristics of deliberative democracy. It extends the 'political'; for example, it involves reaching beyond the individual's effort to protect her rights, e.g. in court, and instead suggests public debate on the values and norms that hold a community together. In other words, when people become engaged in deliberation, they tackle questions of justice, exploitation, and the community's common goals. They therefore become engaged in discussing *socialist* values. It can therefore be claimed that deliberative democracy inevitably raises socialist values for discussion.

Socialist Egalitarianism

Socialist egalitarianism is distinctive from what appears sometimes to be not too distant from it—namely, egalitarian liberalism. The main differences between the two are as follows. First, while for liberals egalitarianism entails primarily equal rights, equality before the law, and so on (rather than economic equality), for socialists, egalitarianism has mainly economic connotations. (This goes hand in hand with the eco-socialist claim that the heart of the environmental problem lies not in our lifestyle but rather in the process of production.) Second, egalitarian liberals assume that we must have liberty, and that politics is about protecting liberty. However, they recognize that traditional liberalism offers liberty to some while being unable to fulfil its promise to others, mainly the poor or worse-off sectors, simply because they lack the economic means to realize the opportunities provided by the political liberal system. Therefore these egalitarian liberals ask: how much liberty can we allow without harming people's chances of enjoying liberty at all? In other words: how little can we limit liberty (so that differences between people are relatively small) and still have everybody benefiting from it? Contemporary socialists, though, start with economic and political equality. They want people to be equal. But recognizing that equalizing (though not equality) might interfere with self-respect, they ask, How much equality should there be to ensure that self respect is not impaired? In other words, How little can we limit equality (so that self-respect and liberty are also enjoyed) and still have everybody being equal? Since liberal egalitarians and socialist egalitarians ask different questions, they also end up recommending different policies.

The question, however, may arise of whether socialism is mainly about egalitarianism, or even whether it is egalitarian at all. Some people argue that, historically at least, not all socialists have been motivated by egalitarianism. Some have had a strong preference for the working classes; they thought that those who contributed more should get more. Those socialists who claimed so differed from liberal-capitalists in their identification of who contributed more. While the capitalist thought that those who initiated and/or owned and/or managed the means of production were contributing more, the socialists believed that the working class—those who physically and actually worked—contributed more. They did not pretend to be strictly speaking egalitarian: they thought that the good-for-nothing, idle bourgeoisie should receive *less*. However, one should not conclude from this that all socialism is anti-egalitarian. In any case, I think that this historical claim (whether or not it is true) is not relevant, because we can firmly state that socialists are egalitarian *to the extent that* they emphasize that distribution should be equal regardless of the contribution, talent, etc.

One of the advocates of the idea that socialism's core value is egalitarianism is John Roemer (1994). To Roemer, the more egalitarian the distribution of company profits, the better: 'People do not deserve to profit differentially from the luck of the birth lottery, which distributes valuable assets (talents, citizenship, parents) in an arbitrary and highly unequal way' (Roemer 1994: 17). Following this line of thought I shall assume that socialism is egalitarian, and that this egalitarianism consists of linking equality of opportunity to welfare measurements, hence requiring people be compensated for handicaps for which they are not responsible, i.e. over which they have no control (Roemer 1994: 12).[12]

---

[12] There are differences between Roemer's and Cohen's formulae. These are marginal differences, so I shall allow myself to ignore them here. However, both Cohen's and Roemer's theories differ from the idea of equality of welfare in that they place a greater burden of

Now we turn to the question of why socialist egalitarianism is good for the environment. That this question is relevant is obvious if we think of the fundamental demand all environmentalists raise: namely, to either limit production or rearrange production relations. If standard of living is measured in terms of income or what is now considered the GNP, then a future world, according to the environmentalists, will be characterized by a lower standard of living (though not necessarily of well-being). A question arises as to how to distribute the cost of this change. Put positively, the question is how to 'ensure that fundamental [environmental] needs are met equitably throughout the world' (Kemball-Cook *et al.* 1991). But this simply tells us why socialist egalitarianism is good for environmentalists: the question still remains of why it is good for the environment.

The answer is related to a structural problem within capitalist society. As many eco-socialist pamphlets and documents claim, the problem is not necessarily pollution, waste, or other environmental wrongs themselves. These are public bads, the inescapable features of society or economy that affect everyone. Societies cannot escape some level of pollution if they wish to manufacture. There will always be waste. However, political means should be available to ensure less pollution and waste in the process of manufacture. Capitalism, I argue, fails to guarantee this, because of its structural problem, i.e. unequal *ecological distribution*. By this, we mean 'social, spatial and temporal asymmetries or inequalities in the human use of traded or non-traded environmental resources and services, with respect to the depletion of natural resources (including the loss of biodiversity) and burdens of pollution' (Martinez-Alier 1997*b*: 91–2; 1995; see also the works of Bullard 1990 and J. O'Connor 1994). Some gross inequalities related to ecological distribution are: dumping toxic and hazardous waste in locations inhabited by poorer or less advantaged ethnic groups or nations, often accompanied by a latent threat (if the poor oppose dumping they stand to lose their jobs, or, in the case of international relations, to lose military and economic aid); unequal vulnerability to heat waves (Davis 1997); ecologically unequal exchange (importing products from poor countries or regions at prices that do not take into account the exhaustion or depletion of resources there); and exploitation of indigenous knowledge without adequate payment (cf. Martinez-Alier 1997*a*: 104–7).

The change in ecological distribution is needed not only in order to rectify injustice, but also because it is a crucial component of any attempt to prevent environmental damage. Capitalist society however is unable to cope with this need. Many activists claim that this is because capitalism 'needs' pollution to sustain the social and economic gaps. I disagree. To see that this

responsibility on the individual for choosing welfare-inducing goals that are reasonable. Here, again, choice comes in, and as I argued above, socialists do not completely ignore choice.

is not the reason for capitalism's failure to cope with a change in ecological distribution all we have to do is recall that in the nineteenth century capitalism was alive and kicking at a time when no such levels of pollution existed. So the reason for high levels of pollution in capitalistic societies is not that pollution is needed to sustain capitalism: rather, it is that capitalism is particularistic and sectarian, and its political thinking is class-oriented. Environmentalists will therefore find themselves in difficulties if they want to promote and advance environment-friendly policies within capitalism. Let me elaborate on this.

Given that every individual is equally affected by pollution (assuming, on average, equal physical and mental vulnerability to toxic waste, etc.), one would expect that all human beings, from all socioeconomic backgrounds, would have the same opinion regarding pollution and its prevention. But classes or groups of people are not equally affected by pollution, because they are not equally exposed to it: not all regions are equally affected, and some people can afford to buy houses in cleaner regions while others cannot. A good example of this would be Israel's main nuclear reactor, which is located near the small desert town of Dimona. Most of the reactor's technicians, cleaners, and service workers live in Dimona; but most of the managers and scientists who work there live quite far away, in a city called Be'er Sheva. In fact, this is a general and universal phenomenon of capitalist democratic societies. The rich can afford to live at a distance from the polluted and risky (in terms of exposure to hazardous materials) places, whereas the poor have to buy their homes where housing is cheap, i.e. near the polluting factories, etc. In the USA, for example, Afro-Americans are 40 per cent more likely to live in a polluted (i.e. above EPA standards) town than white Americans (Field 1997); moreover, excessive exposure to lead poisoning is a particular danger to young children in poor families, largely because of the household paint in common use before the 1940s (Douglas 1985: 10). Interestingly, as geographers have long been arguing, technological changes in this century have meant that some workers no longer need to live near the working place. Consequently, particularly after the Second World War, a culture of suburbs and lower middle-class neighbourhoods emerged (Smith 1988; Field 1997). This implies that living near factories is not a matter of preference or culture type. The preference is to get away from pollution, not to stay near the workplace. Those still living near factories are those who simply cannot afford to move; all those who can afford to have done so. The cost of buying a house near a pollution source is far less than living in an environmentally wholesome location, since not only is there current pollution, but, as is often the case, houses are actually built on old dumping sites (e.g. the case of Love Canal in the USA—see Gibbs 1982), in which case the soil itself is contaminated. So those who are still living in such places will never be able to sell their houses and thereby afford to move to a different place.

The point is that not only is this unjust—i.e. that those who are already poorer are also exposed to greater risks—but also, it imposes a structural constraint on potential efforts to reduce pollution. Mega-firms contract out the more contaminating and riskier (in terms of exposure to hazardous materials) projects to smaller firms (Harvey 1996: ch. 13). The latter cannot afford to locate factories in clean sites, so they go to already polluted ones which are less expensive, and which are populated by poorer people who have to live there. Now these smaller firms cannot afford to control the pollution and handle the toxic waste in the proper (and, therefore, often expensive) manner because this would affect their ability to compete. If we add to this the fact that pollution itself has become a movable commodity (by waste disposal companies), and that it is usually moved to areas where people fail to fight pollution because they do not know how to, then this phenomenon is actually reinforced. Those who are even poorer have to suffer the burial of waste produced far away, sometimes in different countries. These poorer communities could at least be compensated ('selling' room for waste burial), but they are not, since the firms can do what they like without having to pay any compensation. The firms exploit the fact that the poor cannot afford houses in better areas and that they lack the political skills and power to resist this burial. More cynically, those who dare protest against or oppose the burial of waste or of toxic materials at their backdoor are thought to be 'NIMBY' (not-in-my-backyard) activists and no more. We enter, thus, a vicious circle, in which poverty invites pollution, which makes the places where poor people live even less valuable, and their chances of getting out of there even smaller, a fact that is, once again, exploited by the firms creating the pollution. To add insult to injury, poor people trying to exit this vicious circle are criticized for caring only about their own interests (being NIMBYs).

The richer people, however, who do not live by the polluting sources or dumping sites, suffer less from pollution. Moreover, they receive extra benefits. They are compensated for the existence of public bads by the benefits they receive, usually in material terms—e.g. high salaries or profits. However, they are also the ones who enjoy more access to political decision-making centres, since the rationale of politics in capitalist societies is to 'let the economy speak'. In such circumstances, the easier access of rich people to power centres is inevitable. These people are likely to lobby, or to vote for the continuation of the manufacturing process, and hence, actually, for the continuation of pollution. The problem then becomes a question of mentality: these people think as economic agents rather than as citizens who care about the well-being of the whole society. This distinction—the individual as an economic agent versus the individual as a citizen—is reminiscent of the distinction discussed in length by Mark Sagoff (1988), between the individual as consumer versus the individual as citizen. However, I wish to add that the mentality of 'thinking as economic agents rather than citizens' is likely to be common to workers under capitalism as well. When workers look for jobs in a capitalist system, it is as though they were seeking access to a certain good (in this case a source of income). They are asked to tender their offers and compete for this good. They are told that the employer will employ the worker whose offer is cheapest. Under such circumstances, workers are forced to develop a consumer mentality with regard to their jobs: they 'purchase' access to jobs by reducing their demands for higher salaries or by reducing their leisure time by working longer hours.

Thus, the tendency among many workers will be not to raise the issue of pollution, because a reduction in pollution would lead to increased production costs, and privately owned firms would be inclined to fire workers or reduce salaries to compensate for this increased overhead. These workers would prefer jobs and a polluted environment to unemployment and a cleaner environment. Indeed, sociological studies of communities of workers living next to polluting factories show that there is a clear distinction between the workers themselves, who are very reluctant to act against the pollution and tend to let sleeping dogs lie, and their spouses, who are prepared to fight pollution, most likely because they raise the children and because the threat of redundancy is less meaningful to them (Edelstein 1988: 84–118; Hall 1976). There is, therefore, a structural and psychological obstacle to developing an environmental attitude under capitalism, even among those who suffer most from pollution.

There are three reasons for believing that under democratic socialism the above would not occur. First, many socialist theorists believe that socialism would expose the qualities of altruism and caring latent in everyone. There would be no need to speak of a 'new type of person': socialism's more relaxed, less competitive, and more communitarian circumstances would increase the tendency among people to acknowledge that public evils are *public* evils rather than evils besetting others or another, separate, sector of society.

But even if this sounds excessively naive or utopian (I elaborate on this below—see p. 196), under socialism, the problem of the structural inequalities that prevent environmental reform should not arise. Suppose firms' profits are distributed on a more egalitarian basis. Workers would be given opportunities to purchase houses from a wider selection of localities. Housing could be subsidized, so that workers could afford to buy homes in cleaner areas. The change, however, would not be limited to the economy. Workers would be less dependent on the firm for their living because, for example, the state would guarantee their right to work or would compensate anyone losing their job owing to environmental improvement measurements. Workers would therefore be less reluctant to demand such improvements. In fact, they would find it easier to make these demands for another reason: they would now have equal access to the decision-making centres, both within the firm (as owners or participants in a democratic form of management) and at the local and national level.

The workers' growing participation is also related to Mark Sagoff's citizen/consumer analysis mentioned above. Since under socialism more people would have the means to afford to participate in politics (for example, they would have more free time because they could afford to work fewer hours owing to decent pay levels and better welfare services), the circle of participation would be enlarged. Hence more people would take sides on issues not immediately relevant to them: people in Paris, for instance, would consider questions of forest preservation in the French Alps, and villagers in Provence would consider questions of monument preservation in Paris. Citizenship rather than consumerism would enjoy a louder voice than under capitalism. Hence more decisions in favour of environmental protection would be likely.

The third reason why egalitarian socialism would work for the benefit of the environment has to do with the socialist idea of well-being. As Brian Barry claims, socialism differs from other theories or ideologies in proposing that taxes on wealth and income should be seen not only as a means of raising state income, but also as a way of bringing about a fairer distribution of wealth, so that a level of material well-being is defined below which none of its citizens should fall. Equally, the democratic socialist state should define a level of *environmental* well-being below which none of its citizens should fall. For example, a Worldwatch Paper (1989: 33) declares that 'environmental quality' is not a luxury, and the eco-socialist Martin Ryle (1988: 70) suggests that basic needs would be defined as including basic infrastructure requirements (water supply, clean energy, treated sewage) in addition to wealth, health, and education. Ecological distribution would be more egalitarian, at least in the sense that no one would fall beneath the level of environmental well-being considered minimal for a decent life. To this we could add that in many socialist regimes there would be a right to work. If the workers knew that, whatever the government's policy, they would have a place to work, they would be more inclined to vote in favour of environmental policies, even if these imply job losses in certain firms. Workers' fears of losing jobs in the capitalist system because of the introduction of higher environmental standards would be irrelevant in a system where a worker's right to work is protected, or if a mechanism of a basic income (Van Parijs 1992) is practised.

Planning: Rationality in Policies

It is often held against socialists that, although they genuinely care about achieving egalitarian justice or the end of exploitation, they disregard the need for a rational and effective economy and policies. This grievance probably represents two separate claims. First, it is felt that socialists would be less inclined to accept professional decision-making processes in politics and the economy and would instead push for greater participation and equality in access to decision-making centres. Only the market economy, it is believed by many, allows the rare genius to flourish. Any interference with the market serves to limit free competition and thereby, by hindering entrepreneurs from using their talents, inevitably leads to reducing overall welfare. To counter this argument, I think we should resort to Roemer's amazingly simple, yet very illuminating, reply. The wealth of society, claims Roemer, is due not to 'rugged individualists', but rather to the combination of their activism and the planned institutions in which they operate:

It is not correct to characterize modern capitalist firms as instruments by which entrepreneurs capitalize their talents. The profits of firms are distributed to many owners, all or a great many of whom have no direct control over decisions that effect profitability and are in large part not responsible for firms' successes or failures. Firms, in other words, are run by hired agents of their owners, and this suggests that hired agents could as well run firms in a socialist economy, one in which profits would be distributed even more diffusely than they are under capitalism. (Roemer 1994: 5)

So it is feasible to imagine workers owning a firm, controlling the management, but employing experts to run it. Socialism should not imply the exclusion of excellency.

The second branch of the accusation that socialists disregard rationality in policies concerns the belief that socialism may mean less overall growth or utility: 'It is not rational', this claim would go, 'to prefer a certain form of distribution, even if it is more egalitarian, if it also brings about less overall increase in welfare or growth.' Admittedly, socialists often prefer equality to an increase in overall wealth if the increase would mean an increase in socio-economic gaps. But this need not worry socialist environmentalists. On the contrary: all it shows is that people differ in their view of what is rational. The point is that socialists do believe policies should be 'rational'. But, while liberals think that rational policy implies, for instance, letting the market work in order to increase wealth, socialists claim that rational policy implies planning. This is true *in particular* in the environmental era. Planning, in this context, derives from prudence: if in the past technology that went wrong affected only limited areas and few people, in the contemporary world not only is technology not easily controlled, but it also poses new risks (e.g. nuclear leakage, hazardous chemicals, and so on, all of which may harm masses of people) (Beck 1997). In order to try to prevent irreversible damage and ecological disasters, prudence is a must. But prudence is guaranteed only by careful planning inspired by social goals. Therefore, the question to be asked is not whether to plan, but rather what sort of planning contradicts other social goals and values (cf. O'Neill 1993: 175). Thus, planning is rational, even though, admittedly, it may yield less in terms of manufactured goods, wealth, etc. Figure 6.1 illustrates this.

Future circumstances/ politics	Expected, no surprise	Not as expected
Market planning	Affluence, high wealth	Disasters, poverty
Prudence, planned	Moderate wealth	Moderate wealth

FIG. 6.1 The rationality of planning

Let us assume that market advocates are right and that letting the market rule yields the highest wealth. The figure shows nevertheless that, if future circumstances are not known—and they are not[13]—we would be better off if we planned our policies: prudence (planned policies) would yield either moderate wealth (if future circumstances are as we expect them to be) or less moderate wealth (if the future is not as we expected it to be), whereas the market might yield disasters, if we do not prepare for the worse circumstances. (I will elaborate soon on planning as preparing for the worst, and below I elaborate on the difference between prudence and conservative politics, the politics of avoiding change *per se*.)

Interestingly, there is no such thing as a completely planning-free economy. Theoretically there is, but we may assume that it would be so wildly irresponsible that in practice nobody would suggest ignoring the future completely. So when liberals and capitalists say they want the market to work, they actually base their positions on predictions of how the market will affect the economy and the environment, assuming the very optimistic assumption that the environment will not be drastically affected. But this is very risky. For example, it has been argued that excessively rapid growth will inevitably lead to the destruction of ecosystems on which this growth depends for its continuity. This destruction cannot be predicted accurately since ecological processes are too complex, and therefore unpredictable, for us to follow. We are thus left to conclude that the policy of letting the market work is sheer gambling: if the future turns out fine and there is no severe impact on the environment, then such a policy may indeed yield greater wealth than any other. But if the effects of what humans do under such a system get out of hand—if they include floods, the poisoning of animal and human habitats, and so on—then it may also lead to destruction and poverty. It seems that it is much more rational to plan as well as we can, while taking negative scenarios into account, so that in any event we can help ourselves avoid ending up in misery. This mechanism of choice under circumstances of lack of information is called *minimax*. It involves choosing the alternative that yields the best possible results under the

---

[13] They are not known both because data are unavailable and monitoring is not sufficiently intense and because, as many scientists have recognized, their hypotheses are based on evidence that cannot be generalized. See O'Riordan and Jordan (1995: 199).

least positive future circumstances. Obviously, this is no less rational than gambling.

At this point some critics of planning claim that planning rests on several flawed assumptions: that it is possible to integrate varied predictions and evaluations into a single, coherent programme; that society functions according to a deterministic principle, so that, if given sufficient information, society can predict policy consequences (Stirling 1997: 188–9; though Stirling does not sympathize with this attitude). However, even if these criticisms are true, they should not imply that we should let the market decide rather than plan ourselves. A lack of regulations is not a means of overcoming risk but rather a source of new risks. As exemplified by the BSE affair (about which, see Ratzman 1998; also Benton 1997), when individuals work without regulations (there were no regulations about cow fodder and what to do when a cow becomes ill) they tend to think in terms of short-run self-interests. Moreover, this critique misses the nature of planning: planning is not a simple act whereby experts recommend policy A rather than B. Rather, planning—at least, good planning—is a process in which experts, together with the public, speculate about different scenarios and try to prepare various reactions to them: 'if X happens we should do X'; if Y happens, we should do Y'; and if Z happens we should do Z'. In addition, if we want to avoid P we should do P'.' Moreover, it is a process in which people estimate and evaluate the different possible consequences, and decide in advance which consequences are out of the question (thereby implying that the policies leading to them should not be implemented), which are 'risky', i.e. positive outcomes are not guaranteed, whereas negative side effects are likely; and which consequences are welcome (hence the policies leading to them are 'safe'). Seen in this way, it seems that planning is far more rational, from an environmental point of view. Of course, this implies that a structural change, for example via new forms of production, or at least planning, entails investing capital and time in research into means of preventing or reducing pollution.

At this point, another challenge to planning may be raised. According to the counter-argument, even such planning is absurd, since 'we not only have no firm or credible basis for the assignment of probabilities, but no means even to identify a discrete set of possible outcomes', and we cannot 'think of everything in identifying the possible eventualities themselves' (Hajer 1995: 35). But my answer is that we should not think of *everything*, and we should not pretend that planning is a neutral, unbiased, process of 'scientifically' evaluating probabilities. Rather, planning is guided and motivated by values. There are certain possible consequences which we would never accept on moral grounds, and others that we could accept only if we gained something in terms of other values. By planning, we try to avoid such consequences. Planning, then, takes into account the values that are dear to society, and in that sense it is rational.

Notice, however, that until now I have only argued that a planned economy is better for the environment because, by being more prudent, it answers the demand that under circumstances of relative ignorance we should adopt a strategy of maximin: avoid catastrophes, or, in other words, choose the best option out of the worst scenarios. But there is a stronger argument in favour of planning: namely, that to some extent we do know the effect that lack of planning has on the future. Lack of planning means open and free competition, which is one of the reasons why consequent ecological disasters are more likely to happen. If there is unlimited and unregulated competition, the environment will be regarded as resource for short-run success that can be legitimately used and overused. For example, in order to form a monopoly, an entrepreneur will try to flood the market with a certain product so that prices drop immediately and his competitors go bankrupt.[14] The environmental cost, however, is tremendous: natural resources such as open spaces, oil, wood, or clean air may vanish, and more products for which there is no demand will find their way to dumping sites, junk yards, etc.

Even if one does not accept this last argument, it must be noted that by no means do socialists attack rationality. Indeed, environmental socialists must accept Tim Hayward's thesis (1994; 1998) that the answer to environmental problems is not an attack on enlightenment and rationality, but rather a demand for more of it.[15] The problem, argues Hayward, is not that we have been suffering from too much 'enlightenment', but that we have been enjoying too little of it.

Now, there are several environmentalists who seem to believe that the irrationality of a-environmental policies is so clear, evident, and obvious that all it takes to make people environment-friendly is to show them the light: help them become more 'rational', and they will realize how foolishly and irresponsibly they and others have behaved. This position reflects two common failures to grasp the complexity of the political process of change. On the one hand, there are activists who feel uncomfortable debating about the good, or who think that politics should be detached from this debate, and therefore retreat to the arena that seems to them value-free, and hence more 'scientific' and 'objective'. They thus concentrate on preaching for 'rational' rather than 'good' or 'just' politics. The difference is that 'rationality' as such does not relate to the evaluation of goals, but only to the means of achieving given goals. If G is a given goal and W1 and W2 are two ways of achieving G, the

---

[14] Thus, John Barry (1995) distinguishes between a simple claim often made as if the environment has been 'humanized', and a much more sophisticated claim, which he thinks is true, namely that the environment has been 'capitalized' by a small minority of human beings.

[15] Hayward writes: 'There is a challenge . . . to the very rationality and values of enlightenment. But what is especially noteworthy is that the grounds of the objection to enlightenment rationality . . . are that it is precisely not rational, that it is not enlightened. . . . It is enlightenment itself which often provides the standards in terms of which enlightenment is criticized' (T. Hayward 1994: 4).

rational person would calculate the cost (in terms of money, time, pollution) involved in W1 and W2 and would choose the less 'expensive' option. But then the goals are ignored. Environmentalists cannot be satisfied with this because their case is a case in which the good is crucial (see Chapter 3 for this argument). What if the goal is greater material welfare? Should environmentalists ignore their conception of well-being, which challenges the conventional wisdom about material welfare, and show the citizens the more rational way of increasing material welfare? In other words, in a case when environmentalists are faced with a political decision to increase material welfare, should they be satisfied with showing the way to achieve this without causing too much environmental damage? Or should they also challenge the very idea of increasing material welfare, and put forward their notion of well-being?

On the other hand, the position of 'all we have to do is show people the rational way' is mistaken because it fails to understand the importance of institutions. It ignores the structure of society, power relations, and the power of capital (Pepper 1996: 324). For some people, mainly the very rich, it seems highly 'rational' to demand far more development than is sustainable, simply because this will increase their profits. And if this is rational to them, it will also be rational for many politicians to support their claim, for the simple reason that these politicians will not be re-elected without the support of the rich.

We see, then, that rationality, which is very important in the context of environmental policies, is not enough. It should be accompanied by a discussion of the idea of the good, of social goals and values, and of institutions. The same goes for prudence. Taken by itself, prudence can be very conservative, rather than socialist, in its applications and implications. Therefore, it seems to me that the rationale for prudence and careful planning advanced by many environmental activists is often only partial, and therefore misleading. It goes more or less like this: 'Let's try and avoid a possible slippery slope. The consequences of environmental policies are not known, hence we must be careful.' This is true, and I have argued so above; however, it should form only part of the rationale. An explanation of 'Why' should be added.

To see why, consider the argument that, if we need to be cautious when an action's consequences are unknown, then the peace agreements in Ireland, or between Israel and the PLO are wrong because those who have agreed to it have in effect gambled with the unknown future. It is better to play safe than be ambitious and adventurous; it is better to preserve the status quo than to sign peace agreements. This is a typical conservative, right-wing argument. I do not wish to dismiss it here (although I think it is wrong), but rather to draw a distinction between such arguments and the environmentalist (and socialist–environmentalist) rationale for prudence, hence planning, where environmental policies are concerned. The distinction is related to the motivation to be careful. Conservatives are motivated by anxiety, environmentalists by the will to be rational. That is to say that, while both claim to face a set of 'unknown consequences' of a policy, they mean very different things: conservatives mean that 'we shall lose control over the consequences'; if we control everything we know what the results are likely to be; but if we sign a peace agreement we let others affect the consequences as well, and therefore we lose the power to be the only ones determining the future. Environmentalists, on the other hand, mean that we lack enough information about what will happen to ecosystems if we continue to develop haphazardly. They mean that the future is unknown because we lack data, or because we lack the tools to generalize and theorize about the future. And so I think that environmentalists should add this rationale and thereby distinguish themselves from conservatives. Prudence in this context is not a cover-up for the desire for things to stay the same.[16] Prudence would imply, for example, that in each controversial case developers will have to prove the environmental safety of their proposals. At the moment, in many countries, those opposing development proposals have to prove that these controversial cases are not safe (Weale 1992: 79–81).

Eliminating Alienation

According to socialists, alienation—from oneself as a creative person, from other human beings, and from nature—is a key characteristic of capitalist society, and its elimination is one of socialists' major goals. Environmentalists should find this idea attractive, because there is no doubt that alienation is a major contributor to environmental degradation. In the first place, in a capitalist society people become so alienated from themselves as creative individuals (because, rather than being creative, they become part of a manufacturing machine, and because they are so possessive) and from their fellow human beings (since they are alienated from their creative self, they fail to see the creative self in the other, and eventually lose their sense of humanity) that they become indifferent and careless about their surroundings, i.e. the environment. How can they care about it if they lose their sense of subscribing to something greater than themselves?

Secondly, it seems obvious that, if people do not feel related to nature and responsible for it, and if they lose the sense of how much their lives depend on sustainable ecosystems, then they are likely to exploit nature and eliminate 'resources'. In fact, the very term 'resources' reflects an attitude of alienation from nature: the latter is not seen as a whole, it is not seen as it is, and there-

---

[16] This move will help the general public to realize that the environment is a progressive case rather than an ideology of upper-class snobs who don't want things to change. This is a common accusation levelled at environmentalists and Greens.

fore it is not treated with respect.[17] To eliminate alienation between human beings and nature, we must also eliminate alienation between human beings and themselves in the process of production. The goal, then, is to abolish alienation both between human beings and themselves, and between human beings and nature. Since this cannot be achieved by the manipulation of consciousness, institutions that enhance a sense of belonging should be formed.

Contemporary socialists have offered two main theories of how this might be accomplished.[18] These theories relate to mechanisms and institutions that can overcome strict individualism; however, they differ in the moral significance they ascribe to these institutions (socialist community) because they differ in the relationships they see between individualism and alienation. Brian Barry (1996) is interested in reducing competition and enhancing collective action in the economic sphere and in the political arrangements of the economy, because he thinks that individualism and competition cause collective action failures, which he regards as the source of alienation. Hence, to the extent that he offers a community as such an institution, his community is neither holistic nor cultural; instead, it is a community of collective action (see Chapter 4 above). David Miller, on the other hand, thinks that individualism is alienation; therefore he is interested in fostering community for its own sake, as the antithesis of alienation itself, and hence his community is more moral, cultural, and political, although not necessarily more economic. Miller's community is then intrinsically good. I shall now discuss these two theories and how they relate to environmental politics.

Let us start with the claim that the goal is to reduce competition. We have already seen that reducing competition should be considered by socialist environmentalists as rationalizing the political management of the economy. Barry's theory adds to this by arguing that the means to achieve this is by fostering a limited form of community—i.e. collective action. In that sense community is confined to, and justified on the grounds that it is, a method involving collective action in the economic sphere coupled with political arrangements of the economy. Thus, Brian Barry (1996) accepts that socialism is anti-individualistic, not as a methodology (he endorses methodological individualism), nor as simple solidarity, like nationalism. (He dismisses both the liberal claim that obligations derive only from contracts and the solidarity argument that obligations are derived by virtue of being a member.) But he

[17] Alan Holland (1994) elaborates on the concepts used to describe and refer to nature; see also his discussion of whether human-made capital is substitutable for natural capital (Holland 1997) and as his discussion of 'natural capital' (Holland 1999).

[18] I do not impute to contemporary socialism the claim that this leads to the abolition of the state. First, a primary socialist objective has always been the abolition of capitalism, and then, it was argued, the state would wither away. Secondly, contemporary socialists do not necessarily see a future without the state. Quite the contrary: the state—though no doubt a different state from the capitalist one—is a crucial vehicle for socialism. For a discussion of the abolition of the state in socialism and socialist anarchism, and its relations to environmental goals, see Pepper (1996: 31–2, 210–13).

does accept anti-individualism if individualism stands for the idea of the minimal state and the competitive market economy. Indeed, Barry claims that socialism is relevant precisely because it tries to achieve common goals through joint action, monitored and mediated by the state. Thus conceived, Barry thinks that socialism is a theory of citizenship, 'empowering citizens to act collectively in pursuit of the interests and ideals that they share with one another and that can be realized only by collective action'.

Collective action, then, is a characteristic of socialism. How it relates to socialist environmentalists I will leave for the moment and return to later when I discuss citizenship, i.e. the person as a citizen, as opposed to the person as an economic agent. For the moment, suffice to say that the anti-individualistic tendency, which it is claimed would reduce competition and enhance cooperation, would consequently reduce alienation. Of course, by reducing, or overcoming, alienation among human beings, people may become more active in politics and may conduct their collective actions more successfully. Thus, if many environmental problems are problems of collective action failures, socialism may contribute to solving them. In addition, however, people will overcome alienation between themselves and nature, thereby becoming open to ideas and information on how their own well-being depends on that of the environment. I elaborate on these two consequences below.

Rather than regarding community as a means of reducing alienation, David Miller thinks that community is simply the antithesis of alienation, hence, by virtue of being there, community abolishes alienation. The question of how to form such a community then arises: should the abolition of private property be its main component? or direct democracy? perhaps strict egalitarianism? I would like to analyse Miller's theory and compare it with two phases in the history of the kibbutz, the 'old style' and the 'new-style' kibbutz,[19] and show how eliminating alienation may help construct environmental policies.

As David Miller (1989: chs. 6 and 8) puts it, socialism consists of the 'distributive' and the 'quality of life' critiques of capitalism. The former holds that capitalism unfairly distributes wealth income, economic and political power, and freedom within the community. The latter—the quality of life critique—is more relevant to our discussion here. According to this view, capitalism establishes highly competitive relationships which lead people to think of one another in instrumental, rather than genuinely communitarian, terms. Miller claims that the solution to the alienation caused by the 'bads' in capitalism is community socialism. 'At base', he writes, 'socialism is to be identified by its opposition to individualism. It is the idea that the good life consists of living with others, in a way which will contribute to the formation of a collective

---

[19] The new-style kibbutz is the contemporary kibbutz that emerged following drastic ideological and structural changes that took place in the late 1980s and early 1990s (de-Shalit 1992b).

way of living' (Miller 1991: 352). However, two types of socialist community have been offered. The first is ascribed to many radical socialists and was very popular in the 'old-style' kibbutz. This is a conception of community in which each person fully identifies with the social group and its members, accepts the principles of distribution according to need, seeks absolute egalitarianism in all spheres of life, and acknowledges communal relations at all levels of social relations (Miller 1989: 208).

In the old-style kibbutz, each member was supposed to subordinate herself to the general will of the kibbutz and to have empathy for others as an expression of unity between herself and the community, between private and general wills. Social relations were about fraternity, the ultimate response to bourgeois alienation. The institutions needed for this were direct democracy, common culture, partnership, and the abolition of private property. Economic relationships based on public ownership were intended to buttress social fraternity. Envy was to be once and for all eliminated through the formation of partnership and absolute equal distribution, sometimes bypassing the need for distribution by establishing collective ownership of goods such as books, clothes, and shoes (in addition, of course, to the means of production). Furthermore, a system of supply according to the standard of a certain 'average need' was introduced.

And yet, there have been changes in the kibbutz that have not necessarily harmed the sense of community. The main change has been in the recognition that it is possible to overcome alienation by means other than altering the relations of production and abolition of private property. Thus, the kibbutz has allowed the market to enter, permitting members to work outside the kibbutz as lawyers, economic advisors, etc., and has relinquished the idea of community relations in the economic sphere. At the same time, it seeks more intensive community life in the sphere of internal political life and social activities. The most dramatic changes have been towards the concept of collective ownership. This still applies to (most) means of production, but not to distribution. The latter is simply egalitarian. In addition, a more liberal notion of 'need' has emerged. By acknowledging individual needs and making people feel that their needs and individuality are respected, feelings of belonging and community are fostered. The community (as a level of relationships) is achieved, it is claimed in the new kibbutz, not by abolishing differences between human beings (making them equal, transforming their private needs to a standard of 'average needs' and so on), but in the social and political spheres, by encouraging participation, increasing tolerance of exceptional needs, and thereby engendering better communal ties.

Interestingly, similar arguments can be found in Miller's theory. He suggests that the right interpretation of the socialist theory of human nature is that it has 'an ambivalent bearing on the choice between markets and communism' (Miller 1989: 208). Thus, Miller claims, there is no need to abolish private property (see my discussion below of private *v.* public property); neither is there a need to regard the community as the only level of relationship between individuals in societies. The community can be more relaxed in the economic sphere, and at the same time fortified in the spheres of politics, and spiritual and cultural life. Thus, humans can overcome alienation by forming community—as a level of relationships—in politics, culture, and morality.

Socialist environmentalists could emphasize this idea as a more realistic option for overcoming alienation. If alienation is reduced or abolished by changing our poltiical and social institutions, one could go on and argue that alienation towards nature will be abolished as well. That is so because abolishing alienation between people is a precondition for abolishing alienation towards nature. Moreover, as I have argued in this section, reducing or abolishing alienation contributes to the formation of human community, either in a thin sense (as a mechanism of collective action) or in a thick sense (as a community of citizens in David Miller's theory). Both communities can contribute towards the formation of deliberative participatory democracy (see Chapter 5) by fostering social ties and a sense of belonging, care, and empathy. This would lead the way to a more genuine, open, and tolerant deliberation. This brings us to the next political socialist goal, citizenship.

Citizenship

The discussion of the socialist vision of citizenship and its implications for the environment should begin by examining the way socialists (as opposed to liberals) conceive of the person, and particularly the issue of choice. The liberal often ascribes metaphysical status to individuals' choices. Choices reflect the agent's rationality, and therefore, we may say, his moral autonomy. Thus, Scanlon writes:

This term [choice] applies not only to something that an agent does—as in 'she made a choice'—but also to what an agent is presented with—as in 'She was faced with this choice. . . . Choice has an obvious and immediate moral significance. The fact that a certain action or outcome resulted from an agent's choice can make a crucial difference both to our moral appraisal of that agent and to our assessment of the rights and obligations of the agent and others after the action has been performed. (Scanlon 1988: 177, 151)

Most socialists, however, regard choice not necessarily as an expression of 'pure' autonomy, but rather as an expression of preferences that have been shaped by a variety of factors, including the agent's own reflection, but also the socioeconomic circumstances of the time, political events, production relations, etc. No doubt democratic socialists respect choice (thereby distancing themselves from authoritarianism), but the move from respecting choice to awarding it such a lofty moral status is beyond socialism (O'Neill 1998*b*: 165–6).

The implications for environmental policies are clear: when individuals' choices are respected but are not of supreme moral value, there should be less moral constraint on regulations, which are highly necessary if the public wishes to protect the environment through collective action. Thus, when regulations are announced, there is less 'public guilt' for 'imposing' them. In fact, regulations are regarded not as being 'imposed' on individuals, but rather as corrections of behaviour governed by individual rationality; these corrections are introduced by the public on the basis of rational collective action. At this point, the distinction between the person as a consumer and the person as a citizen is put forward by such writers as Mark Sagoff (1988), Brian Barry (1991*a*), Russell Keat (1994), and John O'Neill (1993: 173–81), who modifies, and in my view improves, the use of this distinction. Applying Barry's and O'Neill's arguments to the discussion here, the environmental principle should be that what people want as *citizens* should prevail over what they want as private buyers or sellers.

In order to explain this position, let us consider the opposite position, namely Nozick's famous discussion of the 'Chamberlain example', and its critique by Brian Barry. Robert Nozick, a genuine opponent of socialism, argues that if in a particular community each individual was asked, and everybody agreed, say, to making a voluntary payment to a superstar basketball player (Nozick names Wilt Chamberlain), they cannot afterwards complain of gross inequality in their community, even if, when the agreement is fulfilled, it turns out that this basketball player has become extremely rich. But, as Brian Barry argues, to infer from this example that there are no grounds for complaint would be wrong, because, when people were asked whether they would agree to pay an extra dollar so that the player plays for the town's team, the issue at stake was not in what kind of community they will live. People were asked only whether each of them thought it was worth paying a dollar more in order to watch this player; what others would do, and whether they would be asked at all, was unknown. Thus, the collective action and its meaning was unknown, and had people been informed about it they might have approached the issue as *citizens* (having in mind the effects on their community) rather than as consumers (having in mind whether they as individuals would pay an extra dollar to watch Chamberlain). As a collective, we can change the outcome of an aggregation of individual actions which may seem to us right as individual actions in the sphere of consumerism, but wrong in their implications for society and the community of citizens. That is why the socialist theory, which regards socialism as a way to organize collective action, and which attributes this ability to socialist citizenship, is so important.

I now wish to elaborate on the advantages of socialism in cases related to environmental regulations and people thinking as citizens and not as consumers. To do this, I would first like to distinguish between several types of public and collective goods which may be the objects of environmental policies.

	Rival (what is used by A limits what B may use)	Non-rival
Excludable		Rationed goods: goods that are non-rival but not fully non-excludable, e.g. the university library: available to all within a certain group
Non-excludable (providing it to A makes it available for B)	Collective goods • strictly collective • collective in a looser sense: provision is more efficient when is public	• pure public goods • partly public goods: goods that are non-excludable but not fully non-rival (clean soil)

Fig. 6.2 Different types of public and collective good

Figure 6.2 summarizes the different types of public and collective goods. At first sight, environmental goods appear to be characterized by being pure public goods: they are non-excludable (providing A with the good makes it available for B as well) and/or *non-rival* (that amount of the good that is used by A does not limit what B may use). However, the picture is somewhat more complicated. Let us analyse it. The first type is collective goods. These are non-excludable (providing A with them makes them available to B as well) and yet, they are *rival* (the amount of the good that is used by A is *not* available to B). Often these latter goods are collective in a loose sense; i.e., they are more efficiently provided if undertaken by the public sector, or it is more efficient to supply them collectively than to each individual separately. Public health and education may be good examples. However, sometimes these goods are strictly collective. Clean air for example is non-excludable, but it is potentially rival: providing A with (access to) clean air limits the (access to) clean air available to B—because, for instance, A might pollute it.

The next type of good is the rationed good. This is non-rival, in the sense that what is used by A does not limit what B may use, and yet it is partly excludable, because not everyone can use it. Think, for example, of a park that is open only to members of a certain group, or a beach whose use is exclusive to the inhabitants of the nearby town or village; yet, among this privileged group, access is equally free to all. Of course A's enjoyment of this park, or beach, does not limit B's opportunity to enjoy it as well, provided B and A both live in the nearby village.

Next, we have 'pure public good'. This good is both non-rival and non-excludable. Security is often raised as a good example of a public good.

Environmental goods, however, are often only partly public goods. To understand the difference, consider clean soil v. security. Security is indeed a pure public good. If the south of the country is attacked by foreign armies, then security in the north is affected as well (perhaps not as much, but it is still the case, for example, that the people of, say, Liverpool, felt less secure when Coventry was bombed during the Second World War). However, clean soil is strictly public only within a specific area. If soil in the south is polluted, people in the north may not suffer: on the contrary—people may even benefit from the south being contaminated. For example, the north will become the clean (and more desirable) region; house prices will rise, and northern homeowners will be able to sell at a higher price. So clean soil is a public good whose collectivity is limited to the size of population, region, etc., where it exists.

The question with regard to all these goods is how to attain and then manage them. It seems that, in cases of strictly collective goods, there should not be any difference in the way socialism and liberalism achieve this, i.e. mostly through regulation. However, as mentioned earlier, in the case of socialism, there would be less 'feelings of guilt' about control through regulation, because regulation is not necessarily regarded as contradictory to choice, since choice is regarded as a social act, and preferences are explained by reference to the institutional (and sometimes community) contexts.

The main advantages of socialism, however, emerge where collective goods in the looser sense, as well as pure public goods and partly pure public goods, are concerned. As for goods that are collective in the loose sense, i.e. those whose supply becomes more effective when it is public, Brian Barry's argument about the relevance of socialism is helpful. According to Barry, socialism is the collective effort to bring about the collective good, which if left to individual effort would be achieved at either a much higher cost, or not at all, in either case resulting in injustice for the weaker and worse-off. Socialism, as explained above, is a theory of community as collective action, with citizenship being attuned to this collectivity of action. Thus, if we are interested in environmental security, cleaner energy, or public health, we need to discuss the regulations and to decide how to obtain these goods most effectively. People would then tend to think about these issues from the standpoint of the citizen rather than the consumer. So each person focuses on the most efficient means of achieving these goals, rather than on the cheapest (in his own terms) way. Thus, it is more likely that these goods will be achieved under socialism, and with relatively minimal social side-effects, such as contradicting other social goals.

With regard to public goods, what are the advantages of socialism over liberalism? The point is that a public debate may take place as to why a certain goal is a 'good'. Take, for example, the controversy over the Newbury bypass that took part in England in 1996. Some believed that better transportation facilities were a public good, others thought natural forests a public good. The question, then, was what constituted a public good. But in order for such a debate to be fruitful and productive, people must listen to others and consider their positions. In such cases, a very specific attitude among citizens is needed in order to develop an attitude of care about others' positions. We have already seen that, according to David Miller, such an attitude is likely to emerge under a socialist community. (See the discussion of socialist egalitarianism above.) Miller's theory is that, in order for people to entertain such empathy towards the values expressed by others, they must feel they belong to part of a *just* community which respects its members' values equally. The political order should be able to construct this sense of justice, claims Miller, and in the scheme of socialism this would happen. When people sense that theirs is a just society, they develop greater sensitivity and attentiveness to others' conceptions of the good. Miller assumes that caring is a latent human quality: we just have to expose it, and remove the coating of dust that covers it, dust that has accumulated throughout decades of capitalist individualism and egoism. Socialism thus does not have to invent and create a caring attitude—it just has to unwrap and restore it.

But it seems to me that Miller leaves his argument unfinished, though finishing the job for him will not be difficult, so I shall offer a way to do this. First, a problem may arise if a person thinks that her society is *not* just. Would she lose her good will and her empathy for others? It seems that Miller assumes that this possibility is not plausible in socialism, because justice is done to the vast majority. However, it should be noted that this sense of being a member of a just society is at least partly subjective; so that, even if the society is just, it could well be that many people will not feel it so. It is not absolutely clear that in socialism people will develop this attitude. The answer, however, lies in a combination of socialism and deliberative democracy (see Chapter 5). When people feel that they understand the issue at stake and that they can have an impact, they will feel less alienated and will tend to empathize with others more easily. Thus, in addition to a society being just, the combination of socialism with deliberative participatory democracy is crucial, because it will allow those who do not think that the society is just to express this in a manner that will help them feel a part of the community. This, in turn, will allow them to empathize with others more easily, and others to empathize with them (and understand their position). (I elaborate about this combination in the book's summary.)

Second, it should be explained why other political orders, e.g. ethnicity, cannot provide the solidarity that Miller so rightly sees as a precondition for empathetic consideration of others' values and interests. Miller himself thinks that nationality, for instance, can do just this. However, the answer might be that ethnicity is easy to reject, since ethnicity is almost unthinkable for forming and sustaining an ethics of care and empathy towards others in contemporary multi-cultural and multi-ethnic societies, unless we have in mind very small political units, often single ethnic groups. But what about the liberal notion of justice, whose lack of relevance Miller omitted to explain? Once again, I think the argument is straightforward: the liberal notion of justice fails to engender a sense of *caring*: it offers only fairness. Fairness is motivated not necessarily by care for, and empathy towards, the other, but by care for oneself and one's own interests. Notice that liberal theorists, including Rawls in his *Political Liberalism*, maintain that individuals bargain their way through life, so to speak, in order to guarantee the maximum possible for themselves. Even the 'early' Rawls may be understood as an apologetic explanation for why individuals believe they can be so much better off than others (e.g., because this would have been decided by any rational person who would be in the original position which is designed to be fair), rather than as a justification of a more egalitarian kind of distribution. Socialism therefore has the capacity to remove the dust from altruism, care, and sensitivity, since it offers a theory of justice based on caring for and about the other, rather than a mere justification for why A should be better off than B. Hence the citizens of a socialist society will be helped to feel that theirs is a just society, and will respond with a type of behaviour that is altruistic, sensitive, etc.

Now let us move on to goods that are partly public, such as clean soil. Remember that we are talking about a collective good whose collectivity is limited by the size of population, region, etc., to which it applies. This is not absolutely a public good—not because there are doubts regarding its being a good (everybody wants clean soil), but rather because of the controversy over what constitutes 'public'. This is an important comment, because often people mistakenly think that the debate between developers and conservationists is covered by debate on the good: e.g., is this factory part of the 'good' life? But the truth is that they also argue about whose interests and opinions should count and who should decide on such matters. Often developers claim that environmentalists are nothing but a 'tiny minority representing no one', whereas conservationists may describe developers as 'a small group of rich people whose interests contradict the interests of all, and are therefore illegitimate'. How can socialism contribute to solving this problem?

Liberals transform inputs to the political discourse into the language of interests, and they do so partly out of a reluctance to take sides on whose and which ideas of the good should count. If a particular sub-community feels that cleanliness and lack of contamination in its region is a public good, liberalism will regard this as the sub-community's interest, which must be weighed against the interests of other sub-communities, and could therefore end up being compromised. Thus, the advantage of socialism lies in its breadth of inclusiveness, i.e. in that it regards the entire population (often of a country) as the relevant public. This is because socialists are sensitive to injustice, exploitation, and alienation, and seek to avoid all of them. They therefore try to encourage everyone, including minorities, the poor, or any other group lacking political power, to participate, raise their voices, and contribute to solving such dilemmas. This implies that a socialist society will tend to discuss 'partly' public goods as public goods. If a good is public in one sense and not public in another sense (e.g. clean soils—see above), then under socialism it will be treated as if it were a public good. This brings about a situation in which many more issues are regarded as public goods by the society and therefore by the state. Of course, when goods are regarded as public goods, it is more convenient for the government or any other authority to regulate or legislate with regard to restrictions on their use. Under socialism, then, we are likely to see more environmental regulations and more solutions initiated at the state level. Put differently, an environmental regulation is more likely to be regarded as legitimate under socialism than under any other regime, because the issue is likely to be seen as a public good.

Public or Private Ownership?

In the 'good old days', socialism implied public ownership. Nowadays, many socialists consider this to be a myth or even a fetish. In fact, it is interesting that, among contemporary philosophers, those who define public ownership as the core of socialism (e.g. Dworkin 1991) are critics, rather than advocates, of socialism. So, is public ownership a crucial facet of socialism? And what are the implications of the answer to this question, in terms of the environment? My main interest in the question of public or private ownership here concerns these implications. But first, let us consider why property relations are so important and relevant to environmental issues.

At least prima facie, it seems that property relations are relevant to the environment because of the psychological impact of private/public ownership on the individual's motivation to act and be active in trying to prevent, control, or limit pollution. This motivation can be manifested in two spheres. First, there is a debate over whether people tend to pollute and consume more if property (cars, tractors, machines, land, lakes, etc.) is private. Several activists and scholars have argued that privatizing property makes people feel more responsible for what they and others own and for the way their action affects others' property. This has a tendency to limit pollution and over-consumption. Others, however, claim that only when property is public will people be ashamed to pollute, and therefore reluctant to pollute; and—more importantly—only then will they feel that they have a chance to limit pollution and the extensive use of 'resources'. I discuss these claims below. But I will just remark that in many cases private property rights cannot be defined. Whereas a house or land is stable and fixed in location, and its boundaries can easily be marked, how can we define the boundaries of water? What should we do if animals move? Also, we cannot define stocks of wild animals, or fish, as privately owned (Rose 1997).

The second sphere in which the motivation to act and be active in trying to prevent, control, or limit pollution is manifested—and this is related to the issue of citizenship discussed in the previous section—is in the legitimacy given to regulations and legislation issued by the authorities. It is sometimes suggested that when property is in private hands people are less likely to agree to any legislation or regulation regarding its use, because they regard such acts as interference with their privacy, or as limitations on their liberty. For example, suppose the government decides to impose new pollution taxes which would represent the difference between the private and public cost of a polluting or ecologically significant act. If property is private, many people—especially the polluters—might regard this as an additional limitation on their access to water, soil, etc., and as a measure of public control over their means of production. They may, then, object that this is unfair, or unjust, relying on claims of property rights (Vira 1995: 2). Hence, it is feared, when property is private people will be less likely to tolerate (and later grow accustomed to) decisions concerning the public interest (rather than private, individual interests) with regard to their own or any other property. So, the argument continues, if we wish to ensure that the mechanism for policy decisions is governed by environmental considerations, then property cannot be left in private hands. On the other hand, there is a counter-psychological claim based on strong empirical evidence, according to which, when property is public, people pay less attention to it, to what is done to it, and to the environmental consequences of its use. For example, people tend to litter more readily in public than in private areas, because they do not personally feel the cost of littering.[20]

So far I have presented the arguments that property relations are relevant to environmental issues. But this raises two objections. First, radical environmentalists could argue that we cannot take it for granted that property rights will be an issue at all when dealing with instances of environmental conflict; perhaps the real issue should be which solution is more environment-friendly, *regardless of any commitments we have to certain property rights regimes*. The second, perhaps more sophisticated, objection is that although property relations are relevant, it remains to be clarified in what respect. I wish to elaborate on these two complaints.

Suppose Mr Swan owns a forest, where an endangered species of birds nests. Suppose, further, that Mr Swan hunts these birds. Mr Swan's fellows in the community (not necessarily his neighbours) are shocked by this and ask him to stop hunting these rare birds. Mr Swan answers that the forest is privately owned by him and the birds are nobody's property; therefore he may shoot

---

[20] Although, of course, it does cost them money, because part of their taxes go to the local municipality for collecting the litter.

them as much as he wants. The community splits in its response. The more radicals say: 'OK, we agree, this is your forest. But the reason we, as a community, ask you to stop hunting is not that we care about competing claims over use of a particular property: we do not think that such questions should be guided by considerations of property at all. (Some people in this community think that these considerations are anthropocentric and therefore represent an inferior stage of morality.) Rather, such questions should be decided by considerations of ecological sustainability and environmental harm. In other words, these people ask, What have property rights to do with the morality of hunting?

The other group in this community raises another objection: 'Yes,' they say, 'it is true that you own the forest; but since we too enjoy the fact that these rare birds nest there (or, others say, if these birds cease to exist there will be less good in the world), we think that we are entitled to ask you to stop hunting them, because the question is not who owns the land, but what is right and what is wrong to do with the land. Would you agree that if, for instance, you dumped toxic waste there, and the waste penetrated local water sources, putting the entire area in risk of water contamination, we would have a right to stop you from doing this?' Mr Swan thinks and answers that they would. 'But the reason', he adds, 'is that I would then be harming your property right—your access to your clean water. However, in the case of these rare birds, I harm nobody's property rights. You can't possibly claim that these birds are more important than my liberties.'

Mr Swan's reply is interesting. For some environmentalists it proves that property rights should not be relevant, because their intuition is that what Mr Swan does is simply wrong, and no property right can justify it. These birds *are* more important than his liberties. Perhaps they are right. Perhaps Mr Swan's behaviour is ridiculously egoistic and, even worse, speciesist. But if they stop there, if all they claim is that property is not an issue, they are less likely to change his behaviour. Of course, they could force him to stop; but we are concerned here with philosophical persuasion. They have to find a way of convincing Mr Swan, using his own terminology.

Let us then, examine a third case. Suppose that Mr Swan does not hunt birds, and does not dump poisonous waste. Rather, the stuff Mr Swan is dumping only smells terrible, causing his neighbours unease. Or suppose that he destroys the green-veined orchids that have been there for some years. It seems that it is at least legitimate for the community to ask him to refrain from doing this.

What I argue is this: in cases of environmental conflicts, people often raise the issue of property rights. This empirical fact already makes property relations relevant to environmental matters, but we still want to see whether this should be so. However, I claim, the question is not so much one of possession—who legally owns the property—but a question of the limitations on the use of property resources, whether public or private. We find that in many environmental cases the community, or the state, interferes with regard to what people can and cannot do with their property. Let me now elaborate on this.

Consider, first, an article that appeared in the *BBC Wildlife Magazine* of June 1998. It touches upon an issue that has given rise to debates in Britain recently on whether citizens have a right to roam. George Monbiot, the land rights campaigner, argues that in most areas the costs of free access are minimal, while the public enjoyment to be gained is immense. But he goes even further, blaming the farmers 'who insist that they are the guardians of the countryside' for having engaged in a '50 year orgy of subsidised destruction'. Britain has lost 95 per cent of its flower-rich hay meadows and 40 per cent of its heath-land since the Second World War, he claims, and this is because access to land has been prohibited to the general public, but permitted to landlords—farm-ers and others who have used the land for private profit: grazing and other forms of agriculture. Peter Hall, a gamekeeper, answers that freedom-to-roam legislation would make it even more difficult to protect habitats and wildlife. Indeed, he claims, privatizing land has helped sustain ecosystems because the variety of species on any piece of land depends on a lack of disturbance. He summarizes thus: 'I have looked after the countryside all my life. My fear is that the general public will see any attempt to restrict access as the actions of an arrogant landowner, not that of someone who wants to preserve biodiver-sity' (Lawson 1998: 40–1). Thus, we see that from an environmental point of view the question of public or private property is relevant because the main question is, Who will better care for the environment: the public or the pri-vate owner? However, we also see that the main question here is not whether the property (land, in this case) is privately or publicly owned, but rather, what kind of access the public will be allowed—in other words, how the property is to be managed. George Monbiot may regret that land is privately owned, but his point is not that it has to be nationalized, but rather, that the public should have free access *despite* private ownership. In other words, his argument is about what sort of limitations on property's use are legitimate. My own con-clusion is that this is the crucial question for both the liberal and the socialist society. Even if land is publicly owned, the salient question—from an envir-onmental point of view—is not who owns it, but what the limitations are on its use.

I would now like to examine this question further. Without going into the very complicated question of what it means to own something, I will imme-diately note that 'property' is not an object, but rather an arrangement of *social* relations that exists between the possessor—the property holder—and the good (Christman 1994, ch. 1; Attas 1999). This arrangement includes administration of the good. If this is so, then what do we mean by *public* own-ership? It seems that public ownership may mean one of three things: first, it may mean the abolition of any form of private property. Secondly, it may mean that the public has collective control over, or the right to administrate, transfer, or possess, the use of a certain good. Thirdly, it may mean that goods—especially means of production—are 'owned' publicly, but that individuals have private administrative rights over these goods. Let us now see which of these interpretations of 'public' ownership of property is more environment-friendly.

The first interpretation is that we abolish any form of private ownership. Several socialist environmentalists think this would be a great system:

> With common ownership, what is produced is no longer the property of some individual or group, which has to be purchased before it can be used, but becomes directly available for people to take in accordance with their needs. . . . Common ownership is not to be equated with state ownership . . . Common ownership on a world scale means that there would be no property or territorial rights over any part of the globe nor over any of the instruments of production created throughout the world by human activity. . . . They would simply be there to be used. . . . Gearing production to meeting needs means, in the first instance, making arrangements for individuals to have access to what they need. This access would be free; socialism not being a society in which goods and services are produced for sale, people would not have to buy what they needed. They would be able to decide for themselves what their needs were and then to take from the stock of products set aside for individual consumption. (Socialist Party 1990: 29–31)

In spite of the context of this argument—a pamphlet on environmental politics—this seems to me very anti-environmental. Such a policy implies that a large stock of products must be constantly available. Needs however change; they are flexible. Since there is no way to predict future needs, particularly private needs—which must be met by the available stock of products and goods—there would be a need to produce more than would eventually be used. Many goods cannot be stored for a long time and therefore would need to be thrown away (or, if possible, recycled) after some time. This system, then, leads to a lot of waste both of materials and energy. It is environmentally bad.

The authors of this pamphlet are apparently aware of this problem, for they add that the decision of what to produce would be a function of, among other considerations, 'the protection of the environment and the conservation and the ecological suitability of materials and energy' (Socialist Party 1990: 31–2). But who will decide when environmental considerations overrule the principle of universal free access and the continuous meeting of everybody's needs? There must be a group of people to decide upon this question. This group may be small—something like a government—or large—something like direct democracy. But its existence entails that there is no free access to goods: the situation is far from a genuine abolition of any form of property. Rather, it means that property is collectively owned and administrated. This complicates the picture. However, before I go on to analyse this form of public ownership, it is important to add that there is no historical or sociological evidence that when private property is abolished people become more environmentally sensitive. While there is evidence that often communities with no private property live in harmony with nature, as is the case, for example, of several communes in the USA, there is no indication that their being environment-friendly is a function of their abolition of private property. It could well be the case that people who are already environment-friendly tend to prefer life in communes, or public rather than private ownership of property; so such communes would have been environment-friendly anyway.

Furthermore, if we examine one well known type of commune that did abolish private property—the kibbutz—the evidence concerning the kibbutz's attitude to the environment is illuminating. Until not long ago, the kibbutz represented the vanguard of the Zionist movement's effort to transform the environment (accompanied by slogans such as 'Conquer the desert' and 'Beautify the landscape by paving and building') as a means of overcoming bourgeois Jewish characteristics. It involved development—including irresponsible and irreversible damage to ecosystems—for its own sake, implemented by collective ownership of means of production, and did away with all private property and private interests. Nowadays the kibbutzim are *avante-garde* in their use of alternative and increasingly environment-friendly agricultural technologies, even though they have become accustomed to the system of private property (see above, p. 194). This may imply that total abolition of private property is not necessarily either beneficial or harmful to the environment.

Now let us move to the second interpretation of public ownership, namely that people have collective control over, or the right to administrate, transfer, or possess, the use of this good. In that case, if the common institution in which claims over the administration of goods are legitimized is known as 'property rights', then the right to property is collective, with the restriction that the public is prohibited from selling the good to individuals. How does this idea work in practice? One option is for people to get together and decide whenever something needs to be done regarding the property. However, this would appear to be out of the question in a busy and intense economy such as our current one. We simply cannot afford to do this; and, even if we tried to dedicate ourselves to this full time, we would still be unable to deal with the number of decisions that would arise. So another, less inclusive, option would be for the state to own (at least) all means of production. This would give rise to several problems. Many people claim, following the experience of the communist regimes in East Europe, that such a centralized regime is likely to contradict other goals that socialist environmentalists subscribe to, e.g. participatory democracy, community, public awareness of activity in the public sphere, etc. Moreover, centrism may lead to the emergence of a new elite class, the ruling class. This would be wrong not only socially, but also environmentally. As shown above, a precondition for more environmental sensitivity among those who administrate and conduct policies is egalitarian 'ecological distribution' (see p. 183). If the administrators are not likely to suffer from environmental bads, they will be more likely to turn a blind eye to environmental nuisances. Also, recall the argument in Chapter 5, according to which only democratic deliberation can guarantee environment-friendly policies. A new elite ruling class that would be bureaucratic would be likely to do all it could to prevent this deliberation from taking place.

Thus, let us examine a third, quite radically different, interpretation of 'public ownership'. It may mean no private property, but individuals would still have private administrative rights over goods and publicly 'owned' means of production. These would be rented by individuals (George 1913). The advantage of this system is that, since ownership remains in public hands, there would be no private property rights, and thus limiting the use of any means of production would not mean limiting individual freedom. People would have a contract stipulating the use of means of production; they would thus pay rental (to the community) so that they could have access to the property, and yet they would be limited by society; that is to say, all arrangements of property use would be publicly decided. Often such decisions would relate not to specific objects (e.g. this particular piece of land) but rather to categories of objects (e.g. tractors, agricultural land, print machines). Thus, when I contemplate what I would like to do with the car I use, I will actually need to think of what I want everybody else to do as well, because what is decided with regard to the car I use will be decided with regard to all other cars as well. If I do not limit the use of the car I use, no one else will be limited. If my use of the car is limited, everyone else will be similarly limited. Therefore the use of the property becomes subject to the consideration and reasoning of the 'person as a citizen' rather than a function of the individual's own consumer interests. Thus, environmental considerations enter the picture and form part of the rental contract and its limitations.

However, this system is not as simple is it appears prima facie. What if people start trading their rights? This might affect company profits, forcing them to cut wages or be more reluctant about building filters, investing in recycling, or any other steps toward the proper handling of waste (cf. Roemer 1996: 307). Furthermore, how does the community guarantee that individuals will indeed comply with the terms of the contract? The state would have to form an agency that would be responsible for this. Such an act may be economically and socially undesirable.

It seems difficult to reach a clear-cut conclusion on which form of property—public or private—would be best for the environment. For this reason, Roemer asserts that socialists, and I dare add several environmentalists, 'have made a fetish of public ownership' (p. 307).[21] So, instead of taking this line,

---

[21] However, notice that liberals too have made a fetish of private ownership, at least when it comes to land. As Gary Varner (1994) eloquently argues, even in the USA, as environmental laws and regulations proliferate, the state 'increasingly treats land as a public resource

we must look at property relations in terms of the public goods and public bads, and environmental goods and environmental bads, that they engender.[22]

The immediate implication for environmental policies is that perhaps the best thing would be if, for each case, environmentalists took into account the kind of property relations that would most likely result in more of the goals they seek. Thus, some goods should perhaps be publicly owned, e.g. grazing land or forests, and others privately owned, e.g. computers. Alternatively, it has been argued that objects should be divided into two groups: one consisting of objects whose value is the value assigned to them by individuals whose welfare depends on the use of the good (e.g. a pen, a washing machine, a car), the other consisting of objects whose value can be detached from any particular individual's use and which thus have an 'existence' value (e.g. a wild goose).[23]

Other environmental considerations may lead us to prefer land to be privately owned, and other means of production publicly owned. The criterion would be that land is polluted and contaminated, while other means of production pollute and contaminate. Thus, what is likely to be polluted should be private, whereas what might cause pollution unless controlled should be public. Since individuals tend to defend goods if they own them, they would fight any attempt to pollute their (private) land. However, if land were to be public, they would tend to count on others to fight for it, or would simply ignore the whole issue ('out of sight, out of mind'). On the other hand, means of production such as tractors and fertilizers would need to be public so that their use could be controlled by public interest as a means of preventing them from causing any environmental damage.

But then, one might raise the objection: what if land is privately owned, and you decide to build an atomic reactor on your piece of land? If the land were publicly owned we could have prevented it; now that it is private how can we stop it from happening? Well, we could prevent it by limiting the builders, who will be using public means of production (e.g. trucks, wood). However, this would mean imposing limitations on your right, as a landowner, to do

owned in common and held by individuals only in a stewardship (or trust) capacity'. Indeed, when a society accepts environmental regulations—that is, regulation guided by the interests of 'the environment'—this society *de facto* (at least) restricts private property rights.

[22] In fact, all market socialists admit that public ownership is neither a goal nor a necessary means of what I have called 'feasible' socialism (see e.g. Miller 1988). Roemer (1996: 307–8) begins with the assumption that socialists seek equality of opportunity for (*a*) self-realization and welfare; (*b*) political influence; (*c*) social status. He therefore goes on to claim that '[if] what socialists want are [these three equalities] they should be open minded about what kinds of property rights in the means of production would bring about these three equalities'.

[23] Aldred (1994). Aldred writes that the value of such objects *is* detached from any particular individual's use of them, whereas I write that it *can be* detached. The reason is that if we accept Aldred's version we are in danger of a circular argument: objects that have existence value should not be privately owned. How do we know which objects have existence value? Those that are not privately owned.

what you want with this piece of land. This then becomes even more complicated: the land is yours; nevertheless, the reactor you build is a means of
production and therefore should be owned publicly.

We again reach the conclusion that the key to the solution of these problems is not who has the right to the property, but rather what are the legitimate limitations on its use. This assumes a shift in our thinking on property
rights, and how they relate to rights in general. Rather than seeing property
rights in the liberal way, as being related to human rights, and therefore as
trump cards capable of overriding other social considerations and defending
individuals, we now must acknowledge the communitarian character of property rights. Seen this way, property rights are ascribed to individuals or collect-
ives, but they already consist of restrictions imposed by the community. Thus,
property rights derive from a social process of democratic deliberation by
which the community decides on its environmental goals, but at the same
time decides on what is to be defended as belonging to individuals, on what
constitutes being an 'individual', and on the circumstances in which this
defence can be limited. A socialist state committed to environmental protection can therefore acknowledge property rights while viewing these rights as
limited by definition (i.e. that the use of this property is restricted). This means
that we need a principle that will help us decide how to limit the use of
property—whether public or private—where environmental matters are concerned.

To see how this can be decided, let us look at property relations a little more
deeply. According to Becker (1980: 191), who based his ideas on an earlier
work by Anthony Honore, property rights imply, *inter alia*, the following:[24]

1. the right to possess, i.e. to have exclusive control of a benefit stream;
2. the right to the income that may arise if the owner forgoes personal use
   and allows others access;
3. the right to alienate: to transfer the benefit stream and abandon ownership;
4. the right to transmit: to bequeath an interest in the benefit stream;
5. the right to security: immunity from arbitrary appropriation of the benefit stream;
6. the right to use, for personal enjoyment;
7. the right to manage, including deciding how and by whom the object
   will be used;
8. the right to modify, make changes;
9. the right to consume or destroy.

In general, it can be argued that elements 1, 2, 3, 4, and 5 constitute the *possessive* aspect of property rights, whereas elements 7, 8, and 9 form the *administrative* aspect. As for element 6, it depends on whether the use involves

---

[24] I have changed the order of these elements in order to make my argument clearer.

enjoyment of ownership or any interaction with the property. Indeed, the difference between the possessive and administrative aspects relates to change. If change is introduced to the good, the community is entitled to claim that this alters the status of the agreement between the community and the owner, according to which the owner has property rights over the good.[25]

To sum up the discussion of property rights and their relevance to the environment, it is not obvious whether socialists have a clear position on the abolition of private property, nor is it clear whether the form of property relations makes a difference to the environment. The arguments for public and for private ownership both have their pros and cons, from an environmental perspective. However, what should matter is how the use of property is limited, and whether such restrictions are a function of environmental considerations. To guarantee that they are, the administrative aspects of property rights should be distinguished from the possessive aspects, thereby allowing the community to intervene in the administration of the property. Such a distinction could be based on a combination of socialist and communitarian reasoning. Thus, community would relate to several possible combinations of the possessive and managerial elements of property. Possession may either be public, private, or both. Administration could be public, private, or both. If possession is private, or either private or public, it should not make a difference in terms of impact on the environment; however, if administration is private, or either private or public, environmentalists should be cautious. They must ensure that the administration is founded on environmental considerations, expressed as regulations or legislation, and rationalized by the principle of the person as a citizen rather than as a consumer. There are several mechanisms and institutions that could serve to make public administration of property as environment-friendly as possible, while remaining respectful of individuals and their rights, including encouraging informal local dispute resolutions, administrative boards, open processes of legislation, public gatherings, and media programmes in which policies and regulations are debated. These are all mechanisms associated with the concept of deliberative participatory democracy, as analysed in Chapter 5.

A Short Summary and a Few Challenges

In this chapter I have argued that socialism is a theory and a system that is to be preferred to liberalism in terms of its impact on the environment, but I have pointed out that not all socialist arguments are relevant, or valid, in the context of environmental policies. I have claimed that contemporary, feasible

---

[25] A similar categorization is suggested by Daniel Attas (1999). He suggests that property relations encompass both 'form'—elements that describe the right—and 'content'.

socialism is a theory that seeks a particular form of egalitarian distribution, as well as rationality, prudence, policy planning with regard to policies, the abolition of alienation by the formation of community either as collective action or as a political, moral, and spiritual community, active and equal citizenship, and some form of public control over the use of property. With regard to these goals, I have claimed that they all work for the benefit of the environment. However, with regard to public ownership, I have been more reluctant to make such a claim. I have argued that the crucial aspect of property relations is the way in which the use of property is limited or controlled.

Now, several challenges may be raised against my line of argument. One such challenge is that such a theory of socialism is unrealistic. Bearing in mind that part of my critique of the various animal rights arguments has been that they are alien to real-world politics, that they are therefore confusing to the general public, and that they undermine the case for environmental policies, how can I suggest a rethinking of property rights? These positions, the challenge would continue, are a far cry from what the majority of people would accept. Thus, they also might undermine the case for environmental policies.

In reply, I want first to clarify that, when I criticize the use of animal rights issues in the environmental policies debate, I am really saying that this is a totally new paradigm of thought which is what makes it infertile in the political context. However, the discussion of property rights offered here should not be novel, at least not in the political discourse. In addition, my proposition should not be that difficult for the general public to 'digest'. I do not advise abolishing property rights, but simply differentiating between the possessive and administrative aspects of property. It is not argued that all property should be public: on the contrary, it is suggested that there is no clear indication that public property is better for the environment than private property. So all in all, my argument should not come as a surprise. It has not appeared 'out of the blue'.

Another possible challenge is that at first appearance it seems as if socialism, environmental policies, and democracy do not tie in with each other. Robyn Eckersley and John Dryzek refer to this possibility. If we reject market economy for the sake of a planned economy as described above, then, these authors fear, we will need an ongoing consensus to support the policies that have been decided. Dryzek claims that goal-directed economic systems require a continuing consensus on values in order to yield the desired goal. This is because 'the administrative structure cannot waver in its commitment, for it is only that commitment which can keep the system on course' (Dryzek 1987: 106). Eckersley (1992*a*: 138) quotes him and adds that 'this tells against the feasibility of a well functioning *and* democratic planned economy'. However, I see no reason why socialism, or planned economy, should be seen by definition as demanding continuous consensus. The socialist economy I propose is based upon, and is a continuation of, the community of rational collective reflection (described in Chapter 4) and the model of deliberative democracy (described in Chapter 5). According to this model of community, public life is not about consensus, but rather about engagement in the debate on values. Similarly, the democratic theory advanced in Chapter 5 rests not on an ongoing consensus but rather on an ongoing debate. So planned economy does not necessarily contradict democracy because it does not rest on continuous consensus.

I would like to add one final comment with regard to socialism. Socialism is a theory whose roots lie in humanism, which, unfortunately has been the target of many environmentalist attacks (e.g. Icke 1990). But as David Pepper (1995) rightly claims, socialists are not 'escapist-to-nature' advocates. Nevertheless, because socialism is rooted in humanism, it speaks the language of contemporary people, and it is therefore more likely to appeal to those searching for guidance in their relationships with the environment. I do not suggest that socialism justifies current beliefs or norms, or that it demands whatever people already morally accept; I do, however suggest that it speaks a language that people can understand (basically, anthropocentric arguments), which makes it an accessible philosophy.[26] This brings us back full circle to the chapter that opened this book: the chapter on the social role of the philosopher. I hope that the theory I have advanced will find its way to people's hearts and minds. I hope it succeeds in relating to their intuitions and theories, and I hope that it respects these theories, even though I have been rather critical of most common contemporary attitudes, including those held by both the general public and the politicians. Finally, it is my hope that, having read this book, you will now ask yourself: So what am I to do now?

It remains to analyse the relations between changes in and reforms of the production relations (often a socialist goal) and the changes in and reforms of production forces (an environmental goal). However, readers may recall the opening paragraphs of this chapter, in which I described the questions I would not answer. Instead, my contention has been rather modest: that socialist changes in production relations changes in production forces.

[26] That socialist environmentalists cannot be non-anthropocentric is acknowledged by activists, e.g. the Red–Green Study Group. Defining their 'core value perspectives', they mention the 'intrinsic worth of humans as ends in themselves', whereas the environment is 'important to human well-being' (1995: 8 and 11).

Summary: From Theory to Practice

Even though the approach to this book is academic, it is nevertheless meant to be read by both activists and members of the general public.[1] My goal has been to develop a theory that makes sense philosophically—inasmuch as its arguments follow a consistent and coherent track— while at the same time remaining relevant to activists and those engaged in the politics of the environment. For a theory to be relevant in politics, it must also be consistent with our intuitions about the real world. I hope I have indeed constructed a theory that is valid in this sense.

The first part of the book is a critique of contemporary environmental philosophy, with the major emphasis on environmental ethics. The second part offers no novel paradigms for environmental ethics as such. Instead, it presents a political theory that is structured in such a way as to sustain and justify the institutions responsible for generating environment-friendly policies. I claim that environmental philosophy should encompass this kind of theory as well. I suppose certain readers will feel furious at my claim to have justified the institutions needed for environment-friendly policies. They will accuse my theory of only pretending to be environment-friendly. 'It is not a biocentric theory,' they will say, 'hence it does not form part of environmental thought, nor is it a theory that supports environmental policies. At best, it is a progressive anthropocentric theory.' Others will add that, rather than proposing radically new institutions, all I have done is present more of the same: democracy, community, socialism—an approach they would presumably regard as the 'Western fix'. If community, democracy, and socialism cannot guarantee environment-friendly policies, then we need more of them.

They are right. If the criterion for how friendly a theory is to the environment is its radicalism and/or its non-anthropocentric premises, then my theory certainly fails the test. However, it is not always necessary to strike the most radical pose in order to impact on policies. I would therefore like to defend my political position in this book by meeting such a challenge.

[1] I have therefore applied the mechanism of public reflective equilibrium, as described in Ch. 1.

This challenge is often based on the claim that environmental matters must be tackled with a non-anthropocentric theory, because only a theory such as this will carry 'validity'. The question, of course, is, What do we mean by 'validity'? One way of understanding such a position entails the assumption that only a non-anthropocentric theory can offer an 'authentic' environmental philosophy. In this case, the question of whether or not the theory here is valid becomes important only for the typology of theories, but lacks any normative implications. Indeed, it is my contention that if such a theory has not yet been incorporated within environmental philosophy, then it is about time it is. Alternatively, it could be argued that non-anthropocentrism is the only *right* way of theorizing about the environment. For instance, it has been argued that, while sustainable development is an anthropocentric notion, environmental sustainability is not, and we should therefore use the latter term rather than the former. According to this claim, those who genuinely care for the environment should not be discussing human democracy and justice for human beings: they should instead be discussing ways of incorporating (the interests of) non-human objects in the political system, and ways to ensure that justice is done to animals.

To answer this claim, imagine a world with a growing divergence between the very rich and the very poor. The very rich form about 1 per cent of the population, whereas the remaining 99 per cent are very poor: they consume very little, do not use aeroplanes or cars, etc. The result would be far less industry, transportation, pollution, toxic waste, and so forth. Prima facie, those who wish for 'environmental sustainability' and who would like to care about the environment should favour this world to our current one. It seems however that they will not, and indeed should not. The reason is that we cannot turn a blind eye to injustice to humans when discussing environmental matters. In the same way as we cannot ignore injustice to animals or harm inflicted on them when discussing justice in the context of human beings, so we should not ignore injustice to humans when discussing environmental matters. The fact that the environment is an important political issue does not render other issues marginal or negligible. Moreover, as I showed in Chapter 6 for example, there is a strong correlation between injustice to, and exploitation of, humans and neglect of ecological stability and sustainability. It is therefore legitimate for environmental theorists and activists to use the term 'sustainable development', since it shows that we are not indifferent to the needs of the least advantaged populations, and that sustainability—even environmental sustainability—also involves social and moral sustainability. I would suggest that our line of thought as we contemplate environmental matters should not be monistic. It should not be only anthropocentric, nor should it be merely non-anthropocentric, and it should not consider only the impact of policies—old and new—on nature as well as humans. The opposite is also true: it should not, of course, *neglect* the impact and the environment in general. Elsewhere (de-Shalit 1997*a*) I have called this attitude 'Down to Earth Environmentalism'.

Now one might argue: 'If you are not radical, how can you change anything?' In my opinion, the problem with those who ask such questions is that they have not bothered to study other people's works on changes in politics and in political systems. Philosophy, they think, is a serious business, but politics? We all understand politics. I would say to them it is high time we become more modest and—much more important—more professional about understanding politics. Change requires an understanding of the system one seeks to change. I am therefore interested in building on the basis of research carried out by two political scientists and the model they have developed, in order to suggest at least one option for significant change which is neither extreme nor non-anthropocentric. I refer to the theory of 'maverick issues' developed by Moshe Maor and Gordon Smith (1993). The question confronting us is, How can we transform the issue of the 'environment' into an issue that can change the political system? The reason why Greens and other environmentalists have failed in this[2] is that, at the moment, mainstream political parties translate the issue of the environment from a value issue into an issue of resources.

What does this mean in practice? Parties confront scores of issues. Some of these fit in with the existing party system, either because they fall smoothly into the left–right cleavage, or because the existing parties have already developed a more or less clear normative position on the issue. However, from time to time parties are faced with novel issues, usually value issues, i.e. issues arising from new moral dilemmas. Parties find such issues threatening, mainly because parties are not institutions that can easily deal with new ideological and normative questions.

Robinson analyses the structural constraints which hinder parties in adapting to the wishes of an environmentally aware electorate (Robinson 1992: ch. 6). In addition to the ideological concerns that may clash with environmental values, there are three main spheres in which constraints may emerge. First, party members themselves may be sceptical or unwilling to 'green' the party's positions, policies, and ideology, either because of their position or other interests, or because of their (lack of) comprehension of the issues at stake. Secondly, there are party practicalities. The first problem here is agenda length. 'Global warming, ozone depletion, and soil erosion may have to take a back seat for the MP or local councillor concerned with the imminent closure of a local industry or Mrs Smith's family income support claim' (Robinson

---

[2] See e.g. Robinson (1992), who claims that, while the Greens in Britain have indeed made a strong 'intellectual contribution', they have failed to achieve their goals in the way of a political challenge. Robinson also distinguishes between three levels of 'greening' of political parties. First, there is their changes in rhetoric; second, their support of certain policies. The third level, however, i.e. the integration of normative positions into mainstream parties, rarely happens.

1992: 169). The second problem is procedure, which may in itself delay the introduction of new ideas and issues, and, of course, costs: it is always a problem to introduce new policies and obligations without guaranteeing sufficient financial support for these goals. The third sphere is party policies, mainly, existing and anticipated non-environmental interests. If the party is already committed to such interests or policies, it will find it difficult to commit itself to new ones, particularly if these contradict existing ones. Yet, parties are very important in the democratic system, both inside and outside parliaments. So, if parties are unable to discuss these issues, and in the absence of change, perhaps drastic change, in the party system, it is very unlikely that such value issues will have an impact.

How do parties react when confronted with new value issues? They turn them into resource issues, i.e. issues that can be dealt by distributing and allocating money. This is a language that parties, party members, and members of parliament in particular are familiar with. So, for example, if people raise the issue of bird preservation (e.g. as opposed to road construction in a certain area), parties reduce the question to simple issues, such as how much money should be spent on bird preservation in that area.

For change to occur in this respect, the issues need to be the kind that the parties cannot transform from value-related to resources-related. Smith and Maor have studied many such cases and found that issues need be presented as value-related, and they have to evolve in a 'bottom-up' way. They also need to be non-negotiable:

To the extent that party system change depends on the effects of new issues being put on the public agenda, such a change is most likely to occur when three necessary conditions are met. First, the nature of the issue should be a non-conforming one, that is, an issue which is highly resistant to unilateral ordering [e.g. left-right]. We refer here particularly to value-related issues which point to matters of belief that are absorbed through a person's socialisation as a whole and that lead to a coherent orientation towards a range of specific issues. Second, the issue should evolve in a 'bottom-up' way, that is, emanating from a geographical or socially-defined group. Third, at the level of the party system, the issue should be derived from an unrepresented dimension of party competition. . . . in a context of party competition which cannot 'squeeze' it into one of the existing dimensions of party competition. [Such an issue] is likely to have a disruptive impact on the existing structure of party competition. (Maor and Smith 1993: 40)

I shall first explain this, and then move on to discuss how my theory presents the 'environment' as such an issue.

To begin with, many issues reaffirm the left–right cleavage or any other societal cleavages, even if these issues appear novel. Some issues, however, cannot be absorbed directly into the structure of left–right party competition. These have 'maverick' potential, since 'the parties are neither able to deal adequately with the issues themselves nor yet successfully to exclude them from the public agenda'. Such issues will bring about the following changes: first, they may force a 'new party into the major axis of party competition', and second, they may 'change the content of left–right discourse'.

What determines whether an issue will be nonconforming or 'squeezable'? First, there is the question of whether an issue can be transformed into a resource allocation issue. However, this in itself is not sufficient. Maor and Smith write that even 'the right to enjoy a healthy environment, or women's rights' may be transformed into resource-related issues, if they are treated by parties in terms of 'resource allocation'. Indeed, the authors claim that the secret of the success of existing parties in Western democracies has been 'their ability to sustain a two-stage process: (i) transferring value-related issues into resources related ones; and (ii) subsuming these issues within the most accommodating dimension, i.e. the left–right.'

The second factor, however, determining whether an issue is nonconformist is its evolutionary path. For an issue to shake the system, it should not already be on the political agenda and it should not evolve from the top. The mainstream parties already control the agenda, as well as the rules of party competition. But if an issue evolves from the bottom up, emerging from a geographically or socially defined group, it has a chance of impacting on voters:

By vigorously contesting party elites' attempts to subsume an issue, a viable promotional group may significantly change how the 'concern' of the geographically—or socially—defined population is perceived by citizens and voters. In a broader way, such interest groups may influence the distribution of voters' preferences by bidding up voters' expectation about what is feasible and/or desirable. (Maor and Smith 1993: 46)

The issue, therefore, needs to be value-related and must evolve from the bottom up. Moreover, it must be presented as non-negotiable; in other words, the group that raises the issue does not do so to gain compensation for some wrong it has suffered, but rather because it is a genuine value-related issue.

If you like, this is how I have presented the issue of the environment in this book. In order for environmentalists to make an impact on policies, it is not sufficient to declare 'we are neither left nor right: we are ahead', because the issues—not the parties—must bear the characteristics of being novel and normative. With regard to the issues, then, it is not enough to claim that we must be democratic—other issues imply the same sort of democracy and yet have been unable to either change party competition or force parties to change policies. Neither is it enough to declare 'we are communitarian', and be satisfied with this. And it is not enough to declare that we need (only) socialism. As they stand, such declarations can be absorbed by existing parties and squeezed into the good old cleavages, to avoid disturbing the political system too much. Instead, I argue, the issue of the environment presents a challenge to all existing theories. It needs to be presented as a value-related issue, having to do with several values. I have examined these values and the several ideas related to 'environmentalism' and have argued that, while they include biocentrism (or ecocentrism), the latter is not necessarily a political value, but rather an attitude which serves as the moral ground for environmental attitudes. In politics, I have argued, biocentrism is not necessarily crucial, and it sometimes even prevents change; yet, there are enough values in the environmental issue to be relevant.

However, the fact that an issue is value-related is not enough to change policies. To implement environmental programmes, we need both community and deliberative participatory democracy; without them (held together) there is very little chance of environmental policies being adopted. The two models I propose, namely the collective rational reflection community (Chapter 4) and deliberate, participatory democracy (Chapter 5), emphasize the moral discussion of issues and the process of critical deliberation on policies. The model of democracy allows for more issues to become maverick issues because it attaches an important role to the general public, as opposed to the centre, when it comes to the political agenda. By critically scrutinizing each and every policy, citizens will not allow parties to turn value-related, bottom–top issues such as the 'environment' into resource-related issues. In addition, in Chapters 3 (on liberalism) and 6 (on socialism), I have argued that the issue of the environment cannot be squeezed into models of market behaviour as so many authors, activists, politicians, and economists have suggested. And so, I think, if the call for environment-friendly policies is backed by such a theory (combination of theories), there is a good chance of this call becoming a 'maverick' issue and causing the political system to change and accept the need for genuine environmental sensitivity in its policies.

BIBLIOGRAPHY

Achterberg, W. (1996). 'Sustainability and associative democracy', in W. Lafferty and J. Meadowcraft (eds.), *Democracy and the Environment*. Cheltenham: Edward Elgar, 157–173.

Ajzen, I. and M. Fishbein (1980). *Understanding Attitudes and Predicting Social Behaviour*. Englewood Cliffs, NJ: Prentice-Hall.

Aldred, J. (1994). 'Existence value, welfare and altruism', *Environmental Values*, 3: 381–402.

Anderson, T. L and D. Leal (1991). *Free Market Environmentalism*. San Francisco: Pacific Research Institute for Public Policy.

Arendt, H. (1958). *The Human Condition*. Chicago: Chicago University Press.

—— (1968). *Between Past and Future*. New York: Viking Press.

Arneson, R. J. (1989). 'Equality of opportunity for welfare', *Philosophical Studies*, 56: 77–93.

Arthur, W. (1990). *The Green Machine: Ecology and the Balance of Nature*. Oxford: Basil Blackwell.

Attas, D. (1999). *Liberty, Property and Markets: A Critique of Libertarianism*. To be published.

Attfield, R. (1994). *Environmental Philosophy: Principles and Prospects*. Aldershot: Avebury Press.

—— and A. Belsey (eds.) (1994). *Philosophy and the Natural Environment*. Cambridge: Cambridge University Press.

Bahro, R. (1982). *Socialism and Survival*. London: Heretic Books.

—— (1984). *From Red to Green*. London: Verso.

—— (1986). *Building the Green Movement*, trans. M. Tyler. London: Heretic Books.

—— (1994). *Avoiding Social and Ecological Disaster*. Bath: Gateway Books.

Barber, B. (1984). *Strong Democracy*. Berkeley: University of California Press.

Barry, B. (1991*a*). 'The continuing relevance of socialism', in B. Barry, *Liberty and Justice*. Oxford: Clarendon Press, 274–291.

—— (1991*b*). 'Humanity and justice in global perspective', in B. Barry, *Liberty and Justice*. Oxford: Clarendon Press, 182–211.

—— (1996). 'Does society exist? The case for socialism', in P. King (ed.), *Socialism and the Common Good*. London: Frank Cass, 115–145.

Barry, J. (1995). 'Deep ecology, socialism, and human "being in the world": a part of, yet apart from, nature', *Capitalism, Nature, Socialism*, 6: 33–36.

—— (1998). 'Greening liberal democracy in theory and practice: some thoughts on the right, the good and the sustainable'. Paper presented to the ECPR conference.

—— (1999). *Rethinking Green Politics: Nature, Virtue, and Progress*. London: Sage.

Beck, U. (1992). *Risk Society*. London: Sage.

—— (1995). *Ecological Politics in an Age of Risk*. Cambridge: Polity Press.

—— (1997). 'Global risk politics', in M. Jacobs (ed.), *Greening the Millennium*. Oxford: Blackwell, 18–34.

Becker, C. L. (1980). 'The moral basis of property rights', in J. R. Pennock and J. W. Chapman (eds.), *Property*. New York: New York University Press.

Beiner, R. (1992). *What's the Matter with Liberalism?* Berkeley: University of California Press.

Bellah, R. N. *et al.* (1985). *Habits of the Heart*. New York: Harper & Row.

Benedick, R. E. (1992). *Ozone Diplomacy*. Cambridge, Mass.: Harvard University Press.

Benhabib, S. (1994). 'Deliberative rationality and models of democratic legitimacy'. *Constellation*, 1: 26–52.

—— (1996). 'Toward a deliberative model of democratic legitimacy', in S. Benhabib (ed.), *Democracy and Difference*. Princeton: Princeton University Press.

Benton, T. (1988). 'Humanism = speciesism?' *Radical Philosophy*, 50: 4–18; reprinted in S. Sayers and P. Obsborne (eds.), *Socialism, Feminism and Philosophy*. London: Routledge, 1990, 235–275.

—— (1989). 'Marxism and the natural limits: an ecological critique and reconstruction', *New Left Review*, 178: 51–87.

—— (1993). *Natural Relations: Ecology, Animal Rights and Social Justice*. London: Verso Press.

—— (1996). 'Animal rights: an eco-socialist view', in R. Garner (ed.), *Animal Rights: The Changing Debate*. London: Macmillan, 19–42.

—— (1997). 'Beyond left and right?' in M. Jacobs M. (ed.), *Greening the Millennium*. Oxford: Blackwell, 34–47.

Blowers, A. and P. Leroy (1994). 'Power, politics and environmental inequalities: a theoretical and empirical analysis of the process of "Peripheralisation" ', *Environmental Politics*, 3: 197–228.

Bookchin, M. (1988). *Toward and Ecological Society*. Montreal: Black Rose Books.

Bramwell, A. (1991). *Ecology in the Twentieth Century*. New Haven: Yale University Press.

Brecher, B. (1996). 'Eat your greens', *Radical Philosophy*, 78: 77–78.

—— (1998). *Getting What You Want?* London: Routledge.

Brennan, A. (1988). *Thinking about Nature*. Athens, Ga: University of Georgia Press.

—— (1998). 'Poverty, puritanism and environmental conflict', *Environmental Values*, 7: 305–332.

Brown, L. *et al.* (1995). 'Green taxes', in J. Kirkby *et al.* (eds.), *The Earthscan Reader in Sustainable Development*. London: Earthscan, 343–348.

Brown, P. and E. Mikkelsen (1990). *No Safe Place: Toxic Waste, Leukaemia and Community Action*. Berkeley: University of California Press.

Brundtland, G. H. *et al.* (World Commission on Environment and Development) (1987). *Our Common Future*. Oxford: Oxford University Press.

Bullard, R. (1990). *Dumping in Dixie: Race, Class and Environmental Quality*. Boulder, Colo.: Westview Press.

Caldwell, L. K. (1984). *International Environmental Policy*. Durham, NC: Duke University Press.

Callicott, B. J. (1986). 'The metaphysical implications of ecology', *Environmental Ethics*, 8: 301–317.

—— (1994). 'Moral monism in environmental ethics defended', *Journal of Philosophical Research*, 19: 51–60.

Caney, S. (1992*a*). 'Liberalism and communitarianism: a misconceived debate', *Political Studies*, 40: 273–290.

Caney, S. (1992*b*). 'Liberalism and communitarianism: a reply', *Political Studies*, 41: 657–660.

Capra, F. and S. Charlane (1984). *Green Politics*, New York: Dutton.

Carter, A. (1993). 'Green politics: the state and democarcy', in A. Dobson and P. Lucardie (eds.), *The Politics of Nature*. London: Routledge, 39–62.

Carwardine, M. (1990). *The WWF Environment Handbook*. London: Optima Press.

Castoriadis, C. (1991). *Philosophy, Politics, Autonomy*. New York: Oxford University Press.

Centre for Science and Environment, New Delhi (1992). 'Global environmental democracy (a reaction to the "northern agenda")', *Alternatives*, 17: 261–279.

Chan, J. and D. Miller (1991). 'Elster on self-realization in politics: a critical note', *Ethics*, 102: 96–102.

Chodorow, N. (1979). *The Reproduction of Mothering*. Berkeley: University of California Press.

Christiano, T. (1995). 'Voting and democracy', *Canadian Journal of Philosophy*, 25: 395–414.

—— (1997). 'The significance of public deliberation', in J. Bohman and W. Rehg (eds.), *Deliberative Democracy*. Cambridge, Mass.: MIT Press, 243–279.

Christman, J. (1994). *The Myth of Property*. Oxford: Oxford University Press.

Christoff, P. (1995). 'Market-based instruments: the Australian experience', in R. Eckersley (ed.), *Markets, the State and the Environment: Towards Integration*. London: Macmillan, 157–193.

Clark, S. (1984). *The Moral Status of Animals*, Oxford: Oxford University Press.

—— (1986). 'Icons, sacred relics, obsolescent plants', *Journal of Applied Philosophy*, 3: 201–210.

Cohen, G. A. (1992). 'Incentives, inequality and community', *The Tanner Lectures on Human Values*, xiii. Salt Lake City: University of Utah Press.

—— (1995). *Self-Ownership, Freedom and Equality*. Cambridge: Cambridge University Press.

Cohen, J. (1986). 'An epistemic conception of democracy', *Ethics*, 97: 27–40.

—— (1989). 'Deliberation and democratic legitimacy' in A. Hamlin and P. Pettit (eds.), *The Good Polity*. Oxford: Blackwell.

—— and J. Rogers (1995). 'Secondary associations and democratic governance', in E. Wright (ed.), *Associations and Democracy*. London: Verso (first published in *Politics and Society*, 20 (1993): 393–472.

Cohen, M. (1996). 'Economic dimensions of environmental and technological risk events: towards a tenable taxonomy', *Industrial and Environmental Crisis*, 9.

Collard, A. and J. Contrucci (1988). *Rape of the Wild*. London: Women's Press.

Cotgrove, S. (1982). *Catastrophe or Cornucopia*. New York: John Wiley.

Crick, B. (1993). *In Defence of Politics*. London: Penguin. First published 1962.

Dahl, R. (1989). *Democracy and its Critics*. New Haven: Yale University Press.

Daly, H. (1991). *Steady State Economics*. Washington: Island Press.

—— and J. Cobb (1989). *For the Common Good*. Boston: Beacon Press.

Daniels, N. (1996). *Justice and Justification*. Cambridge: Cambridge University Press.

Davis, M. (1997). 'The radical politics of shade', *Capitalism, Nature, Socialism*, 8: 35–36.

d'Entreves, M. P. (1992). 'Hannah Arendt and the idea of citizenship', in C. Mouffe (ed.), *Dimensions of Radical Democracy*. London: Verso, 145–169.

de-Shalit, A. (1992*a*). 'Community and the rights of future generations', *Journal of Applied Philosophy*, 9: 105–115.

—— (1992*b*). 'David Miller's theory of market-socialism and the recent reforms in the kibbutzim', *Political Studies*, 40: 116–123.

—— (1993). European liberalism and the environment', in B. Brecher (ed.), *Liberalism and the New Europe*. London: Avebury Press.

—— (1994*a*). 'Environmental attitudes and progressive attitudes', paper delivered at the Israeli–Palestinian Conference on the Environment, Bethlehem.

—— (1994*b*). 'Urban preservation and the judgement of King Solomon', *Journal of Applied Philosophy*, 11: 3–13.

—— (1995*a*). *Why Posterity Matters*. London: Routledge.

—— (1995*b*). 'From the political to the objective: the dialectics of Zionism and the environment', *Environmental Politics*, 4: 70–87.

—— (1996). 'Ruralism or Environmentalism?' *Environmental Values*, 5: 47–58.

—— (1997*a*). 'Down to earth environmentalism', in N. Fotion and J. Heller (eds.), *Contingent Future Persons*. Boston: Kluwer, 123–137.

—— (1997*b*). Environmentalism for Europe: one model?' *Journal of Applied Philosophy*, 14: 177–186.

Devall, B. and G. Sessions (1985). *Deep Ecology*. Salt Lake City: Gibbs Smith.

Die Grunen (the German Green Party) (1980). *The Basic Programme*, Bonn: Die Grunen.

—— (1983). *Purpose in Work-Solidarity in Life*, Bonn: Die Grunen.

di-Zerga, G. (1992). 'Social ecology, deep ecology and liberalism', *Critical Review*, 6: 305–370.

—— (1995). 'Empathy, society, nature and the relational self: Deep Ecology and liberal modernity', in *Social Theory and Practice*, 21: 239–271; reprinted in R. Gottlieb (ed.), *The Ecological Community*. London: Routledge, 1996, 56–81.

Dobson, A. (1990). *Green Political Thought*, London: Harper-Collins.

—— (1993). 'Afterword', in A. Dobson and P. Lucardie (eds.), *The Politics of Nature*, London: Routledge, 229–234.

—— (1997). 'Representative democracy and the environment', in J. Meadowcraft (ed.), *Democracy and the Environment*, Cheltenham: Edward Elgar, 124–140.

—— (1998). *Justice and the Environment*. Oxford: Oxford University Press.

—— (ed.) (1999). *Fairness and Futurity*. Oxford: Oxford University Press.

—— and P. Lucardie (eds.) (1993). *The Politics of Nature*. London: Routledge.

Douglas, M. (1966). *Purity and Danger*. London: Routledge.

—— (1985). *Risk Acceptability according to the Social Sciences*. New York: Russell Sage.

—— and A. Wildawsky (1982). *Risk and Culture: An Essay on the Selection of Technological and Environmental Dangers*. Berkeley: University of California Press.

Dryzek, J. (1988). *Rational Ecology*. New York: Blackwell.

—— (1995). 'Political and ecological communication', *Environmental Politics* (Special Issue: Ecology and Democracy, ed. F. Matthews), 4: 13–31.

—— (1996). *Democracy in Capitalist Times: Ideas, Limits and Struggles*. New York: Oxford University Press.

—— (1997). *The Politics of the Earth: Environmental Discourses*. New York: Oxford University Press.

Dworkin, R. (1981*a*). *Taking Rights Seriously*. London: Duckworth.

—— (1981*b*). 'What is equality? Part I', *Philosophy and Public Affairs*, 10: 185–246.

—— (1981*c*). 'What is equality? Part II', *Philosophy and Public Affairs*, 10: 283–345.

Dworkin, R. (1986). 'Liberalism', in R. Dworkin, *A Matter of Principle*. Oxford: Clarendon Press.

—— (1991). 'Confronting the end of the socialist era', *Economy and Society*, 20: 341–350.

Eckersley, R. (1992*a*). *Environmentalism and Political Theory*. London: UCL Press.

—— (1992*b*). 'Green versus ecosocialist economic programmes: the market rules OK?' *Political Studies*, 40: 315–334.

—— (1993). 'Free market environmentalism: friend or foe?' *Environmental Politics*, 2: 1–20.

—— (1995*a*). 'The political challenge of Left–Green reconciliation', *Capitalism, Nature, Socialism*, 6.

—— (ed.) (1995*b*). *Markets, the State and the Environment: Towards Integration*. London: Macmillan.

Edelstein, M. (1988). *Contaminated Communities: The Social and Psychological Impacts of Residential Toxic Exposure*. Boulder, Colo.: Westview Press.

Ekins, P (1986). *The Living Economy*. London: Routledge & Kegan Paul.

Elster, J. (1985). 'Rationality, morality and collective choice', *Ethics*, 86: 136–155.

—— (1986). 'The market and the forum: three varieties of political theory', in J. Elster and A. Hylland, *The Foundations of Social Choice Theory*. Cambridge: Cambridge University Press.

—— (ed.) (1998*a*). *Deliberative Democracy*. Cambridge: Cambridge University Press.

—— (1998*b*). 'Deliberation and constitution making', in J. Elster (ed.), *Deliberative Democracy*. Cambridge: Cambridge University Press, 97–123.

Erikson, K. (1994). *A New Species of Trouble: Explorations in Disaster, Trauma, and Community*. New York: W.W. Norton.

Ezrahi, Y. (1990). *The Descent of Icarus: Science and the Transformation of Contemporary Democracy*. Cambridge, Mass.: Harvard University Press.

Faber, D. and J. O'Connor (1989). 'The struggle for nature: environmental crisis and the crisis of environmentalism in the US', *Capitalism, Nature, Socialism*, 2: 12–40.

Feinberg, J. (1974). 'The rights of animals and unborn generations', in W. T. Blackstone, *Philosophy and the Environmental Crisis*. Athens, Ga: University of Georgia Press.

Ferencz, B. and K. Keyes (1988). *PlanetHood: the Keys to Your Survival and Prosperity*. Coos Bay, Ore.: Vision Books.

Field, R. (1997). 'Risk and justice: capitalist production and the environment', *Capitalism, Nature, Socialism*, 8: 69–94.

Fiorino, D. (1990). 'Can problems shape priorities? The case of risk-based environmental planning', *Public Administration Review*, 50: 82–90.

—— (1996). 'Environmental policy and the participation gap', in W. Lafferty and J. Meadowcraft (eds.), *Democracy and the Environment*. Cheltenham: Edward Elgar, 194–213.

Fishkin, J. (1991). *Democracy and Deliberation: New Directions for Democratic Reform*. New Haven: Yale University Press.

Foreman, D. (1991). *Confessions of an Eco-Warrior*. New York: Harmony Books.

Fox, W. (1986). 'Approaching Deep Ecology: a response to Richard Sylvan's Critique of Deep Ecology', *Environmental Studies Occasional Paper*, no. 20. Hobart: University of Tasmania.

—— (1995). *Towards a Transpersonal Ecology*. Totnes, Devon: Green Books.

Francis, L. P. and R. Norman (1978). 'Some animals are more equal than others', *Philosophy*, 53: 507–527.

Frankel, B. (1988). *The Post-Industrial Utopias*. Cambridge: Polity Press.

Freeden, M. (1978). *The New Liberalism*. Oxford: Clarendon Press.

—— (1991). *Rights*. Milton Keynes: Open University Press.

Galston, W. (1991). *Liberal Purposes*. Cambridge: Cambridge University Press.

Gambetta, D. (1998). ' "Claro!" An essay on discursive machismo', in J. Elster (ed.), *Deliberative Democracy*. Cambridge: Cambridge University Press, 19–43.

Garner, R. (1993). *Animals, Politics and Morality*, Manchester: Manchester University Press.

—— (1996a). *Animal Rights: The Changing Debate*. London: Macmillan.

—— (1996b). *Environmental Politics: An Introduction*. Hemel Hempstead: Harvester-Wheatsheaf.

Gaus, G. (1997). 'Reason, justification and consensus: why democracy can't have it all', in J. Bohman and W. Rehg (eds.), *Deliberative Democracy*. Cambridge, Mass.: MIT Press, 205–243.

Gauthier, D. (1986). *Morals by Agreement*. Oxford: Clarendon Press.

George, H. (1913). *Progress and Poverty*. London: J. M. Dent. First published 1897.

Gibbs, L. (1982). *Love Canal: My Story*. Albany, NY: SUNY Press.

Giddens, A. (1995). *Beyond Left and Right*. Cambridge: Polity Press.

Gille, Z. (1997). 'Two pairs of women's boots for a hectare of land: nature and the construction of the environmental problem in state socialism'. *Capitalism, Nature, Socialism*, 8: 1–23.

Goldsmith, T. *et al.* (1972). *Blueprint for Survival*, London: Tom Stacey.

Goodin, R. (1985). *Protecting the Vulnerable*. Chicago: Chicago University Press.

—— (1988). *Reasons for Welfare*. Princeton: Princeton University Press.

—— (1992a). 'The high road is green', *Environmental Politics*, 1: 1–8.

—— (1992b). *Green Political Theory*. Cambridge: Polity Press.

—— (1996). 'Enfranchising the Earth, and its alternatives', *Political Studies*, 44: 835–850.

—— and J. Dryzek (1977). 'Risk sharing and social justice: the motivational foundations of the post-war welfare state', in J. Le Grand, *Not Only the Poor: The Middle Classes and the Welfare State*. London: Allen & Unwin, 37–73.

Gorz, A. (1980). *Ecology as Politics*. Boston: South End Press.

—— (1982). *Farewell to the Working Class*. Cambridge: Pluto Press.

Gottlieb, R. (1995). 'Spiritual Deep Ecology and the left', *Capitalism, Nature, Socialism*, 6.

Grubb, M. *et al.* (1993). *The Earth Summit Agreements*. London: Earthscan.

Grundmann, R. (1991). *Marxism and Ecology*. Oxford: Clarendon Press.

Gunn, A. (1983). 'Traditional ethics and the moral status of animals', *Environmental Ethics*, 5: 133–154.

Habermas, J. (1994). 'Three normative models of democracy', *Constellations*, 1: 1–11.

Hajer, M. (1995). *The Politics of Environmental Discourse*. Oxford: Clarendon Press.

Hall, I. (1976). *Community Action versus Pollution*. Cardiff: University of Wales Press.

Hardin, G. (1968). 'The tragedy of the commons', *Science*, 162: 1243–1248.

Hare, R. M. (1982). 'Ethical theory and utilitarianism', in A. Sen and B. Williams (eds.), *Utilitarianism and Beyond*. Cambridge: Cambridge University Press, 23–39.

Hargrove, E. (1992). *The Animal Rights/Environmental Ethics Debate*. Albany, NY: SUNY Press.

Harvey, D. (1996). *Justice, Nature and the Geography of Difference*. Oxford: Blackwell.

Hayward, B. (1995). 'The greening of participatory democracy: reconsideration of theory', *Environmental Politics*, 4 (Special Issue): 215–236.

Hayward, T. (1994). *Ecological Thought*. Cambridge: Polity Press.

—— (1998). *Political Theory and Ecological Values*. Cambridge: Polity Press.

Hefferman, J. (1982). 'The land ethic: a critical appraisal', *Environmental Ethics*, 4: 235–247.

Herman, B. (1996). 'Pluralism and the community of moral judgement', in D. Heyd (ed.), *Toleration*. Princeton: Princeton University Press, 60–81.

Holland, A. (1994). 'Natural capital', in R. Attfield and A. Belsey (eds.), *Philosophy and the Natural Environment*. Cambridge: Cambridge University Press.

—— (1997). 'Substitutability', in J. Foster (ed.), *Valuing Nature*. London: Routledge, 119–134.

—— (1999). 'Sustainability: should we start from here?' in A. Dobson (ed.), *Fairness and Futurity*. Oxford: Oxford University Press, 46–68.

Holmes, S. (1999). 'Liberalism and weak states', in D. Avnon and A. de-Shalit (eds.), *Liberalism and its Practice*. London: Routledge, 31–50.

Horton, J. and S. Mendus (1985). *Aspects of Toleration*. London: Methuen.

Icke, D. (1990). *It Does Not Have To Be Like This*. London: Green Print.

Ingelhart, R. (1977). *The Silent Revolution: Changing Values and Political Styles among Western Publics*. Princeton: Princeton University Press.

Irvine, S. and A. Ponton (1988). *A Green Manifesto*. London: Optima Press.

Jacobs, M. (1995*a*). 'Sustainability and the market: a typology of environmental economics', in R. Eckersley (ed.), *Markets, the State and the Environment*. London: Routledge.

—— (1995*b*). *Sustainability and Socialism*, London: Socialist Environment and Resources Association.

—— (ed.) (1997*a*). *Greening the Millennium*. Oxford: Blackwell.

—— (1997*b*). 'Environmental valuation, deliberative democracy and public decision-making institutions', in J. Foster (ed.), *Valuing Nature*. London: Routledge, 211–232.

—— (1997*c*). 'The quality of life', in M. Jacobs (ed.), *Greening the Millennium?* Oxford: Blackwell, 47–61.

Jaising, I. and C. Sathyamala (1993). 'Legal rights . . . and wrongs: internationalizing Bhopal', in V. Shiva (ed.), *Close to Home*. London: Earthscan.

Jameison, D. (1988). 'Animal liberation is an environmental ethic', *Environmental Values*, 7: 41–57.

Jamison, A., Eyerman, R. and Cramer, J. (1990). *The Making of the New Environmental Consciousness*. Edinburgh: Edinburgh University Press.

Jasper, J. (1996). 'The American animal rights movement', in R. Garner, *Animal Rights: The Changing Debate*. London: Macmillan, 129–143.

Jay, A. (1997). *The Oxford Dictionary of Political Quotations*. Oxford: Oxford University Press.

Johnson, H. D. (1995). *Green Plans*. Lincoln, Neb.: University of Nebraska Press.

Kahaneman, D. and A. Tversky (1982). 'Subjective probability' in D. Kahaneman and A. Tversky, *Judgement under Uncertainty*. Cambridge: Cambridge University Press.

Keat, R. (1994). 'Citizens, consumers and the environment', *Environmental Values*, 3: 333–351.

—— (1997). 'Values and preferences in neo-classical environmental economics', in J. Foster, *Valuing Nature?* London: Routledge, 32–48.

Kemball-Cook, D. *et al.* (eds.) (1991). *The Green Budget*. London: Green Print.

Kenny, M. (1996). 'Paradoxes of community', in B. Doherty and M. de Geus (eds.), *Democracy and Green Political Thought*. London: Routledge, 19–36.

Ketab, G. (1989). 'Democratic individuality and the meaning of rights', in Rosenblaum N. (ed.), *Liberalism and the Moral Life*. Cambridge, Mass.: Harvard University Press, 183–206.

Kinrade, P. (1995). 'Towards ecologically sustainable development: the role and shortcomings of markets', in R. Eckersley (ed.), *Markets, the State and the Environment: Towards Integration*. London: Macmillan, 86–112.

Kirkby, J. *et al.* (eds.) (1995). *The Earthscan Reader in Sustainable Development*. London: Earthscan.

Kymlicka, W. (1989). 'Liberal individualism and liberal neutrality', *Ethics*, 99: 883–905.

Lafferty, W. and J. Meadowcroft (eds.) (1997). *Democracy and the Environment*. Cheltenham: Edward Elgar.

Lawson, T. (1998). 'Is it our right to roam?' *BBC Wildlife Magazine*, June: 40–41.

Leopold, A. (1949). *A Sand County Almanac*. New York: Oxford University Press.

Light, A. (1992). 'The role of technology in environmental questions: Martin Buber and Deep Ecology as answers to technological consciousness', *Research in Philosophy and Technology*, 14.

—— (1994a). 'Is wilderness a natural kind?' *Society for Philosophy and Geography Newsletter*, 1.

—— (1994b). 'Hegemony and democracy: how politics in restoration informs the politics of restoration', *Restoration and Management Notes*, 12: 140–144.

—— (1995). 'Materialists, ontologists, and environmental pragmatists', *Social Theory and Practice*, 21, 315–332; reprinted in R. Gottlieb, *The Ecological Community*. London: Routledge, 1996.

—— (1996). 'Environmental pragmatism as philosophy or metaphilosophy', in A. Light and E. Katz (eds.), *Environmental Pragmatism*. London: Routledge, 325–338.

—— (2000). 'Ecological restoration and the culture of nature: a pragmatic perspective', in P. Gobster and B. Hall (eds.), *Restoring Nature: Perspectives from the Social Sciences and Humanities*. Washington: Island Press.

—— and E. Katz (eds.) (1996). *Environmental Pragmatism*. London: Routledge.

MacLean, I. (1987). *Public Choice*. Oxford: Blackwell.

Maor, M. and G. Smith (1993). 'On the structuring of party competition: the impact of maverick issues', in T. Bryder (ed.), *Party Systems, Party Behaviour and Democracy*. Copenhagen: University of Copenhagen Press, 40–51.

Marquand, D. (1997). *The New Reckoning: Capitalism, State and Citizenship*. Cambridge: Polity Press.

Martinez-Alier, J. (1993). 'Distributional obstacles to international environmental policy: the failures at Rio and prospects after Rio', *Environmental Values*, 2: 97–124.

—— (1995). 'Political ecology, distribution conflicts, and economic incommensurability', *New Left Review*, 211: 70–89.

Martinez-Alier, J. (1997*a*). *Varieties of Environmentalism*. London: Earthscan.
—— (1997*b*). 'Environmental justice', *Capitalism, Nature, Socialism*, 8: 91–109.
Mathews, F. (1988). 'Conservation and self-realization: a Deep Ecology perspective', *Environmental Ethics*, 10: 347–357.
—— (1995). 'Community and the ecological self', in F. Mathews (guest ed.), *Environmental Politics*, 4 (Special Issue: Ecology and Democracy): 66–101.
May, J. (1989). *The Greenpeace Book of the Nuclear Age*. London: Victor Gollancz.
Merchant, C. (1992). *Radical Ecology*. London: Routledge.
—— (1995). *Earthcare: Women and the Environment*. New York: Routledge.
Milbrath, L.W. (1984). *Environmentalists; Vanguard for a New Society*. Albany, NY: SUNY Press.
Mill, J. S. (1990). *Principles of Political Economy*. New York: Coloral Press. First published 1848.
Miller, D. (1988). 'The ethical significance of nationality', *Ethics*, 98: 647–662.
—— (1989). *Market, State, Community*. Oxford: Clarendon Press.
—— (1991). 'The relevance of socialism', *Economy and Society*, 20: 350–363.
—— (1992). 'Deliberative democracy and social choice', *Political Studies*, 40 (Special Issue): 54–66.
—— (1999). 'Social justice and environmental goods' in A. Dobson (ed.), *Fairness and Futurity*. Oxford: Oxford University Press, 151–172.
Mills, M. (1996). 'Green democracy: the search for an ethical solution', in B. Doherty and M. de Geus (eds.), *Democracy and Green Political Thought*. London: Routledge, 79–97.
Moberg, D. (1991). 'Environment and markets', *Dissent*, Fall: 508–515.
Mulhall, S. and A. Swift (1992). 'Liberalism and communitarianism: whose misconception? *Political Studies*, 41: 650–656.
Naess, A. (1973). 'The shallow and the deep, long-range ecology movement: a summary', *Inquiry*, 16: 95–100.
—— (1989). *Ecology, Community and Lifestyle*, trans. D. Rothenberg. Cambridge: Cambridge University Press.
—— and G. Sessions (1984). 'Basic principles of deep ecology', *Ecophilosophy*, 6: 3–7.
Nagel, T. (1975). 'Rawls on Justice' in N. Daniels, *Reading Rawls*. Oxford: Basil Blackwell, 1–16.
—— (1986). *The View from Nowhere*. New York: Oxford University Press.
—— (1991). *Equality and Partiality*. New York: Oxford University Press.
—— (1997). *The Last Word*. New York and Oxford: Oxford University Press.
Nash, R. (1989). *The Rights of Nature*. Madison: University of Wisconsin Press.
Norton, B. (1984). 'Environmental ethics and nonhuman rights', *Environmental Ethics*, 4: 17–36; reprinted in E. Hargrove (ed.), *The Animal Rights/Environmental Ethics Debate*. Albany, NY: SUNY Press, 1992, 71–94.
—— and B. Hannon (1997). 'Environmental values: a place-based approach', *Environmental Ethics*, 19: 227–245.
Nozick, R. (1974). *Anarchy, State, Utopia*. Oxford: Blackwell.
O'Connor, J. (1994). 'Socialism and ecology', in C. Merchant (ed.), *Ecology*. Atlantic Highlands, NJ: Humanities Press, 163–174.
O'Connor, M. (1994). 'Introduction' and 'On the misadvantages of capitalist nature', in M. O'Connor (ed.), *Is Capitalism Sustainable?* New York: The Guilford Press, 125–152.

O'Neill, J. (1993). *Ecology, Policy and Politics: Human Well-Being and the Natural World*. London: Routledge.

—— (1994). 'Humanism and nature', *Radical Philosophy*, 66: 21–29.

—— (1998*a*). 'Whose environment? Which nature? (Reply to Avner de-Shalit's 'Everybody is talking about the environment—but what is it?') Paper given at University College, London.

—— (1998*b*). *The Market*. London: Routledge.

Ophuls, W. (1977). *Ecology and the Politics of Scarcity*. San Francisco: W. H. Freeman.

—— (1986).'On Hoffert and the scarcity of politics', *Environmental Ethics*, 8: 287–288.

—— (1992). 'Leviathan or oblivion?' in H. E. Daly (ed.), *Toward a Steady State Economy*. San Francisco: Freeman, 215–229.

—— (1997). *Requiem for Modern Politics*. Boulder, Colo., and Oxford: Westview Press.

O'Riordan, T. (1981). *Environmentalism*. London: Pion.

—— and A. Jordan (1995). 'The precautionary principle in contemporary environmental politics', *Environmental Values*, 4: 191–212.

Paehlke, R. (1988). 'Democracy, bureaucracy, and environmentalism', *Environmental Ethics*, 10: 291–308.

—— (1989). *Environmentalism and the Future of Progressive Politics*. New Haven: Yale University Press.

—— (1996). 'Environmental challenges to democratic practice', in W. Lafferty and J. Meadowcraft (eds.), *Democracy and the Environment*. Cheltenham: Edward Elgar, 18–39.

Parkin, S. (1991). *Green Futures*. London: Harper Collins.

Pateman, C. (1970). *Participation and Democratic Theory*. Cambridge: Cambridge University Press.

Pearce, D. (1992). 'Green economics', *Environmental Values*, 1: 3–15.

Pepper, D. (1993). *Eco-Socialism*. London: Routledge.

—— (1995). 'Misrepresenting Deep Ecology and the left', *Capitalism, Nature, Socialism*, 6: 39–41.

—— (1996). *Modern Environmentalism*. London: Routledge.

Pepperman Taylor, B. (1996). 'Democracy and environmental ethics', in W. Lafferty and J. Meadowcraft (eds.), *Democracy and the Environment*. Cheltenham: Edward Elgar, 86–107.

Picon, S., Gill, D. and M. Cohen (1997). 'The Exxon Valdez oil spill as a technological disaster: conceptualising a social problem', in S. Picon, D. Gill and M. Cohen (eds.), *The Exxon Valdez Disaster*, [name of town]: Kendalm Hunt, 3–23.

Plumwood, V. (1988). 'Women, humanity and nature', *Radical Philosophy*, 48: 16–24; reprinted in S. Sayers and P. Osborne (eds.), *Socialism, Feminism and Philosophy*. London: Routledge, 1990, 211–235.

—— (1991). 'Nature, self, and gender: feminism, environmental philosophy, and the critique of rationalism', *Hypatia*, 6: 3–27.

Podgorodnikov, M. J. (1993). 'Ecological crisis in Russia', *Man and Nature Working Paper*, no. 18, Odense University (Denmark).

Popper, K. (1945). *The Open Society and its Enemies*. London: Routledge & Kegan Paul.

Porritt, J. (1984). *Seeing Green*. Oxford: Basil Blackwell.

—— (1988). *The Coming of the Greens*. London: Fontana.

Porritt, J. (1998). 'Comment', in *BBC Wildlife Magazine*, (March).

Porter, G. and J. Brown (1991). *Global Environmental Change*. Boulder, Colo.: Westview Press.

Price, B. (1983). *The Friends of the Earth Guide to Pollution*. London: Friends of the Earth.

Radner, D. and M. Radner (1996). *Animal Consciousness*. Arhest, NY: Prometheus Books.

Randall, A. (1986). 'Human preferences, economics, and the preservation of species', in B. Norton (ed.), *The Preservation of Species*. Princeton: Princeton University Press, 79–110.

Ratzman, S. (ed.) (1998). *The Mad Cow Crisis*. London: UCL Press.

Rawls, K. (1997). 'Conservation and animal welfare', in T. D. Chapell (ed.), *Philosophy of the Environment*, London: Chapman Hall.

—— (1998). 'Philosophy and the environmental movement', in D. Copper and J. Palmer (eds.), *Spirit of the Earth*. London: Routledge, 133–146.

Rawles, J. (1973). *A Theory of Justice*. Oxford: Oxford University Press. First published 1971.

—— (1993). *Political Liberalism*. New York: Columbia University Press.

Raz, J. (1980). 'Liberalism, autonomy and the politics of neutral concern', *Midwest Studies in Philosophy*, 7: 89–120.

—— (1986). *The Morality of Freedom*. Oxford: Clarendon Press.

Red–Green Study Group (1995). *What on Earth is to be Done?* London: Red–Green Study Group.

Regan, T. (1988). *The Case for Animal Rights*. London: Routledge. First published 1984.

Renn, O. (1992). 'Concepts of risk: a classification', in S. Krimsky and D. Golding (eds.), *Social Theories of Risk*. London: Praeger, 53–83.

Riker, W. (1982). *Liberalism against Populism: A Confrontation between the Theory of Democracy and the Theory of Social Choice*. San Francisco: W. H. Freeman.

Robinson, M. (1992). *The Greening of British Party Politics*. Manchester: Manchester University Press.

Roemer, J. (1994). *A Future for Socialism*. London: Verso Press.

—— (1996). *Egalitarian Perspectives*. Cambridge: Cambridge University Press.

Rolston, H. (1988). *Environmental Ethics*. Philadelphia: Temple University Press.

—— (1994*a*). *Conserving Natural Value*. New York: Columbia University Press.

—— (1994*b*). 'Value in nature and the nature of value', in R. Attfield and A. Belsey (eds.), *Philosophy and the Natural Environment*. Cambridge: Cambridge University Press.

—— (1996). 'Feeding people vs. saving nature', in W. Aiken and H. LaFollette (eds.), *World Hunger and Morality*. Englewood Cliffs, NJ: Prentice-Hall.

Rose, C. M. (1997). 'Property rights and responsibilities', in M. R. Chertow and D. Esty (eds.), *Thinking Ecologically*. New Haven: Yale University Press, 49–60.

Rosenblaum, N. (1998). *Membership and Morals*. Princeton: Princeton University Press.

Roszak, T. (1978). *Person/Planet*. Garden City, NY: Doubleday.

Routley, R. (1979). 'Against the inevitability of human chauvinism', in K. Goodpaster (ed.), *Ethics and the Problems of the 21st Century*. South Bend, Ind.: Notre Dame University Press.

Ryder, R. (1996). 'Putting animals into politics', in R. Garner, *Animal Rights: The Changing Debate*. London: Macmillan, 166–194.

Ryle, M. (1988). *Ecology and Socialism*. London: Radius Press.

Sagoff, M. (1984). 'Ethics and economics in environmental law', in T. Regan (ed.), *Earthbound*. Prospect Heights, Ill.: Waveland Press, 147–178.

—— (1988). *The Economy of the Earth*. Cambridge: Cambridge University Press.

—— (1994). 'Four dogmas of environmental economics', *Environmental Values*, 3: 285–311.

Sale, K. (1984). 'Mother of all: an introduction to bioregionalism', in S. Kumar (ed.), *The Schumacher Lectures*, ii. London: Blond & Briggs.

Salleh, A. (1994). 'Nature, woman, labour, capital', in M. O'Connor (ed.), *Is Capitalism Sustainable?*, New York: Guilford Press.

—— (1997). *Ecofeminism and Politics*. London: Zed Books.

Sandel, M. (1982). *Liberalism and its Limits*. Cambridge: Cambridge University Press.

Sandilas, M. (1995). 'From natural identity to radical democracy', *Environmental Ethics* 17: 75–92.

Saward, M. (1993). 'Green democracy?' in A. Dobson and P. Lucardie (eds.), *The Politics of Nature*. London: Routledge, 63–81.

Scanlon, T. (1988). 'The significance of choice', *The Tanner Lectures in Human Values*, viii. Salt Lake City: University of Utah Press.

Schrecker, T. (1991). 'Resisting environmental regulations', in R. Paehlke and D. Torgerson (eds.), *Managing Leviathan*. London: Belhaven Press, 165–199.

Schumacher, E. F. (1973). *Small is Beautiful*. London: Blond & Briggs.

Scoville, J. (1995). 'Value theory and ecology in environmental ethics: a comparison of Rolston and Niebuhr', *Environmental Ethics*, 17: 115–135.

Seabrook, J. (1990). *The Myth of the Market*. London: Green Books.

Shiva, V. (1989). *Staying Alive*. London: Zed Books.

Shrader-Frechette, K. (1985). *Risk Analysis and Scientific Methods*. Boston: Reidel.

—— (1991). *Risk and Rationality*. Berkeley: University of California Press.

—— (1993). 'Science, democracy and public policy', *Critical Review*, 6: 255–265.

—— and E. D. McCoy (1994). 'How the tail wags the dog: how value judgments determine ecological science', *Environmental Values*, 3: 107–120.

Singer, B. A. (1988). 'An extension of Rawls's theory to environmental ethics', *Environmental Ethics*, 10: 217–231.

Skolimowsky, H. (1992). *Living Philosophy*. London: Arakana.

Slicer, D. (1995). 'Is there an ecofeminism–Deep Ecology debate?' *Environmental Ethics*, 17: 151–170.

Smith, M. (1988). *City, State and Market: The Political Economy of Urban Society*. Oxford: Blackwell.

Socialist Party (1990). *Ecology and Socialism*. London: Socialist Party of Great Britain.

Spretnak, C. and F. Capra (1985). *Green Politics*. London: Paladin.

Steidlmeier, P. (1993). 'The morality of pollution permits', *Environmental Ethics*, 15: 133–150.

Steiner, H. (1983). 'The rights of future generations', in D. MacLean (ed.), *Energy and the Future*. Totowa NJ: Rowman & Littlefield.

Stirling, A. (1997).'Multi-criteria mapping', in J. Foster (ed.), *Valuing Nature?* London: Routledge.

Sylvan, R. and D. Bennet (1994). *The Greening of Ethics*. Cambridge: White Horse Press/Tucson: University of Arizona Press.

Talshir, G. (1998). *The Political Ideologies of the German and British Green Parties: Reconceptualising Ideology?* D.Phil. thesis, Oxford University.

Taylor, C. (1975). *Hegel*. Cambridge: Cambridge University Press.

—— (1991). *The Ethics of Authenticity*. Cambridge, Mass.: Harvard University Press.

Taylor, P. (1981). 'Frankena on environmental ethics', *Monist*, 64: 313–324.

—— (1986). *Respect for Nature*. Princeton: Princeton University Press.

Taylor, R. (1993). 'The environmental implications of liberalism', *Critical Review*, 6: 265–283.

Thero, D. (1995). 'Rawls and environmental ethics: a critical examination of the literature', *Environmental Ethics*, 16: 93–106.

Thompson, D. (1970). *The Democratic Citizen*. Cambridge: Cambridge University Press.

Tickle, A. and I. Welsh (eds.) (1998). *Environment and Society in Eastern Europe*, London: Longman.

Turner, J. (1998). 'Reinventing the wolf'. *BBC Wildlife Magazine*, May.

Van Parijs, P. (ed.) (1992). *Arguing for Basic Income*. London: Verso Press.

Varner, G. (1994). 'Environmental law and the eclipse of land as private property' in F. Ferre and P. Hartel (eds.), *Ethics and Environmental Policy*. Athens, Ga: The University of Georgia Press, 142–160.

Vira, B. (1995). 'Rights, property rights and their protection: implications for the analysis of environmental policy', *Oxford Centre for Environment, Ethics, and Society Research Paper* no. 2.

—— (1998). 'Environmental regulation and economic deregulation: is there a conflict?' in A. Qureshi, G. Parry and H. Steiner (eds.), *The Legal and Moral Aspects of International Trade; Freedom and Trade* iii. London: Routledge, 147–162.

Vogler, J. and M. Imber (eds.) (1995). *The Environment and International Relations*. London: Routledge.

Walker, K. (1989). 'The state in environmental management', *Political Studies*, 37: 25–38.

Walzer, M. (1983). *Spheres of Justice*. Oxford: Blackwell.

—— (1987). *Interpretation and Social Criticism*. Cambridge, Mass.: Harvard University Press.

—— (1988). *The Company of Critics*. New York: Basic Books.

—— (1994). *Thick and Thin: Moral Argument at Home and Abroad*. Souoth Bend, Ind.: University of Notre Dame Press.

Warren, M. A. (1992). 'The rights of the non-human world', in E. Hargrove, *The Animal Rights/Environmental Ethics Debate*. Albany, NY: SUNY Press, 185–210.

Warren, K. (1994). *Ecological Feminism*. London: Routledge.

Weale, A. (1984). 'Social choice versus populism? An interpretation of Riker's political theory', *British Journal of Political Science*, 14: 369–385.

—— (1992). *The New Politics of Pollution*. Manchester: Manchester University Press.

Weber, M. (1968). *Politics als Beruf*. Berlin; Dunker & Humboldt.

Weston, A. (1996). 'Before environmental ethics', in A. Light and E. Katz (eds.), *Environmental Pragmatism*. London: Routledge, 285–307.

Westra, L. (1993). 'The ethics of environmental holism and the democratic state', *Environmental Values*, 2: 125–136.

—— (1994). *An Environmental Proposal for Ethics: The Principle of Integrity*. Lanham Md: Rowman & Littlefield.

—— (1995). 'Ecosystem integrity and sustainability: the foundational value of the wild', in L. Westra and J. Lemons (eds.), *Perspectives on Ecological Integrity*. Dordrecht: Kluwer.

White, S. (1997). 'What egalitarians want?' in J. Franklin (ed.), *Equality*. London: Institute for Public Policy Research, 59–83.

Williams, C. B. (1964). *Patterns of Balance in Nature*. London: Academic Press.

Wissenburg, M. (1998). *Green Liberalism*. London: UCL Press.

—— (1999). 'An extension of the Rawlsian saving principle to liberal theories of justice in general', in A. Dobson (ed.), *Fairness and Futurity*. Oxford: Oxford University Press, 173–198.

Witherspoon, S. (1997). 'Democracy, the environment and public opinion in Western Europe', in W. Lafferty and J. Meadowcroft (eds.), *Democracy and the Environment*. Cheltenham: Edward Elgar, 39–71.

Wolfsfeld, G. (1988). *The Politics of Participation*. Albany, NY: SUNY Press.

Worcester, R. (1997). 'Public opinion and the environment', in M. Jacobs (ed.), *Greening the Millennium*. Oxford: Blackwell, 160–174.

Worldwatch (1989). *Action at the Grassroots: Fighting Poverty and Environmental Decline, a Worldwatch Paper*. New York: Worldwatch Institute.

Wright, A. (1987). *Socialisms*. Oxford: Oxford University Press.

Yearley, S. (1991). *The Green Case*. London: Harper Collins.

Young, R. (1995). 'Monkeywrenching and the processes of democracy', in F. Mathews (guest ed.), *Environmental Politics*, 4 (Special Issue: Ecology and Democracy): 199–215.

Young, S. (1997). 'Local agenda 21', in M. Jacobs, *Greening the Millennium?* Oxford: Blackwell, 138–147.

INDEX